ALABAMA RAILROADS

ALABAMA
RAILROADS

Wayne Cline

THE UNIVERSITY OF ALABAMA PRESS
Tuscaloosa and London

Jacket and interior designed by Erin Toppin Bradley

∞

The paper on which this book is printed
meets the minimum requirements of American National
Standard for Information Science-Permanence of Paper
for Printed Library Materials, ANSI Z39.48-1984.

Library of Congress Cataloging-in-Publication Data

Cline, Wayne.
     Alabama railroads / Wayne Cline.
          p.   cm.
     Includes bibliographical references and index.
     ISBN 0-8173-0812-1 (cloth : alk. paper)
     1. Railroads—Alabama—History.   I. Title.
TF24.A2C58   1996
385'.09761—dc20   95-51241

British Library Cataloguing-in-Publication Data available

Maps prepared by The University of Alabama Cartographic
Research Laboratory, Craig Remington, Supervisor,
unless otherwise noted.

On the cover: Alabama train crew, ca. 1930s.
(Courtesy of William Stanley Hoole Special Collections Library,
The University of Alabama, Tuscaloosa)

On pages ii–iii: Southern Railway 2-8-8-2 articulated Mallet type locomotive
at Birmingham on July 25, 1931. (From the author's collection.)

FOR MY MOTHER AND FATHER

CONTENTS

MAPS

ALABAMA RAILROADS

Woodward Iron Company ore train near Birmingham, ca. 1940s. (Courtesy of William Stanley Hoole Special Collections Library, The University of Alabama, Tuscaloosa)

INTRODUCTION

Known as the "Heart of Dixie," the state of Alabama occupies a strategic geographical position in the Deep South. Surrounded by Florida, Georgia, Tennessee, and Mississippi, the state has always exerted a strong economic, cultural, and political influence upon this region; but Alabama has also earned the title "Heart of Dixie" because it is the mineral heartland of the Deep South. From this bosom of the South, the lifeblood of industry—coal and iron—issued forth to provide energy and building material for the world. Initially, the coal and iron fed the Confederate war machine. Then, after the true value of Alabama minerals was established, these natural resources ultimately fueled much of the Industrial Revolution in America. In the center of the state, great mountains arise that contain every mineral needed for making iron. This unique feature of Alabama geology enabled the state to produce iron at such a low cost that Alabama eventually dictated its price to the rest of the country.[1] Good-quality, inexpensive Alabama iron allowed manufacturers throughout the United States to keep their costs down and profits up, but this great stimulus to American industry would have been impossible without the indispensable railroad arteries that brought the minerals from the mines to the furnaces and carried the furnace products to far-flung markets. Until the railroads came along, Alabama's abundant store of natural resources was practically worthless. Realizing this need, a few visionary Alabamians fought against monumental odds to develop a viable railway system that they knew would bring pulsating vitality to the state.

These pioneer Alabama railroad promoters were cast from remarkably similar molds. They were practical builders, not unrealistic dreamers or speculators, and they possessed an indomitable confidence that enabled them to persevere tenaciously in the face of extreme adversity. When these resourceful men came to Alabama in antebellum times, they had no initial intentions of developing coal and iron, however. Almost nothing was known of the mineral regions when these men ventured South, and the riches of the state were not considered coal black or iron red but snowy white. With cotton prices rapidly advancing after the invention of the cotton gin, the plantation and slave system ascended in the South and attracted these adventurers to Alabama, where they were determined to accumulate wealth in the cotton trade.

Though sowing baneful seeds, these ambitious planters soon harvested the expected treasure and turned their thoughts to ways to make their plantations even more profitable.

As cotton culture flourished, the South became the export engine of the United States, and planters sought more efficient means to get the cotton bales to trade centers where they could be exchanged for cash, grain, groceries, merchandise, and farm implements. A handful of prosperous Alabama planters believed that the newly invented iron horse could be the answer to these growing transportation needs and pledged their fortunes to lay the state's first railroad tracks.

Indeed, Alabama's first railroads could never have been built without these men of wealth. Unlike voters in other states, the fiercely individualistic citizens of antebellum Alabama steadfastly refused to provide state financial aid for railroad construction. After all, the State Bank had recently failed and burdened the taxpayers with a great levy. Why should they expect state-supported railroads to fare any better? Also, the average rural Alabamian reasoned that railroads would only benefit the rich agricultural and merchantile interests of the state. At the beginning of the nineteenth century, there was some truth in such thinking, since the earliest railroads in the state were exclusively constructed to circumvent river hazards and bring the planter's cotton to river wharves where it could be shipped to Mobile or New Orleans for export. Therefore, only the most affluent planters were left to become Alabama's railroad trailblazers.

But railroad construction is expensive, and most of Alabama's antebellum railroads were stillborn or died in infancy because planters alone could not provide adequate financing. Moreover, the planters were restrained by their own economic system—a system that was so labor intensive that the greater part of their income went into the pocket of the slave trader, leaving little money for railway investment. Also, the slaves were needed to till the fields and harvest the crops, and since the slave system discouraged immigrant labor, it was almost impossible to find the hands needed to lay and maintain the track.[2] Consequently, the story of Alabama's earliest railroad enterprises turned out to be one of frustration and failure.

But the more ardent of the men behind Alabama's antebellum railroads did not give up. They persevered through many extreme difficulties until a great rush to build railroads overwhelmed the country at midcentury. By then, Alabamians were beginning to change their minds about government aid to railroads. Previously, any type of government involvement, state or federal, had been vigorously opposed. In fact, at least one early Alabama railroad charter contained a provision requiring its forfeiture if the company even *asked* for federal aid.[3] But as demand for railroads steadily increased, states' rights activists began to view the federal role in a brand new light and cast a longing eye toward the vast expanse of virgin wilderness that comprised the public domain. This shift of attitude soon brought the state of Alabama to the forefront of the national railway scene.

In Washington, United States senator Stephen Douglas of Illinois also had designs on these great tracts of unused federal land, and he introduced a bill that proposed to appropriate a portion of the public domain to help finance the Illinois Central Railroad. Douglas didn't get very far, however, until he enlisted the support of Alabama lawmakers. Led by twenty-five-year Senate veteran William R. King, the Alabamians attached an amendment to the Douglas measure that called for an equivalent land grant for the proposed Mobile & Ohio Railroad. Reacting to agitation for federal aid back home, Senator King joined Douglas as cosponsor of the new land-grant bill and exercised considerable influence among his colleagues to help secure passage of historic land-grant legislation.[4]

The land-grant bill was written into law in 1850, but it was not until 1861 that the M&O and Illinois Central finally joined to form the longest railroad in the world. Nevertheless, Americans from the Great Lakes to the Gulf could place Alabama legislators near the top of their list of railway benefactors. The precedent-setting legislation that the Alabamians were so instrumental in framing eventually provided over 131 million acres of public land to the nation's railroads and gave impetus to the great transcontinental roads that opened the American West and welded the country together.[5] The land-grant effort was among the first of many pivotal roles the state of Alabama would play in the national railway drama. As the Civil War soon demonstrated, Alabama railroads were becoming an integral part of the nation's destiny.

One of the first railroads ever built in America stretched across northern Alabama and eventually became a segment of the Memphis & Charleston Railroad. The Memphis & Charleston Railroad led from Memphis to Chattanooga, where it connected with Georgia's famous Western & Atlantic Railroad and, in conjunction with other southern lines, constituted the only east-west rail route running entirely across the Confederate states during the Civil War. This vital trans-Confederate line could be reached directly by rail from the Ohio River via the Nashville & Chattanooga Railroad, which joined the Memphis & Charleston at Stevenson, Alabama, just outside Chattanooga. The importance of the Memphis & Charleston Railroad and the junction at Stevenson did not go unnoticed by Union strategists. By capturing the Nashville & Chattanooga Railroad as well as the portion of the M&C leading from Stevenson into Chattanooga, the Federal army could not only cut off rail movements across the South but also could assure a supply line for Sherman's Atlanta campaign. The Union army wasted no time in accomplishing this objective. By holding Chattanooga and the vital railroad through north Alabama, Sherman's victory was certain. In Sherman's own words, "The Atlanta campaign was an impossibility without those railroads." Sherman's conquest was one of the signal events that saved the Union. Coming at a time when the North was so weary of war that Lincoln's reelection was in jeopardy, it convinced many who were ready to sue for peace that a complete U.S. triumph was within reach.[6]

The Memphis & Charleston's route through northern Alabama was a strategically vital key to victory, but the rest of Alabama's Civil War rail system was incomplete, and prewar neglect of the state's railroads and natural resources haunted the Confederacy throughout the conflict. Even though enough iron ore lay in Alabama's hills to supply the South adequately, these resources remained undeveloped, and the Confederate army could never find a sufficient amount of iron with which to wage war. Only a small portion of Alabama's vast deposits of iron ore was turned into iron, and this process was possible only because of the diligent efforts of men like the transplanted Georgia railway engineer John T. Milner. Devoted to his adopted state, Milner would spend his life fighting to develop its railroads and mineral industry. With a single locomotive, Milner aided the Confederate cause by resourcefully operating a little railroad that transported iron products from a primitive Jefferson County furnace to the rebel arsenal at Selma. This railroad, like all others in the state, was almost obliterated at war's end, but Milner saved enough of it to keep the spark of this enterprise alive. He did not know that the maelstrom of war had placed events in motion that would eventually kindle this spark into a flaming beacon of Alabama's iron industry.

Many obstacles blocked the path to mineral development in Alabama, not the least of which was the ravaged railroad system left in the wake of the Civil War. Nothing in the state was more devastated than the railroads. The equipment of all the roads was burned, destroyed, or scattered across the South in wretched condition. With only worthless Confederate currency in an otherwise empty treasury, Alabama's railroad rebuilders were forced to look northward for help. Unfortunately, the postwar investment climate was rife with corruption and rampant speculation. Northern capital markets were dominated by the likes of Daniel Drew, James Fisk, and Jay Gould—the infamous "Erie Ring."[7] The Civil War had cut a yawning void in the capital base of the Deep South. Against this backdrop, Alabama's decimated railroads desperately fought for survival through the early Reconstruction days, and were easy marks for the unscrupulous.

The struggling roads of Alabama's mineral regions, including the one built by John T. Milner in Jefferson County, soon became popular targets of mercenary politicians and financiers; and Milner was compelled to wrestle with intrigues that threatened not only his promising little mineral line but Alabama's whole mineral industry as well. Just when it appeared that Alabama's cause was lost, a redeemer appeared and the course of Deep South railroad history was forever changed. That rescuer was the Louisville & Nashville Railroad, which was bidding to become the Deep South's first real railroad superpower.

The Louisville & Nashville Railroad had tried to remain neutral during the early months of the Civil War, but when the rebels assailed the road, L&N officials accepted federal protection and placed the railroad at the disposal of the Union army. The Louisville & Nashville became a vital link in the Union's supply line and hauled great numbers of men, weapons, and sustenance in support of the Yankee invasion of the South. Wartime profits and the generosity of a grateful government made the Louisville & Nashville one of the most powerful and profitable railroads in the nation at war's end.[8] But the L&N wanted to reign over the entire mid-South by extending its tracks throughout the region—to Pensacola, to Mobile, and to New Orleans. In order to accomplish this expansion, the L&N had to penetrate Alabama, and the company did not miss the opportunity when it came.

John Milner's troubled, underfinanced railway ran in a north-south direction through Alabama's most prolific mineral district and could potentially be extended to connect with the Louisville & Nashville's southbound main line. The L&N decided to absorb this beleaguered little line, make the extension, and bring the full weight of its financial strength to bear in making it a first-class road that could spur development of the mineral region. The L&N gambled in Alabama, and although at times it seemed to be a loser, the investment eventually made the Louisville & Nashville Railroad the predominate system in the mid-South. With the L&N forging the way, Alabama coal soon found its way to the Southwest, to be used in the fireboxes of almost all the railroads in that part of the country; coal mines and blast furnaces proliferated near the infant city of Birmingham; Alabama iron was cast into car wheels that rolled over the tracks of every major railroad in the country; and Alabama steel eventually found its way into structures from coast to coast. Working hand-in-hand, the iron furnace and the iron horse secured a place for Alabama on the world's industrial map.

The commercial success of Alabama minerals quickly attracted other railroads. The Southern, Central of Georgia, Seaboard, Atlantic Coast Line, Illinois Central, and others coupled their fate to Alabama's industrial star and watched it rise to worldwide fame. In short order, these railroads built Alabama and steered the state's history with an impact that extended far beyond the state's boundaries. In a prelude to the great westward expansion of America, the railroads came to Alabama, and settlers followed closely behind. The great city of Birmingham and scores of small Alabama communities owe their very existence to the railroads. Indeed, railways wove the fabric of the state, and the railroad story is truly the story of Alabama.

Consequently, when Alabama's railroad story is told, it must encompass a sweeping panorama of momentous events in the state's history. *Alabama Railroads,* the first comprehensive history of the formation of the state's railway system, traces these events, from land-grant legislation and the strategic importance of Alabama's railroads in the Civil War to the founding of Birmingham and the development of the state's mineral regions. The following pages will explore Alabama's railway system and introduce the men who built it. From David Hubbard, who planned the first railroad west of the Alleghenies, to Charles T. Pollard, who mapped out many of the main-line routes through the South; from John T. Milner, whose railroad through Jefferson County led to the founding of Birmingham, to Milton H. Smith, cantankerous and pragmatic president of the L&N Railroad, who played a major role in developing Alabama's mineral districts, we

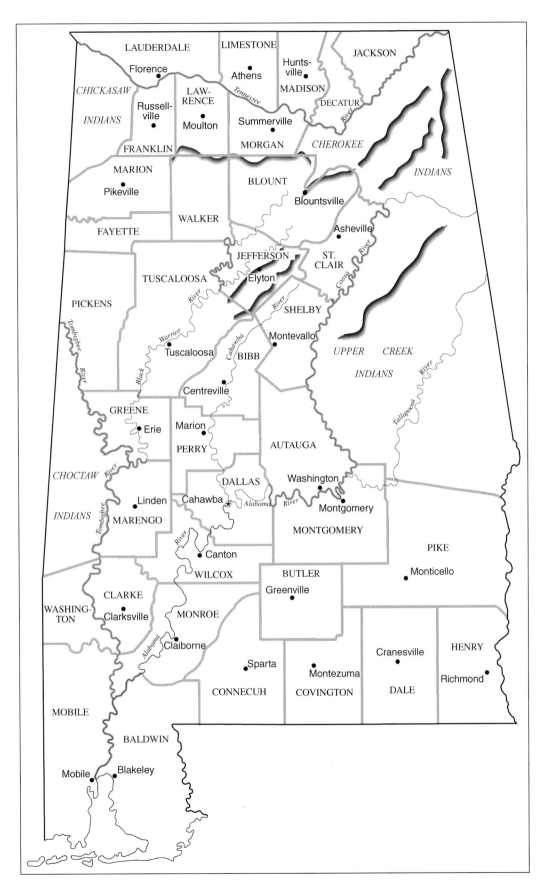

LAUDERDALE

Florence

CHICKASAW

LAW-
RENCE

Russell-
ville

INDIANS

Moulton

FRANKLIN

MARION

Pikeville

WALKER

FAYETTE

LIMESTONE

Athens

Hunts-
ville

MADISON

Tennessee

DECATUR

Summerville

MORGAN

BLOUNT

Blountsville

Asheville

JACKSON

CHEROKEE

INDIANS

River

JEFFERSON

Elyton

ST.
CLAIR

Coosa

River

TUSCALOOSA

PICKENS

Tombigbee

River

Warrior

River

Black

Tuscaloosa

SHELBY

Montevallo

Cahawba

BIBB

Centreville

River

UPPER CREEK

INDIANS

Tallapoosa

River

GREENE

Erie

Marion

PERRY

AUTAUGA

CHOCTAW

INDIANS

River

Tombigbee

Linden

MARENGO

DALLAS

Cahawba

Washington

Alabama

River

Montgomery

MONTGOMERY

River

Canton

WILCOX

BUTLER

Greenville

PIKE

Monticello

CLARKE

Clarksville

MONROE

Claiborne

Alabama

WASHING-
TON

Sparta

CONNECUH

Montezuma

COVINGTON

Cranesville

DALE

HENRY

Richmond

MOBILE

BALDWIN

Mobile

Blakeley

Alabama in 1827

will follow the footsteps of these pioneers as they shaped the history of the state and influenced the direction of railway progress in America.

In order to observe this history from the perspective of those who actually lived it, many personal accounts, newspaper articles, and other contemporary documentation relevant to important events in Alabama's railroad story are quoted liberally throughout the text. These echoes from the past will, I hope, complement the equally liberal use of period photographs and illustrations to make our journey through the early years of Alabama railroading more intimately meaningful. Moreover, every effort has been made to present this story from a decidedly nontechnical point of view. Beginning with Alabama's first railroad and continuing until the rail system reaches maturity in the early part of the twentieth century, all of the major lines and the most important short lines, including many quaint old logging railroads, will be surveyed. In the final chapter we will extend our time horizon and ride the passenger trains that highballed through Alabama until Amtrak assumed full control of the nation's passenger train service.

Alabama Railroads is about "old-time" railroading, so the photographs selected for the volume generally depict pre-1930 scenes, and most are from the turn of the century. For passenger trains, the cutoff date is extended to 1970, when Amtrak was formed. Illustrations and photographs are integrated chronologically into the text.

So now, let us begin our exploration of Alabama and the railroads that forged this wonderful state. Let us give free rein to our imaginations and become early-nineteenth-century pioneers, as we trek through the Cumberland Gap, descend the Holston and Tennessee rivers, and enter the western frontier, where we will discover the lush forests, rolling mountains, and untamed rivers of the Alabama Territory—and the dawn of Alabama railroads.

1

THE
TUSCUMBIA
TRIO

IN 1813, FOLLOWING THE bloody Creek Indian War, a large part of the Alabama Territory was opened for settlement. With the Indians subdued and confined to areas east of the Coosa River and in western sections of the Territory, an ever-increasing number of settlers migrated to the rich land vacated by the Native Americans. During the decade from 1810 to 1820, the population of the region increased from slightly more than 9,000 to over 127,000. This great influx of settlers propelled Alabama to statehood in 1819.[1]

Settlements, family farms, and plantations established by these newcomers were primarily located in the fertile river valleys of the state. Cotton was king, and planters needed reliable ways of moving this product to both foreign and domestic markets. Blessed with many nearby navigable rivers, planters shipped their cotton by steamer to ports at Mobile and New Orleans. From Mobile, the Alabama River was navigable to Montgomery, and steamboats could ascend the Tombigbee as far as Demopolis.[2] Tennessee River Valley planters were faced with a formidable obstacle, however. Although cotton could be shipped from Florence to New Orleans and the North via the Tennessee-Mississippi River system, access to the upper reaches of the Tennessee Valley was impeded by the treacherous Tennessee River rapids known as Muscle Shoals. These rapids, near Florence and Tuscumbia, were impassable for much of the year. Canals were popular at the time, and one was proposed to overcome this obstruction to transportation. Meanwhile, an enterprising Tuscumbia resident named David Hubbard correctly thought that a canal would prove ineffectual and sought some other means of circumventing the shoals.[3]

Born in Tennessee in 1792, Hubbard was the son of a Revolutionary War officer. During the War of 1812 young Hubbard followed in his father's footsteps and enlisted as a quartermaster in General Andrew Jackson's army at New Orleans. He attained the rank of major, but resigned his commission after being wounded in the leg and moved to Huntsville, where he worked as a carpenter and studied law. Hubbard was elected solicitor at Florence, but soon moved across the river to Lawrence County, where he became a merchant and a popular political figure. He was elected state senator in both 1827 and 1828 before beginning a seven-term appointment to the state legislature.

In 1829, while buying and selling Chickasaw Indian Land near the Tennessee Valley town of Courtland, Hubbard became preoccupied with the problem of circumnavigating Muscle Shoals.[4] He had heard of an innovative system for hauling coal in Pennsylvania and decided to make the long, arduous trip to the Keystone State to observe its operation. The young legislator wanted to know if the experimental invention, known as a railroad, might be adapted to haul cotton around the shoals. When Hubbard arrived at Mauch Chunk, Pennsylvania, he was shown a switchback railroad operated by a stationary steam engine.[5] Hubbard was so impressed that he returned to Alabama determined to organize the first railroad west of the Allegheny Mountains.[6]

Hubbard's railroad around Muscle Shoals was to be built in stages. First, two miles of track would be laid to connect the town of Tuscumbia with the river landing. The road would then be extended eastward to Decatur. The first phase of Hubbard's plan began on January 16, 1830, when the state legislature granted a charter to the Tuscumbia Railway Company, with an authorized capital of $20,000, to construct a line from Tuscumbia to Tuscumbia Landing on the Tennessee River. Hubbard solicited investment from prominent Tennessee Valley planters, and stock in the railroad was soon sold. On May 1, 1830, a board of directors was elected and ground was broken a little more than a year later, on June 5, 1831.

The track of the Tuscumbia Railway was built using crude contemporary construction techniques. First, cedar cross-ties, called "sleepers," were laid five feet apart. Then the rails, called "stringers," made of five-inch-square lengths of oak, were nailed to the sleepers. The four-foot-nine-and-one-half-inch-gauge track was finished by capping the rail with long strips of flat iron that were two inches wide and half an inch thick. Although Tennessee Valley topography was relatively level,

David Hubbard as he appeared in the 1830s when he organized Alabama's first railroad. (Courtesy of the Alabama Department of Archives and History, Montgomery, Alabama)

the terrain near the river was quite rugged and presented many engineering challenges. Curves as tight as four hundred feet in radius wound through the hills, and a 274-foot-long truss bridge was required to breach a thirty-six-foot-deep ravine.[7]

Alabama's first railroad depot, a quaint three-story structure measuring seventy-five feet long and sixty feet wide, was erected on a hillside overlooking the Tennessee River at Tuscumbia Landing. The lower floor was made of strong rubble masonry, while brickwork constituted the upper stories. The railroad track led to the upper floor, where cargo was loaded onto the cars after being pulled up an inclined plane from the river. The inclined plane was powered by horses hitched to a gear mechanism behind the depot and was accommodated to varying river levels by a floating wharf. Chutes transferred freight from track level to storage areas within the lower floors and thence onto the wharf.[8]

Although long-term plans called for the eventual use of modern locomotive power, the iron horse made no appearance on the Tuscumbia Railway. Real horses did the work instead. Nevertheless, completion of the railroad on June 12, 1832, was cause for great celebration. The Huntsville *Southern Advocate* gave the following account of the opening ceremonies:

> On the 12th inst. the Tuscumbia Railway was opened in conformity with previous arrangements. At an early hour a large concourse had assembled to witness the first railroad in Alabama.
>
> The cars were in motion throughout the day for the accommodation of visitors. A procession was formed at eleven o'clock a.m. of the cars drawn by one horse, crowded with the beauty and the fashion of the County and accompanied with a band of music. The procession passed to the foot of the road where an extensive collation had been prepared for the occasion. Several thousand persons partook of the hospitality of the railroad company. The utmost harmony and good humor prevailed. The whole scene was gay and animating and the celebration creditable to the company. It was truly novel and interesting to witness the rapid and graceful flight of the 'majestic cars' in a country where but yesterday the paths of Indians were the only traces of human footsteps.[9]

The railroad proved to be of great advantage in hauling freight. It was found that one horse walking down a graveled path alongside the track could pull a car containing forty bales of cotton. Passenger business was also competitive with existing conveyances, and the line was profitable from its inception.[10] Round-trip fares were set at twenty-five cents, a considerable sum for the era. Reduced monthly and yearly rates were available, however.[11]

Before the first car rolled over the Tuscumbia Railway's track, the company's promoters worked diligently to extend the road to Decatur. The company held several organizational meetings, culminating in a convention at Courtland on October 8, 1831, during which a committee was formed to publicize and promote the railroad extension.[12] With the support of Governor Samuel B. Moore, the Tuscumbia, Courtland & Decatur Railroad was chartered on January 13, 1832, with a capitalization of $1,000,000.

Strangely, David Hubbard had not served on the board of directors of the Tuscumbia Railway, but was added to the board of the Tuscumbia, Courtland & Decatur, along with the respected and prosperous planter, Benjamin Sherrod.[13] The orphaned son of North Carolina pioneers who had emigrated from Britain, Sherrod had been raised by his grandfather and educated at Chapel Hill before moving to Wilkes County, Georgia, to become a cotton planter. In 1818, at the age of 32, Sherrod migrated to Alabama and established a plantation near Courtland that he called "Cotton Garden."[14] Soon, Sherrod had accumulated great wealth, which at that time was measured largely in slave holdings. Like a great army, formations of up to seven hundred slaves plowed Sherrod's cotton fields under his direction. He continuously sought innovative ways to increase production and was one of the few planters in Alabama to practice crop rotation.[15] On the strength of his widely acknowledged administrative abilities, Sherrod was promptly elected president of the Tuscumbia, Courtland & Decatur Railroad. Hubbard became secretary.

The initial contract for roadbed grading was awarded in May 1832. The complete line to Decatur was to be relatively straight and level, requiring only six and one-half miles of curves and a maximum grade of just twenty-five feet per mile. Contractors would use essentially the same construction practices as were employed on the Tuscumbia Railway, except that the sleepers had a four-foot separation and some stringers were made of cedar rather than oak. Horse power continued to be used when the first section of the line opened from Tuscumbia to Leighton on August 20, 1833. A steam locomotive had been ordered from E. Bury of Liverpool early in 1833 but did not arrive until June 1834. This locomotive, called the *Fulton,* was put to use immediately upon its arrival from New Orleans and was in operation when the railroad reached Courtland in July 1834.[16]

What a marvelous spectacle this machine must have presented to the agrarian populace as it chugged through the Alabama countryside!

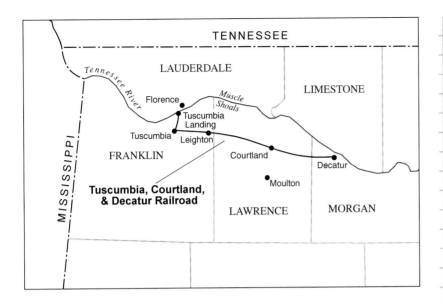

Alabama's First Railroad. The Tuscumbia, Courtland & Decatur Railroad was built in the northwestern corner of the state in 1834 to bypass the river rapids called Muscle Shoals that blocked navigation of the Tennessee River east of Florence and Tuscumbia.

David Deshler, the company engineer, was certainly impressed with the little four-wheeled engine. "Performance is such as has determined the Board of Directors to dispense with horses altogether so soon as a sufficient number of engines for their business can be procured," Deshler announced. "With a light load this engine has at divers times attained a velocity of 40 miles an hour. Pine and ash wood has been used as fuel; but so soon as the road is finished to Decatur, it is contemplated coal will be used exclusively, as that can be obtained cheap, and is entirely safe from sparks."[17] Deshler's comments were prophetic. After the Civil War, coal would supplant wood as locomotive fuel, and abundant Alabama coal would provide energy for steam engines around the world.

Deshler's praise of the *Fulton* was not uniformly endorsed by others, however. One observer noted in the *Leighton News* that the locomotive was "a rude structure, wanting in speed and power. . . . Its average speed was only about 4 miles per hour."[18]

Tennessee Valley residents were less concerned with the engine's speed, however, than with its potential to overcome the frustrations of Muscle Shoals. Anxious shippers could not wait to try out the new invention, and long before the track approached Decatur, great quantities of cargo bound for the upper Tennessee River began to accumulate at Courtland in anticipation of the road's completion. On December 15, 1834, the railroad was completed to Decatur and the *Fulton* finally pulled a train of freight and pleasure cars over the entire forty-three miles of gently undulating terrain. Dignitaries, dressed in their finest regalia, crowded into the passenger cars and waved to the cheering throngs that lined the track.[19] The Tuscumbia, Courtland & Decatur

Railroad received immediate public acceptance, but the excitement and unbridled enthusiasm for the iron horse in Alabama would prove to be short-lived.

When Hubbard, Sherrod, and Deshler began to grapple with the overwhelming volume of commodity and merchandise traffic awaiting shipment at the depots, they found that the company was critically short of motive power and freight cars. Deshler estimated that fifty to seventy-five cars were needed to handle all the freight that had piled up at Courtland, but only fifteen lumber cars and three pleasure cars were listed on the company's roster of rolling stock. Additional cars and locomotives had been ordered, but since they were still in transit over fretfully slow water routes, Deshler had to improvise as best he could until they arrived. "Owing to the disappointments in motive power we were in 1835 compelled to resort to the only alternative left to us—horses to do the business," the engineer reported, "and in the use of this kind of power the want of cars was much more seriously felt owing to the limited speed of horses. Besides this, owing to the fact that the roadbed was so newly completed, as the winter set in and the horse path not being graveled, the path soon became almost impassable."

Deshler breathed a sigh of relief when a secondhand locomotive, purchased from the Philadelphia, Germantown & Norristown Railroad, was delivered in February 1835. Unfortunately, this engine was too heavy to negotiate the road's light rail, so it was relegated to stationary duty in the machine shop while the horses continued to labor over the muddy roadway. It was midsummer before the next locomotive, the *Comet,* arrived from the West Point Foundry. By then the Tuscumbia, Courtland & Decatur had also obtained enough cars to efficiently handle the anticipated traffic, and Sherrod looked optimistically to the future. "From all reports of the different departments we may safely predict the future prosperity of the company," he sanguinely asserted.[20]

But, as company officials are wont to do, the enthusiastic Sherrod overstated the road's prospects for success. Mechanical difficulties kept the locomotives in the repair shop almost as much as they were on the road, and delay after delay eventually wiped out public confidence. Red ink soon flowed, and the TC&D would struggle unprofitably into an increasingly dim and uncertain future.

What was it like to witness this pioneering railroad in operation?

Mr. S. R. Burford, who lived near the track in Lawrence County, offers his recollections.

> I remember riding on the cars one time in 1836 with my mother, from our home to Courtland and return, and seeing them many times running through our farm, the track being only about two hundred yards north of our house. The cars were not as large as an average street car and had no platform at the end. There was only one step about one foot above the ground for getting in and out. The wheels were low and I suppose there were not springs, as the car bed was low down. . . .
>
> In 1849 or 1850 my father sent me to LaGrange College, and I traveled over the road from Tuscumbia to Leighton (ten miles). Then passenger trains had ceased to run. I suppose that they did not pay. Something like an old fashioned coach body, which would carry about a dozen passengers, with a large boot behind for trunks, and bannistered overhead for lighter baggage, was used upon car trucks.
>
> Two horses worked, one in front of the other, constituting the motive power. When all was ready, the agent who collected the fares took a pry on a hind wheel with a crowbar, thus assisting the horses to start, and pretty soon they were in a lope between the stringers; which gait they kept up to Leighton, where fresh horses took their places, other changes being made on to Decatur.[21]

Track problems incessantly plagued the fledgling road. Not only was the rail too light to adequately support the locomotives, but the iron straps frequently worked loose and curled up at the ends, forming what were called "snakeheads." Engine drivers kept a sharp vigil for snakeheads and when one was seen, the train stopped to let passengers and crew scramble down to clamp the rail back in place.[22]

Although failing financially, the TC&D made significant contributions to railway science, and instituted a number of "firsts." Among these was a fundamental improvement in locomotive design. The second locomotive delivered to the TC&D, the *Pennsylvania,* had four wheels of equal size, but only two of them were powered (a 2-2-0 wheel arrangement).[23] In 1836 David Deshler offered an innovative proposal regarding this engine. He suggested "putting her on eight wheels, carrying the front part on four small wheels, and using four adhesion or driving wheels, by means of outside cranks and connections." Deshler noted that his modification "causes her to take the curves much better."[24] Little did he realize that this original idea would be adopted by railroads throughout the world. Outside cranks and rods would become standard features of future steam engines; and the 4-4-0 wheel arrangement evolved as the most widely used configuration in nineteenth-century locomotive design.

Another Deshler innovation was the sand dome. Here is his description of how it was used to overcome adhesion problems of the *Triumph,* the fourth and final engine to be added to the company's locomotive roster. "Being placed on six wheels she is very easy on the road, but the want of sufficient adhesion in slippery weather, is frequently felt through her driving wheels, although an apparatus is attached by means of which part of the weight of the tender is brought to bear on the driving wheels. A plan to obviate the want of adhesion is being worked out and a simple apparatus will likely remove this difficulty. My plan is to let a sort of hopper be arranged just forward of the driving wheels and above the frame of the engine from which a tube will be projected downward to within a small distance of the rail. The hopper will feed dry sand through the tube, a cock will control the stream of sand. Water may be used to the same advantage."[25] This invention was a resounding success, and the sand dome became another standard feature of future locomotives—yet another manifestation of Deshler's remarkable creativity, vision, and pioneering spirit.

Although Deshler, Hubbard, and Sherrod faithfully persevered, none of these men would achieve their ambitious long-term goals. This trio of visionaries hoped to extend the TC&D to Memphis and make it a vital link in a great integrated railway system connecting the eastern seaboard with the Mississippi River. But their dreams crumbled with the economic depression of 1837.[26]

Hubbard and Sherrod desperately fought for the line's survival and personally offered financial support when money could not be raised elsewhere. Indeed, at the depths of the depression, the Tuscumbia, Courtland and Decatur Railroad found few other sponsors.[27] Even the state of Alabama was unsympathetic and demanded repayment of a bond issue. Sherrod answered this call by writing a personal check for $300,000. Ultimately, the venture cost Hubbard and Sherrod a large portion of their personal fortunes.[28] In 1847 the Tuscumbia, Courtland & Decatur Railroad was sold to a group of investors who reorganized it as the Tennessee Valley Railroad, and in a sad irony, the Memphis & Charleston Railroad would soon build from Memphis to Tuscumbia, and by absorbing and extending the Tennessee Valley Railroad, bring the Tuscumbia trio's grand vision to fruition by connecting the Mississippi River with the Atlantic Ocean.[29]

2

PIONEER
POLLARD

A MANIA FOR RAILROADS arose across America in the early 1830s, and state governments throughout the country enthusiastically supported their development. Railroad fever also pervaded Alabama, and many communities demanded rail connections that would stimulate economic development. Alabamians generally acknowledged that projects of such magnitude could not be financed solely with private capital, and considerable sentiment existed favoring the use of state, federal, and county taxes to supplement investment provided by wealthy planters. In antebellum Alabama, unlike other states, however, broad-based support for public aid to railroads never gained a firm footing.

Although the state legislature granted more than twenty-five charters to railroad companies in the 1830s, most of them never got beyond the planning stages, and the panic of 1837 effectively brought an end to all of them.[1] The panic also reversed the trend toward public assistance to railroads. Economic recovery slowly brought renewed enthusiasm for the iron horse, but popular support for governmental aid in building railroads was greatly diminished. The trauma produced by the failure of the State Bank and concomitant fear of higher taxes caused Alabamians to be divided on the question of state aid to railroads for many years to come.[2]

Thus, planters were left virtually to their own resources as they sought to break steamboat company monopoly of the cotton trade and reduce their transportation costs. If any governmental support were to be secured, it would probably come from the federal government in the form of the Two and Three Percent Funds. When Alabama became a state, Uncle Sam set aside five percent of the proceeds from the sale of federal land within her boundaries to be used for internal improvements. Two percent of the money was to be used for construction of roads leading into adjoining states while the other three percent was to be used for intrastate roads. Hence, these appropriations became known as the Two Percent and Three Percent Funds. But antebellum conservatism would make access to even these relatively small funds difficult at best, and until the 1850s most of the capital for the state's railroad ventures continued to come from wealthy individuals.[3]

A group of such men from Montgomery and Mobile initiated Alabama's second railroad as they sought to tap the resources of Georgia and the eastern seaboard. Led by the wealthy fifty-three-year-old planter Abner McGehee, they organized the Montgomery Railroad Company, which was chartered on January 20, 1832, to lay track through the sandy, infertile pine barrens of east Alabama and connect Montgomery with the navigable portion of the Chattahoochee River opposite Columbus, Georgia.[4] McGehee, descended from seventeenth-century Virginians, was no stranger to investments. A well-educated man, he had used his business acumen to become a successful planter, tanner, and trader.[5] Little was accomplished under his original charter, however, and on January 15, 1834, another charter was granted to McGehee and his associates for the construction of a line from Montgomery to West Point, Georgia. This charter was taken out by essentially the same group of promoters, with the important addition of Charles T. Pollard, another affluent Montgomery planter.[6]

Pollard, born in Virginia in 1805, was also of pioneer stock. Like McGehee, his ancestors were among the first settlers of Virginia. Pollard's grandfather had achieved fame as a scout in Aaron Burr's regiment during the Revolutionary War, having been captured no less than three times, and escaping in each instance through his innate ingenuity and strength. As a young man Charles Pollard was ambitious and attained a good reputation as a bookkeeper, but admitted that his abilities were seldom challenged as he settled into a life of "ease and indulgence" that was "the way with your Virginians of good family." Therefore, the restlessly energetic Pollard was quick to accept an invitation to accompany his uncle to South Carolina, where he hoped to begin a new life and accumulate a fortune. Pollard headed south in 1824, and a few years later he ventured into Alabama.[7] When he settled in the boisterous frontier town of Montgomery the iron horse was just another peculiar new invention, but Pollard instinctively knew that the railroad could make Montgomery the focal point of southern commerce and welcomed the opportunity to become a manager of the Montgomery Railroad. Pollard was destined to be instrumental in assuring the survival and ultimate success of this company, and although faced with adversities that would have discouraged most, he tenaciously pressed forward a vision that eventually defined the map of railway development in Alabama.

Before the Montgomery Railroad was conceived, merchandise bound for Montgomery was loaded onto horses and wagons at Charleston or Savannah and freighted through the Creek Indian Nation. The roads through this forbidding wilderness, if they could be labeled as such, were in a desperate state of disrepair, and the Indians exacted exorbitant tolls.[8]

Left: Charles T. Pollard (portrait ca. 1840s). Right: *Abner McGehee (portrait ca. 1830s). (Courtesy of the Alabama Department of Archives and History, Montgomery Alabama)*

The Montgomery Railroad was designed to bring this Eastern trade efficiently to Montgomery and, via the Alabama River, to the wharves of Mobile. A Georgia railroad was also proposed to connect the Tennessee River with the Chattahoochee. If this happened, or if a branch of the Montgomery Railroad could be built to the Tennessee River, substantial Tennessee Valley commerce could also be directed over this route to Mobile.[9]

Until the advent of the railroad, trade between north and south Alabama had been restrained by mountain ranges that thrust into the heart of the state. Considerable stretches of the river routes through these mountains were unnavigable, and trade was only possible using muddy turnpikes that wound tortuously through the rugged landscape. The Tennessee Valley was effectively cut off from Alabama's seaport, and consequently its commerce was deflected to New Orleans. This division not only inhibited Alabama's economic development but caused the two regions to be culturally isolated and politically polarized. A direct rail link serving the common interests of both north and south Alabama would not only facilitate trade but also help dissipate much of the sectionalism that the physical separation had caused.[10] Thus, the railroad promised to unify the state by bringing Tennessee Valley commerce to Montgomery and Mobile. Such a connection would greatly enhance Mobile's competitive position as a major Gulf seaport, and Mobile investors subscribed to almost half of the Montgomery Railroad stock when it was offered to the public in October 1835.

The Montgomery Railroad was to be constructed in the typical manner, using wooden stringers capped with strap iron. The strap iron measured 2 3/16 inches in width and 5/8 inches in thickness, just slightly larger dimensions than those found on the Tuscumbia, Courtland & Decatur Railroad.[11] The original investors had paid in one dollar for each of the 100,000 shares subscribed, allowing grading of the line to begin in February 1836.

The standard practice in financing early railroads was to raise equity capital in installments, and under the Montgomery Railroad's charter, shareholders were to be assessed for construction costs as they progressed. Failure to pay an assessment could result in the forfeiture of stock. In March 1836 the Montgomery Railroad stockholders were called upon to invest another installment of five dollars per share.[12]

At this time, however, trouble was brewing in "New Alabama," the Indian lands through which the proposed route was projected to run. When the second Creek Indian War erupted in 1836, alarm spread among the shareholders, and their confidence in the company's prospects was shaken. For this and other reasons, the anxious stockholders hesitated in making further investment in the enterprise. Mobilians were especially reluctant to make their installments, as they were preoccupied with other railways they were projecting to the west.

Chief Engineer A. A. Dexter urged continued support for the project when he sent a reassuring letter to the Mobile shareholders on June 3, 1836. "As the present situation of this work is not generally understood in this city, and some fears appear to be entertained lest the progress of the operation shall be interrupted by the Indian War, I presume that a few facts regarding the undertaking will be acceptable to you at this time," he wrote. "We have now an entire force of about one hundred hands engaged upon the work; a portion near Montgomery and the balance in two parties, seven and twelve miles above Line Creek. As the Indians are friendly in this part of the Nation, we apprehend no interruption to our operations in this quarter." As proof that the project was advancing as scheduled, Dexter alluded to a $20,000 expenditure the contractors had made to purchase more slave labor. "As soon as crops are laid by they expect to withdraw from their plantations and put upon their contracts an additional force of about one hundred hands," the engineer warranted. He went on to enumerate many reasons to expect a favorable return on an investment in the Montgomery Railroad. In addition to a potentially huge freight business, Dexter optimistically surmised that the federal government would almost certainly award the new road a lucrative mail contract.

While considering Dexter's appeal, Mobile investors soon found another compelling reason to come to the aid of the Montgomery Railroad. A keen rivalry existed between Mobile and Pensacola as each aspired to be the leading Gulf seaport, and warnings of a move by Pensacola to appropriate the benefits of the Montgomery Railroad to herself appeared in Mobile newspapers. The Columbus & Pensacola Company reportedly intended to buy all of Mobile's forfeited stock and obtain a charter allowing the road to be rerouted to Pensacola.[13]

But neither Dexter's assurances nor the threats from Pensacola could regain the support of the Mobile shareholders, and calls for their installments continued to go unheeded. Management chose not to force forfeiture, however, hoping that the stockholders would shortly regain their faith in the company and come forward with their installments. The delinquent shareholders were indulged until March 1837, when another installment fell due. By then, management's forbearance had reached its limit and payment was demanded. The timing could not have been worse. The panic of 1837 soon struck, bringing with it economic depression and a complete loss of confidence in the enterprise. Consequently, all of the Mobile stock and almost one third of the Montgomery stock was forfeited.

Through the diligent efforts of Colonel Pollard, the company survived until 1839, when it became evident that the road could not be finished without governmental aid. Almost miraculously, Pollard had doubled subscriptions to the company's stock, but much more money would be needed. Encouraged by Pollard, the remaining shareholders gradually regained confidence in the project, and by 1839 they stood ready courageously to support their company. When the stockholders asked the state legislature to grant a loan guarantee of $900,000, they offered to secure it not only with a mortgage on the railroad but by the pledge of up to $1,200,000 of their own personal real estate as well. Even with such liberal security and the bold expression of the owner's confidence it represented, the legislature refused to commit state funds.

Though disappointed in their failure to obtain state aid, management felt that financing could be arranged if the company could show some tangible results demonstrating the effectiveness of the railroad. With a short section of track ready for operation, the company purchased its first locomotive in July 1839 and promised that this part of the line would soon be opened to the public.[14] The locomotive had four leading wheels and two driven wheels (a 4-2-0 type), and was named *Abner McGehee* in honor of the road's founder.[15] To finance a demonstration, the railroad was mortgaged for $50,000 on October 9, 1839. The promoters hoped that this small section of line would provide enough revenue to finance the building of another small section. In this manner, the entire line might be completed using the profits from continuing operations.[16]

After careful preparation, a group of invited dignitaries boarded the train at Montgomery on June 6, 1840, for the inaugural twelve-mile trip of the Montgomery Railroad. The train stopped seven miles from Montgomery, where the public had gathered for a company-sponsored dinner and grand-opening celebration.[17] A second 4-2-0 type locomotive, the *West Point,* was put on the road in September, and by November a daily mixed train was carrying freight and passengers thirty-three and one-half miles between Montgomery and Franklin.[18] The schedule called for the train to leave Montgomery at 8:00 A.M. and return at 2:00 P.M., but for various reasons, including accidents, ill workmen, and mechanical problems, the line seldom met this schedule. At times, horses had to be substituted for malfunctioning locomotives.[19]

These operating difficulties did not inspire public confidence, and the amount of revenue generated by the railroad proved insufficient to cover operating costs. Abner McGehee tried to keep the line afloat by leasing it in 1842, but revenues continued to lag expenses, and soon the company could not meet its loan obligations. Finally, on July 5, 1842, the railroad was auctioned under mortgage foreclosure.

Little change in management resulted from the sale. Pollard, McGehee, and other former owners simply purchased the company and changed its name to the Montgomery & West Point Railroad Company. This reorganization was a turning point for the struggling road, however. A major victory was about to be achieved in the battle for vital state aid.[20]

Even though much sympathy could be found in the Alabama legislature for aid to the railroad, there was still too much opposition to the use of state funds to push through a direct loan. Instead, the legislature authorized a loan from the federally sanctioned Two Percent Fund. The charter was transferred to the Montgomery & West Point Railroad on February 13, 1843, and the next day the legislature granted a loan of $120,000 from the Two Percent Fund. The loan was secured by a mortgage on the railroad and by the personal bonds of Pollard and the other directors.[21]

In 1845, the company obtained another loan from the Two Percent fund for almost $117,000. This time, many of the directors succumbed to the state's onerous demands for personal security and were forced to sell their interest in the railroad to wealthier colleagues. This left only Pollard, McGehee, and three others as the sole remaining stockholders who were able to secure the loan by mortgaging their personal property. A large part of this loan, in accord with standard antebellum business practice, was used to purchase slaves. Pollard's analytical tone in his 1850 report to shareholders betrayed a starkly pragmatic attitude toward the use of chattel labor. "Upon the receipt of this money," Pollard stated, "vigorous measures were adopted to push forward the work; and, for the purpose of doing so in the most economical manner, the Board concluded to invest a portion of the loan in negroes. An agent was forthwith dispatched to Virginia, who purchased eighty-four negroes, at a total cost of $42,176.20. With these negroes, for several years, the Company had great trouble. At one time as many as ten had run off. Some were found in Kentucky, some in Indiana, some in the mountains of Georgia, and two have never been heard from. But of this purchase there still remains a valuable force of 53 men, 7 women, and 11 children."[22]

These slaves were put to work immediately, and interest in the road mounted as it made slow but steady progress. Newsmen regularly visited the right-of-way in order to chronicle the line's advance, and in April 1847 one of these correspondents reported that the road had been opened to Notasulga, approximately forty-nine miles east of Montgomery, and was "doing a profitable business which is steadily increasing every year." The reporter also observed "a very handsome passenger car, with very convenient accommodations, and private apartments for ladies at each end," and noted that another passenger car had been ordered from Boston, "the finish and furniture of which will be superior in style to any used here before."[23]

On July 8 the scribe returned to the construction camp and found that another four and a half miles of track had been spiked into place. This brought the road to within five miles of Auburn, and it was estimated that the line would reach this little village by September 1, just in time for the cotton season. With nicely rising profits, the company relayed the happy tidings that "new cars are in preparation for the coming season, and built with especial eye to the convenience and comfort of the passengers."[24]

One would hope that these cars were an improvement over the spartan coaches that carried the famous English geologist, Sir Charles Lyell, over this road in 1846. Rumors that vast mineral resources lay in Alabama's hills had prompted Lyell to come to the state to investigate, and he gave the following account of an eventful ride over the Montgomery & West Point Railroad:

> The railway cars between Chehaw and Montgomery consisted, like those in the North, of a long apartment, with cross benches and a middle passage. There were many travelers, and among them one rustic, evidently in liquor, who put both of his feet on one of the cushioned benches, and began to sing. The conductor told him to put his feet down, and afterwards, on his repeating the offense, lifted them off. On his doing it a third time, the train was ordered to stop, and the man was told, in a peremptory tone, to get out immediately. . . . We left him seated on the ground, many miles from any habitation, and there was no prospect of another train passing for many a long hour. . . . Although we had now penetrated into regions where this school master had not been much abroad, we observed that the railway cars are every where attended by news boys, who in some places, are carried on a whole stage, walking up and down "the middle aisle" of the long car. Usually, however, at each station, they, and others who sell apples and bisquits, may be seen calculating the exact speed at which it is safe to jump off, and taking, with the utmost coolness, a few cents in change a moment before they know that the rate acquired by the train will be dangerous. I never witnessed an accident, but as the locomotive usually runs only fifteen miles an hour, and is some time before it reaches half that pace, the urchins are not hurried as they would be in England.[25]

As planned, the road's receipts increased with every mile of track that was opened. Revenues from 1847 through 1851 were, respectively: $55,787.97, $79,706.83, $95,665.90, $123,781.61, and $140,057.09.[26] Construction was completed to West Point on April 28, 1851, where a 50-by-150-foot freight depot was built to accommodate the great volume of freight that was anticipated to flow over the Montgomery & West Point Railroad after it reached the Chattahoochee River. A passenger station at West Point was delayed pending completion of the connecting Atlanta & LaGrange Railroad. When this railroad reached West Point, a depot serving the mutual

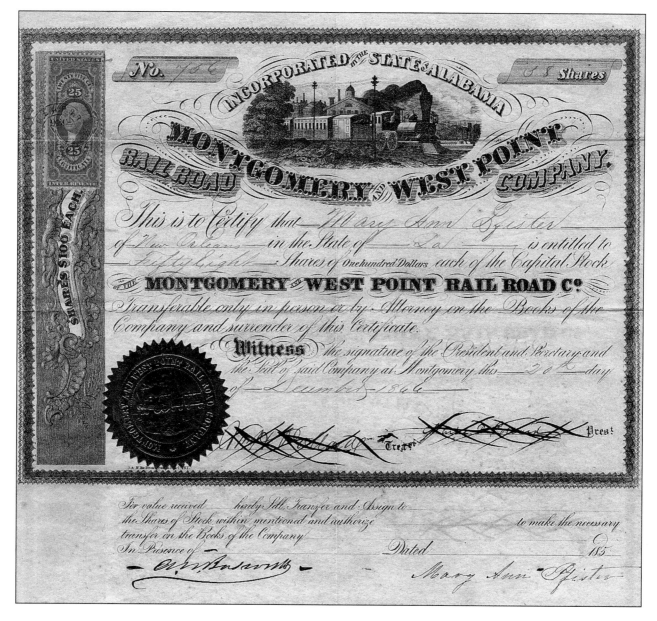

needs of both companies was to be erected as a joint venture. In 1854 a twenty-nine-mile branch leading from Opelika to the west bank of the Chattahoochee River near Columbus, Georgia, was completed. A bridge across the river was built the following year giving access to Columbus.[27] By 1857 only Pollard and William Taylor remained of the original promoters, but under their guidance the enterprise kept making good progress. The road suffered during the severe winter of 1856, and more bonds had to be issued to put it in good order, but the company continued to thrive, and intermittent dividends were paid.[28] On the eve of the Civil War, every car on the Montgomery & West Point had been built in the railroad's own shops, where an innovative spirit of experimentation produced some rather distinctive equipment. Many of the cars manufactured at these shops used rubber springs, and a unique "dumping car" was said to function "by cast iron arc-dumping wholeload."[29] The joint passenger station, with dimensions of 75 by 200 feet, was finally erected at West Point in 1857–58.

In 1860 the future appeared bright. The company earned a net income of $195,960.54 and paid a pair of three-percent dividends as well as a stock dividend of five percent. But Charles T. Pollard's dreams extended beyond the Montgomery & West Point Railroad. He envisioned a railway hub at Montgomery with tracks radiating outward to connect with the great main lines of the country, and he would not rest until he achieved that goal.[30]

While Pollard toiled in the pine barrens and Indian Territory of east Alabama, another railroad enterprise was underway at the opposite end of the state, where trackwork on the Alabama & Mississippi Rivers Railroad was crawling slowly between Selma and Uniontown en route to Meridian, Mississippi. This railroad had been planned since 1841, when money from the Two and Three Percent Funds was reserved to build a line connecting Cahawba, the former state capital, with Uniontown. It was chartered on February 7, 1850, with an authorized capital stock of $1,000,000. The original charter was amended in 1852, changing the eastern terminus to Selma and awarding a right-of-way reaching to the Mississippi state line. The legislature further promised a loan of $100,000 from the Two Percent Fund whenever thirty miles of track was completed. This proved to be wishful thinking, however, and two years later the legislature scaled back its conditions and offered the money if only fourteen miles could be completed.[31]

Pollard was determined to extend his tracks from Montgomery to Selma, where a connection with the Alabama & Mississippi Rivers Railroad would provide a continuous line across the state. The first step to consummate this plan was taken on February 16, 1854, when the Montgomery & West Point Railroad was consolidated with the proposed Selma extension to form a new company under Pollard's management called the Western Rail Road Company of Alabama. Pollard was joined as an incorporator by Bolling Hall, Daniel Pratt, and John Whiting, all of whom were to be associated with other efforts to develop a viable system of railways in Alabama.[32]

Daniel Pratt, born in New Hampshire in 1799, had already achieved worldwide fame as an inventor. He founded the town of Prattville on the Alabama River just outside Montgomery, where he established the largest gin factory of its kind in the world. In a supreme tribute to his inventive genius, his ginning process was used everywhere cotton was grown throughout the world. In Pratt's case, fortune followed fame, and he was counted among the richest men in the state.[33]

Pratt's wealth and renown notwithstanding, work was not started on the Western Rail Road of Alabama within the time limits imposed by the charter, and the charter was forfeited. But Pollard, Hall, Pratt, and Whiting were undeterred. On February 23, 1860, the Western Rail Road Company was rechartered. This time, Pollard enlisted the assistance of the Central Railroad and Banking Company of Georgia, and the line from Selma to Montgomery was soon surveyed.[34]

As war loomed, the Alabama legislature recognized the strategic importance of this route across the center of the state and redirected a portion of the Two Percent Fund to aid in the construction of the Alabama & Mississippi Rivers Railroad. The act appropriating this money stipulated that the loan would become an outright gift if the line were completed to Meridian by 1864. Regardless, if the money had to be paid back, it would be interest free. These incentives were negated by the Civil War, however, and hostilities erupted before significant progress could be made on the trans-Alabama project. This vital route was left as a concern of high priority for Confederate government strategists.[35]

Meanwhile, Pollard was having greater success with a southern route. As the Montgomery & West Point Railroad neared completion, Pollard turned his attention to a rail connection with the Gulf. Such a road had been contemplated since 1836, when the Alabama & City of Montgomery Railroad Company was chartered to build a line from Montgomery to Pensacola. This pioneer company fell victim to the panic of 1837, but was renewed in 1850 as the Alabama & Florida Railroad Company.[36] Actually, two organizations assumed this name, one incorporated in Alabama and the other in Florida. Since the entrenched southern precept of states' rights required that each state should bear the responsibility for improvements within its own borders, the construction crews of the Alabama company were to work southward to meet the advancing Florida company at the state line. Neither company accomplished anything of note, however, until Pollard and his chief engineer, Colonel Samuel G. Jones, became interested in the project.

Jones, a well-respected engineer of national stature, joined the Montgomery & West Point in 1850 and soon became an enthusiastic champion of the Alabama & Florida Railroad. Like Pollard, he was a determined man who could seize opportunities and make the most of them. Both men recognized the vast potential the proposed railroad could unlock as it passed through the fertile agricultural land and virgin forests south of Montgomery. Cotton culture was already taking hold in this productive region known (because of its dark, fertile soil) as the Black Belt, but the riverboat landings of the Alabama River were as much as 150 miles away from these new plantations. A reliable railway was needed to move the cotton. Also, as the final link in a railway chain from the Atlantic to the Gulf, the road would bypass the caprice of the river and speed thru traffic between the two shores.[37]

Pollard and Jones campaigned to convince the directors of the Montgomery & West Point to lend assistance to the Alabama & Florida Railroad, and by 1853 they had succeeded. Directors of the Montgomery & West Point Railroad agreed to provide financial support through stock subscriptions and bond endorsements. On May 3, 1853, a stockholder's meeting was held at the Exchange Hotel in Montgomery. At this meeting, Col. Thomas J. Judge was elected president and Samuel Jones was appointed chief engineer of the rejuvenated Alabama & Florida Railroad Company.[38]

Samuel Jones, a Virginian by birth, was a wise and pious man and a good judge of talent. Many of his employees had gone on to be famous railroaders, including Samuel Spencer, who became the highly respected first president of the Southern Railway System. Spencer had served as a surveying rodman under Jones's direction when both men were employed on the Memphis & Charleston Railroad.[39] Jones continued to exercise sagacity in his hiring practices when he gave the responsibility for locating the route of the Alabama & Florida Railroad to his protégé, John Turner Milner, a young Montgomery & West Point engineer.

Milner was talented and experienced. Born in Pike County, Georgia, in 1826, he had worked for his father, a railroad contractor, since he was twelve years of age. He had also served a number of years on Georgia railroads under the supervision of the distinguished civil engineer George Hazelhurst. In 1842, Milner drove an ox team to California, where he was appointed city surveyor for the state's capital city, San Jose. Ten years later he rejoined his father, who was now employed with the Montgomery & West Point Railroad.[40]

Milner's survey was influenced greatly by a notable supporter of the road, Frank Gilmer. Frank Gilmer, who could trace his lineage to prominent lawyers and physicians of Scotland and London, moved with his family to Kentucky in 1813, when he was three years old. Abner McGehee had married Gilmer's aunt, and when Frank was twenty years old, McGehee urged him to accept a position as clerk in his store at Hayneville, near Montgomery. Young Frank accepted McGehee's offer and set out on horseback for Alabama. At Hayneville, he worked hard, both in the store and as an instructor at the local school. Within a year, Gilmer had bought the business, and began developing it into an immensely profitable enterprise. Soon, Gilmer was able to purchase a partnership in Charles T. Pollard's cotton warehouse. Gilmer skillfully cultivated his business interests, continued to prosper, and invested in some large plantations in the Black Belt.[41] Naturally, he wanted the Alabama & Florida Railroad to be located near his plantations, so he exerted his influence to have the line projected to Fort Deposit and Greenville, rather than by the more direct and level route through Hayneville that was favored by Pollard and Jones.[42]

But Gilmer's avarice belied nobler ambitions. When Gilmer rode to Montgomery from Kentucky in 1830, he was fascinated by the red dust and rock he encountered in Alabama's mountains. He filled his saddlebag with some samples and later found the curious material to be iron ore. Gilmer resolved to exploit this mineral resource someday, and this dream still burned brightly when he met John T. Milner. The two men eventually were to be instrumental in the conquest of Alabama's vast mineral wealth, and both remained deeply committed to the state's railroads throughout their lives.[43]

Pollard soon became president of the Alabama & Florida Railroad and immediately summoned every available resource to finance the company. Montgomery landowners were urged to invest in the road, and in 1854 they empowered the city of Montgomery to subscribe to $500,000 in stock, but no money was ever appropriated to allow the transaction to be consummated.[44]

Meanwhile, momentous legislation was being enacted in Washington. With the support of Alabama congressmen, an act was passed allowing federal land grants to railroad companies. The Alabama & Florida Railroad was routed through undeveloped land owned by the U.S. government, and under the terms of the new law, was eligible to receive alternate sections of land that could be sold to finance construction. In December 1857 the Alabama & Florida Railroad secured its land grant, amounting to nearly 400,000 acres.[45]

Both the *Montgomery & West Point* and the *Alabama & Florida* railroads were operational by 1861, and efforts were being made to construct a continuous rail line from Montgomery to the Mississippi River.

With the land grant in hand, work began in earnest. Under Jones's personal supervision, the road pressed relentlessly southward, and the persistence of Pollard and Jones was resoundingly rewarded with every spike driven. In 1861, as work crews in Alabama converged upon the gandy dancers working their way north from Pensacola, a suitable site for building a town was selected just inside the Alabama boundary. This junction point was called Pollard, in honor of the road's indefatigable president.[46] In November, a locomotive appropriately named the *Perseverance*[47] triumphantly rolled over the tracks of the first continuous rail line between the Atlantic and Gulf. The route surveyed by John T. Milner was finished, but Milner was just beginning to make his mark in Alabama.

3

LAND
GRANTS

THE LAND GRANT that assured the success of Pollard's Alabama &
Florida Railroad stemmed from the original land grant for railroad
construction obtained jointly by the Mobile & Ohio and Illinois Central Railroads. The Mobile & Ohio was the brainchild of M. J. D.
Baldwyn of Mobile, who in the 1830s saw his city's status as a commercial center steadily erode while New Orleans monopolized the growing midwestern commerce brought by the Mississippi River. But steamboats to New Orleans were slow, inefficient, and vulnerable to river
hazards that raised insurance rates, and Baldwyn was confident that
trains could compete effectively with the Mississippi steamers by cheaply
channeling midwestern traffic to Mobile's fine harbor. Thus, he hoped
to restore Mobile's prosperity by building a rail artery to America's
heartland. Moreover, Baldwyn visualized an easy airline route through
the relatively level terrain of Mississippi, Tennessee, and Kentucky that
could be put through to the confluence of the Mississippi and Ohio
rivers at comparatively modest cost.

Baldwyn first advanced his grand scheme in 1838, but almost ten
years of diligent effort was required before he garnered enough support
to take action. A plan of such great scope could only be implemented
through the coordinated mobilization of a complex of political and
economic factors. These factors coalesced in 1848, when the Mobile &
Ohio Railroad was chartered in the states of Alabama, Mississippi, Tennessee and Kentucky. Private capital was supplemented by state and
municipal aid as the state of Tennessee and the city of Mobile each
subscribed to $600,000 in Mobile & Ohio Railroad stock. A
groundswell of public sponsorship soon buoyed the project, and it was
ultimately embraced by the federal government.[1]

The U.S. government owned millions of acres of unimproved land along the Mobile & Ohio Railroad's proposed route through Alabama and Mississippi. Even though it had been offered for sale for many years, this land remained sparsely settled because of its isolation. But the railroad promised to end this isolation, bring an influx of settlers, and raise the value of all these tracts of public land. Therefore, the federal government stood to reap a huge windfall at the expense of localities that used their own tax revenue and private capital to finance the Mobile & Ohio Railroad. This was deemed unfair by many Alabamians, especially the more extreme advocates of states' rights. They already resented federal ownership of property within the state and demanded concessions benefiting local citizens.[2]

In 1848, the state legislature agreed that it was time for the federal government to lend a hand with internal improvements, and legislators sent an appeal to the U.S. Congress calling for a land grant for the Mobile & Ohio Railroad. The legislators emphasized that the M&O would provide an indispensable service by bringing highly sought products of the West Indies to the midwestern farmer's door while supplying the South with his staple commodities at low cost. In addition, the Alabama lawmakers reminded Congress that the road "would be of inconceivable importance, enabling the Government at short notice and at comparatively small cost in time of war, to transport a large force to the defense of any assailable point on the Gulf coast." According to the Alabamians, the U.S. government could reap all these benefits by simply awarding the M&O with the alternate sections of federal land along its route, as they were requesting.[3]

Concurrently, Senator Stephen A. Douglas of Illinois was fighting for a similar land grant in aid of a railroad joining the northern and southern parts of his state. In 1849 he placed a bill before the U.S. Congress seeking a land grant for this line, the predecessor of the Illinois Central Railroad. Alabama and Mississippi legislators pledged to the M&O opposed the bill, however, and concurred with the majority in the House of Representatives in voting down the competing proposal. Douglas was determined to change their minds and went to Mobile to solicit support for an even more sweeping land-grant measure. He persuaded the representatives to join him in the quest for simultaneous land grants for both roads and returned to Washington assured of the assenting votes of the Alabama and Mississippi delegations. During the next congressional session, Douglas and Alabama senator William R. King, now allies instead of adversaries, cosponsored a new piece of legislation that sought aid for both the Illinois Central and the Mobile & Ohio. Through skillful political maneuvering, the pair pushed this legislation through and inaugurated federal land grants for railroads.[4] This legislative success greatly enhanced King's résumé, and he went on to become vice president of the United States.

The landmark law provided public land in Alabama and Mississippi for the construction of a railroad connecting Mobile with the Illinois Central Railroad at Cairo, Illinois. Alternate sections of unsold federal land six miles on either side of the ceded right-of-way were given in trust to each state, and any of these tracts could be sold to finance the M&O. If all sections within six miles had already been sold, the law further stipulated that land could be appropriated up to nine miles away from the road. The total land grant to the Mobile & Ohio within Alabama was 419,528.44 acres.[5]

Columbus, Kentucky, was selected as the northern terminus of the M&O because this site could be conveniently reached by steamer from both Cairo and St. Louis. Construction began at Mobile on February 1, 1852, with two locomotives immediately in service, the *Mobile* and the *Chicago*.[6] By July 23 a regular schedule was being run between Mobile and Citronelle, Alabama. Meanwhile, the northern section of the road was being built southward from Columbus.[7]

The M&O was destined to enjoy a public and private munificence unknown to any other railroad venture within the state. On February 17, 1854, a rare act aiding the Mobile & Ohio was written into Alabama law when the state authorized a two-year loan to the M&O amounting to $400,000, which was to be secured by a mortgage on the road or by personal property, or both, as the governor saw fit. With relatively few money worries, the Mobile & Ohio pressed forward and in April 1861 the two ends of the line were joined at Corinth, Mississippi, to complete the longest railroad under a single charter in the country. Mobile now had the distinction of being the only Gulf port with a direct rail connection to the Midwest.[8]

But the work had not been without difficulty. The M&O had been resisted in the state of Mississippi by supporters of a competing road from New Orleans, and had incurred "violent opposition" from citizens of Memphis because it had bypassed that city. As stated in a subsequent annual report, "Towns and villages, a short distance from the track of the road, put themselves in hostility to it because it did not change its location and send its cars directly to their doors." Nevertheless, "by energy and perseverance," an M&O official wrote, "when the last rail was laid in the track, the company had a road of the first class, built in the most substantial manner with rails and fastenings and other material unsurpassed in the United States and supplied with rolling stock amply sufficient to meet all the requirements of its extensive business."[9]

Alabama legislators continued to pursue similar land grants for transportation improvements within the state. Through a combination of land grants and outright sales, they hoped to eventually extinguish the sixteen million acres of federally owned land in Alabama. Further requests for land grants were received favorably in Washington, and more and more land was forthcoming. In 1857 Alabama accepted the donation of federal land in aid of Pollard's Alabama & Florida Railroad. Another early beneficiary of the land grant legislation was the Alabama & Tennessee River Railroad—the first legitimate attempt to unite north and south Alabama by scaling the mountains that divided the state.[10]

No internal improvement was more valued than a railroad unifying north and south Alabama, and, like the Mobile & Ohio and Alabama & Florida Railroads, the Alabama & Tennessee River Railroad was considered important enough to receive one of the first land grants in the United States. But unlike the other roads, this line did not require the land grant to ensure its survival. Its survival would be achieved through the resolute will of its promoters.

The genesis of this first serious attempt to forge a direct north-south intrastate rail connection can be traced to a railroad convention held in Knoxville, Tennessee, in 1836. This meeting was attended by a Selma resident, John Beene, who listened as the discussion focused on a railway running from Knoxville to the Gulf Coast. Beene fancied Selma as a station on this line and called a meeting in Selma to cultivate patronage for the scheme. Knoxvillians soon abandoned their plan, but the conference in Selma aroused enough interest to beget the Selma & Tennessee Railroad Company. On December 22, 1836, despite opposition from Huntsville and Mobile, the Alabama legislature chartered this company to build its road from Selma to the Tennessee River. The legislature authorized $1,200,000 of capital, and the company could elect officers and complete its organization upon the subscription of $500,000 of stock.

The required $500,000 was soon raised and the company demonstrated its resolve by appointing Alfred A. Dexter as chief engineer. Dexter was the highly regarded engineer who had guided the Montgomery & West Point Railroad through its formative years. Dexter went to work immediately, and by December 1838 he had located the line as far as Montevallo and accomplished twenty miles of grading out of Selma. By then, $602,000 of stock had been subscribed, but Dexter estimated that $1,700,000 would be required to complete the road, so the incessant search for capital continued.

Despite the recent panic, management was optimistically determined. Citizens of Huntsville and Mobile were beginning to see the advantages the road could bring to their cities, and a rally was held in Mobile at which Dexter exhorted Port City investors to support the company. Following this convocation, Dexter estimated that $100,000 in stock subscriptions could be collected from Mobilians. More money might also be obtained from the U.S. government in the form of the Two Percent Fund. The company even approached the state for assistance but was turned away by a government bent upon maintaining its intransigent opposition to railroad aid.

Although the company had worked valiantly to make the road a success during times of extreme economic hardship, the depression relentlessly deepened and so gripped the country by 1839 that the venture was doomed to failure. Neither the state nor federal government took action, and private capital dried up as investor confidence faltered. Management followed the familiar path of making optimistic assessments regarding the company's prospects while cajoling shareholders to maintain their investment. All inducements were predictably futile, however, and in 1840, management called for a temporary suspension of work. This "temporary" construction halt would last for more than ten years.[11]

As the country slowly recovered from the downturn, Selma residents regained interest in the railroad. Renamed the Alabama & Tennessee River Railroad Company, the railroad obtained a new charter in March 1848. The new company was permitted to construct a line from a point at or near Selma to some convenient point on another newly chartered railroad called the Tennessee & Coosa Railroad, which was authorized to run between its namesake rivers.

The Alabama & Tennessee River Railroad Company convened an organizational meeting at Talladega in September 1849. Montgomery did not send a delegation to this gathering, but if it had, the route might have been changed to go to Montgomery rather than Selma. When representatives chose between the two towns, a tie vote resulted. The tie was broken by the chairman, Phillip Phillips, who cast his vote in favor of Selma.

This meeting was attended by a Talladega County planter named James Mallory, who was so interested in the railroad that he kept a diary recording its progress. Mr. Mallory expresses cautious optimism in his early entries.[12]

> [September 26, 1849:] Have been in a convention for three days in Talladega Town for the purpose of fixing on some route for the construction of a railroad connecting the waters of the Tennessee with Mobile. It was ably and largely attended. The route was fixed to begin at Selma and run to Gunter's Landing.
>
> [February 25, 1850:] There is quite a railroad spirit at work amongst us, books will soon be open to test the sincerity of the people.
>
> [March 13, 1850:] The meeting was well attended at Wewakaville and about $40,000 was subscribed. I took a thousand dollars worth, think the prospects are now good for the enterprise.
>
> [May 4, 1850:] The engineers are in the neighborhood running different routes for the Alabama and Tennessee River Railroad.
>
> [May 25, 1850:] There was a railroad barbecue at Tallasahatchie today, the attendance was good and speaking interesting, the friends of the enterprise are quite sanguine, hope they may not be deceived for such a work is much needed to bring us nearer to market, but fear, it will take longer than its friends expect and the cost to be large from want of experience.[13]

Meanwhile, the Two Percent Fund had been released to the state, and on February 4, 1850, the Alabama legislature authorized payment of up to one half of the entire amount to the Alabama & Tennessee River Railroad. The next day, they approved a bill allowing the city of Selma to subscribe to A&TRRR stock. To pay for the stock, a $50,000 bond issue financed by a new property tax came to market on September 1, 1852.

Tracklaying began in 1851, and the road reached Montevallo by July 4, 1853, an event that was celebrated with a big dinner held in Shelby County. After some delay, construction resumed and the railroad reached the Coosa River in 1855.[14] Mr. Mallory described the great impact the railroad had on the community in his journal entry of December 12, 1855. "Finished picking cotton; nearly done ginning, baling and hauling to the railroad," he writes. "Making a trip every three days. Five and six bales to the load. It often took seven days to make a trip to Wetumpka with four bales." Over two more years were required to build a long bridge across the Coosa River, but on January 17, 1857, a train finally rolled across the bridge into Talladega County. There was "great rejoicing at the event," Mallory's diary discloses. "For 20 years have the people suffered for a conveyance to market. The neighborhood is making preparations for celebrating the occasion."

By 1857 planters were routinely bringing their cotton each day to the railhead, and a little over a year later, the first one hundred miles of track work was completed to a place near Alpine, where a depot was established that was suitably referred to as "100 Mile Station." This event was commemorated with another grand celebration on July 15, 1858, and once again the festivities were duly recorded in Mr. Mallory's diary. "The morning was clear and fair," he penned. "People began pouring in from every road in a living stream until acres were covered with the crowd. The cars arrived, adding between one and two thousand to the vast crowd, from eight to ten thousand being present. Addresses were made. Two silver pitchers were presented, one to Thomas Walker, President of the road, the other to our county man, Walker Reynolds, one of the directors, for their great efforts in forwarding the work. The dinner was ample. The very best order prevailed. Not a single accident occurred. Efforts are being made to extend the road."[15]

On January 20, 1858, the Alabama & Tennessee River Railroad received its land grant. The grant was of little use, however, since only a few more miles of track were laid before the Confederate rebellion intervened. A few years later, the war-ravaged company would plead with the United States Congress to have the land grants reinstated.[16]

On June 18, 1859, President Thomas A. Walker reported that he anticipated completion of the entire line to Talladega by the following September. He also confidently predicted that the road would soon reach Gadsden, since approximately thirty-three miles of the full fifty-eight-mile distance was completely graded and nearly nine more miles were partly graded. Right on schedule, the railroad entered Talladega in the fall of 1859. Talladega had supported the road through a 2.5 percent property tax, and its arrival was gratefully celebrated on October 13 with yet another barbecue.

The state authorized more financing on December 17, 1859, allowing Selma to subscribe to as much as $300,000 in stock; and on February 7, 1861, the legislature donated the total remaining amount of the

Two Percent Fund.[17] With this money available, construction continued until the outbreak of the Civil War. Tracklaying halted abruptly at Blue Mountain, and since no progress had been made on the Tennessee & Coosa Railroad, the dream of consolidating the state by rail would be delayed. But much progress had been made, and the Alabama & Tennessee River Railroad proved to be a valuable asset when the state became embroiled in war.[18]

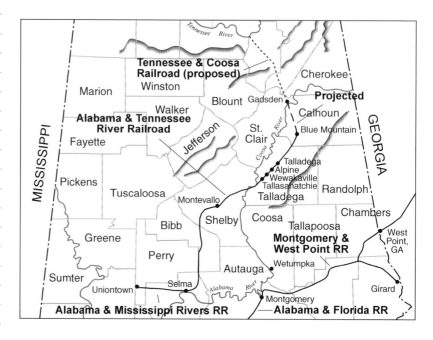

From Selma, the Alabama & Tennessee River Railroad snaked northward through Shelby County, crossed the Coosa River, and reached Talladega on the eve of the Civil War. Trackwork abruptly stopped at Blue Mountain, in Calhoun County, when the Civil War cut short plans of reaching the Tennessee River via a connection with the proposed Tennessee & Coosa Railroad.

Another major land grant was secured by the North East & South West Alabama Railroad, which was chartered in 1853 to connect Meridian, Mississippi, with Chattanooga. University of Alabama professor L. C. Garland was elected president of the NE&SW, and he immediately initiated merger negotiations with the Wills Valley Railroad. Garland hoped to use the Wills Valley Railroad, projected to thread through the mountain ranges of northeast Alabama between Chattanooga and Jefferson County, Alabama, as the eastern portion of his route.[19]

Garland did not want the North East & South West Alabama Railroad to encounter the same problems that his contemporaries had faced and vowed that the company would not lift a spade to begin construction of the road until "the means to secure its prosecution to a successful issue" had been obtained. "The ground of such assurance," said Garland, "shall not be less than subscriptions in work adequate to grade and prepare the roadbed for the ties and iron in its entire length, including subscriptions in money to this amount of six hundred thousand dollars."[20]

Within a year, the necessary $600,000 cash subscriptions were obtained. As Garland suggested, landowners along the route in Tuscaloosa, Greene, and Sumter counties were to pay for additional stock subscriptions by providing labor to build the road. The proposed labor contracts would allow these planters to pay for any or all of their stock subscriptions by assigning five slaves per mile to a designated portion of the line until the roadwork along that portion was completed. Unfortunately, cotton prices soon rose and caused the price of labor to become so high that this plan could not be implemented. So, despite this company's determination to avoid financial pitfalls, the North East & South West Alabama Railroad was overtaken by the same problems that plagued its sister railroads. Individual contractors agreed to do the work for part cash and part stock, however, and by 1859 considerable grading had been prosecuted.

The company appealed to the state's congressional representatives in Washington for a land grant and were rewarded with a grant of over 227,000 acres on June 3, 1856. Including a grant to the Wills Valley Railroad, this amount was later increased to 652,956 acres. In 1860, partly because of the influence of Charles T. Pollard, the North East & South West Alabama Railroad was also able to secure a loan of $219,000 from the Three Percent Fund. The city of Tuscaloosa contributed a $40,000 bond investment as well.

The company sorely needed all of these investments. It would not take possession of the land grant properties until 1860, and at the outbreak of the Civil War only twenty-seven miles of line from Meridian to York were complete. But most of the heavy grading had been done between York and Tuscaloosa, and the war only brought a temporary halt to this important road. It was destined eventually to rise again to play a dramatic role in Alabama's railroad story.[21]

The land grants were vital, and helped insure the survival of many Alabama railroads—not because the land was immediately sold to finance construction, but because of the credit the roads could obtain by using these assets as collateral. Altogether, the state's railroads ultimately received 2,747,479 acres in land grants—far more than any other southern state, and, except for Wisconsin and Michigan, more than any state east of the Mississippi River.[22]

4

MINERALS AND MILNER

BY 1850 THE SPECULATIVE BUBBLE of railroad promotion was expanding at a rapid rate. Seventy-three railroads were chartered in Alabama during the decade preceding the Civil War, but because of inadequate financing, only a few of them made notable progress.[1] Among these was the Memphis & Charleston Railroad, which was chartered in Alabama in 1850 to become part of the great rail route between Charleston, South Carolina, and Memphis, Tennessee. This road had strong backing from prominent entrepreneurs both outside and within Alabama. Many investors along the line contributed to its construction, including citizens of Huntsville, who invested $50,000 in the company. Under the able hand of its president, Sam Tate, the well-financed Memphis & Charleston repaired and upgraded the old Tuscumbia, Courtland & Decatur properties and integrated them into its line through north Alabama. These tracks were then extended to Stevenson, Alabama, where the M&C connected with the Nashville & Chattanooga Railroad to enter the city of Chattanooga.[2] The line was then extended westward from Tuscumbia and reached Memphis in 1858. Meanwhile, enterprising Georgians had voted to appropriate state funds to construct the Western & Atlantic Railroad. At Chattanooga, the state-owned Western & Atlantic was to link the Memphis & Charleston Railroad with other lines running to Charleston and Savannah, thus forming a continuous chain of railroads between the Atlantic coast and Memphis.[3] On May 1, 1858, the opening of this great southern route to the West was celebrated with a "Railroad Jubilee" in Memphis. Tate and other luminaries made speeches, and water from the Atlantic Ocean was symbolically poured into the Mississippi River to commemorate the "Marriage of the Waters" that the Memphis & Charleston Railroad had helped make possible.[4]

Meanwhile, another Tennessee Valley resident, Col. James Withers Sloss of Lauderdale County, was making his mark on the railroad industry in Alabama. Of Irish stock, Sloss was a native Alabamian, born in Limestone County in 1820. With limited formal education, he had worked his way up from humble beginnings to become one of the wealthiest and most influential men in the Tennessee Valley.[5] Sloss was always on the lookout for investment opportunities and decided that none could be better than a railroad leading from the Tennessee Valley to Nashville. In 1853 he obtained a charter for the Tennessee & Alabama Central Railroad, which was to run from Decatur to the Tennessee state line, where it would connect with southbound lines out of Nashville.[6] The connecting lines in Tennessee, like those of the Western & Atlantic in Georgia, were subsidized by the state. While Sloss had to use his own resources to build his road, Tennessee was generously providing $10,000 for each mile of track laid in the Volunteer State.[7] But the distance from Decatur to the state line was relatively short, so Sloss had the Tennessee & Alabama Central in full operation by 1860 and was making plans to extend it southward to Montevallo, Alabama.[8]

Compared to the celerity with which Sloss and Tate prosecuted their ventures, railroad building in south Alabama proceeded at a glacial pace. By 1861 the Mobile & Girard Railroad had laid several miles of track from the Chattahoochee River in the direction of Mobile, and in west Alabama some work was underway on the Cahaba, Marion & Greensboro Railroad. The Alabama & Mississippi Rivers Railroad had only advanced as far as Uniontown, and no trackwork at all had been done on the Mobile & Great Northern Railroad, which was to connect Mobile Bay with the Alabama & Florida Railroad at Pollard. Unlike their state-supported counterparts in Georgia, Tennessee, and many other states, all of these Alabama roads suffered from the same malady, inadequate financing.[9]

Alabama investors were holding back for several reasons. In the 1850s railroads were not considered a primary means of transportation. Instead, in the agrarian economy of antebellum Alabama, they were projected to haul farm and plantation products to river landings, where the steamboats took over. Therefore, capital investment came mostly from river towns and planters wishing to reach them. But the planter

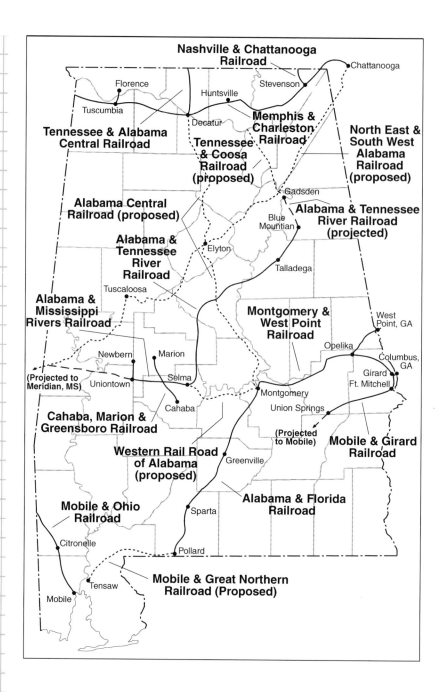

Alabama's Antebellum Railway System, 1861

was often in debt for other expenditures, including the purchase of slaves, and could seldom muster enough cash to build a railroad.[10] Moreover, the iron horse was still viewed as a novelty by many Alabamians, and the general public did not place full confidence in the new mode of locomotion. This attitude was manifested in a September 1854 edition of the *Huntsville Democrat.* Even though there is little evidence to suggest that Alabama roads were uniquely hazardous, the paper addressed the safety concerns of Tennessee Valley citizens by publishing the following "Rules for Safe Travel": "(1) Never sit in an unusual place or posture. (2) An excellent plan in railway traveling is to remain in your place without going out at all until you arrive at your destination. (3) Never get out until the train is fully stopped. (4) Never get out on the wrong side. (5) Never pass from one side to the other unless it is indispensably necessary. (6) Express trains are more dangerous. (7) Special trains and excursions are more dangerous. (8) In case of accident, causing irregular stoppage, it is better to quit the train. (9) Beware of yielding to the sudden impulse to spring from the carriage to recover your hat. (10) Select carriages near the center of the train if possible. (11) Do not attempt to hand an article into a train in motion. (12) Travel by day, if possible, not in foggy weather."[11]

John T. Milner, engineer on the Alabama & Florida Railroad, could not fathom the abounding distrust of railroads that he found among Alabama's citizens, and noted that there seemed to exist "a holy horror . . . of railroad corporations."[12] Still, the unquestioned utility of railroads caused demand for them to grow inexorably, even though battle lines were being drawn over the question of state financial aid for their construction. Lingering memories of the State Bank failure made many voters reluctant to risk supporting railroad schemes with public funds. Alabamians scattered over the thinly populated state also saw little reason to pay taxes that they reasoned would benefit only wealthy planters and river towns. The migratory nature of Alabama residents of this period only served to reinforce their resistance to making tax payments that they perceived as unlikely to yield benefits. But the primary reason for opposition to state aid to railroads was the philosophy of rugged individualism espoused by most of the state's people.[13] This caused the public to view the motives of promoters, speculators, and visionaries with suspicion. Milner characterized Alabamians as "the most cautious in the United States," with an "indispostion . . . to embark in any new enterprise."[14]

All these factors added up at the ballot box in 1853 when opposition to state aid to railroads culminated in the election of Governor John Winston.[15] In his address to the 1855 session of the general assembly, Winston congratulated the electorate for having the wisdom to place candidates in office who would keep the state's purse strings tightly drawn. "The propriety of the State loaning its credit, or raising the means from the people, to aid in the construction of railroads," said Winston, "appears not to have received the approbation either of the people, or those seeking place in the councils of the State. I look on it as a most fortunate circumstance for the country, that the sober common sense of the people pervaded the minds of many, but a few months since. We should rejoice that for the future there is hope that the acts of the State will be confined to the few simple, legitimate purposes of a republican government."[16]

Winston maintained his firm opposition to state aid throughout his administration and killed so many railroad bills in his second term that he became known as the "Veto Governor."[17] His attitude may have saved the treasury from folly on occasions; but Winston probably did considerably more harm to the state by withholding support for worthy ventures that could have projected Alabama into the mainstream of the country's economic growth at a critical period in railroad development.

One of the more enlightened actions of the Winston administration was approval of an appropriation to hire a full-time state geologist. Michael Tuomey, a geology professor at the University of Alabama, had been appointed state geologist in 1848 by Governor Chapman, but lawmakers did not feel his position was important enough to warrant a salary. The university recognized the value of Tuomey's work, however, and supported him with a stipend as he toiled tirelessly to prepare an exhaustive survey of the state's mineral resources. When the state finally decided to pay him for his work, he was able to resign from his teaching duties and devote all his energy to the survey. Tuomey died in 1857, but not before completing a thorough two-year geological survey. His study was comprehensive and accurate, and confirmed what had been rumored for many years—that the industrial future of Alabama lay in coal and iron.[18]

John T. Milner was strongly influenced by Tuomey's work, and in later years he offered the following tribute to Tuomey: "I can see Tuomey now, as hammer in hand, he travels over our rough mountains, along our rugged streams, his soul full of the future of Alabama! His reports are the first guide books of the mineral regions of our State. Simple, earnest old man! Fate hurried him prematurely away only a few short years before the veil was lifted from the hidden treasures he alone knew lay buried in the bosom of his adopted State."[19]

Tuomey showed the world that Alabama possessed enormous mineral resources, but it was clear that these resources were worthless unless a viable transportation method could be put in place to haul them to market. In 1840, when Alabamians were in a more liberal frame of mind, they had voted to build macadamized roads. But the electorate continued to balk at railway investments, and the old wagon roads were of little utility in the heavy industries of iron and coal. As *DeBow's Review* succinctly put it, "God may have given you coal and iron sufficient to work the spindles and navies of the world, but they shall sleep in your everlasting hills until the trumpet of Gabriel shall sound unless you can do something better than build turnpikes."[20]

As the debate over state aid heated up, Frank Gilmer honed his railroading skills on Pollard's Alabama & Florida Railroad. Since his first encounter with the dusty ores of Red Mountain, Gilmer's fascination with Alabama iron had become an obsession. He knew that railroads were the key that could transform the state's latent mineral wealth into a commercially viable iron industry, and decided to tackle simultaneously the twin priorities for economic progress in Alabama: mineral development and unification of the southern and northern regions of the state. Together with his colleague John T. Milner, Gilmer formulated a visionary plan for uniting the state by building a railroad through north Alabama's mineral district.

The right-of-way for their road was projected from Montgomery to Decatur, where it would connect with Sloss's Tennessee & Alabama Central Railroad. In Montgomery, Gilmer worked hard to marshal support for this great state road, which he called the Alabama Central. On February 17, 1854, the legislature granted the Alabama Central Railroad its charter, and soon thereafter politics turned in its favor. Governor Winston was succeeded by Andrew B. Moore, who had a better appreciation for the riches in Alabama's mountains, and in 1858 the state appropriated $10,000 from the Three Percent Fund to survey a route for the Alabama Central.[21]

Governor Moore now sought a man with enough talent and enthusiasm to successfully conduct the survey. That man was John Turner Milner. Milner was working on a muddy right-of-way thirty-five miles south of Montgomery when he received word of his appointment. Overcome with excitement and anticipation, Milner didn't hesitate long enough to change his soiled and tattered work clothes; instead, he immediately mounted his horse and galloped straightway to the state capitol where he presented himself to Governor Moore. Moore scrupulously looked Milner over, then put his hand on the young man's shoulder and observed: "Is this the man I have appointed chief engineer of our great State railroad? Well, it looks to me, Mr. Milner, as if the first thing we'd better do is get you some new breeches."[22]

Thus Milner embarked upon a dramatic odyssey that would lead through twists and turns to some of the most momentous developments in the state's history. Years later, he reflected upon this beginning:

When I look back and see the magnitude of the interest placed in my hands, I often wonder at the accidents that carried me through. I had no commissioners or advisers to aid me or advise me in this great work. The matter of connecting the two sections of the State, and at the same time developing the mineral regions in the best possible way, was left in my hands alone. The legislature of Alabama was not then aware of the results depending on my actions, as time has clearly shown, or they never would have left this matter in the hands of any one man. The governor of Alabama gave me the law without any instructions. He could give none. The mineral regions were then an unknown quantity. Michael Tuomey was dead. He alone had any just conception where they were, or what they were. If ever a man was surrounded by a sea of difficulties, endless, boundless, I was that man. There was no chart, and no compass, but there was a never-ending show of blue lights all over Alabama saying, Come here, or Go there.[23]

At the time of the survey the great city of Birmingham was only a seed in Milner's mind. From the crest of Jefferson County's iron-rich Red Mountain, the engineer paused in the midst of his work to savor the pastoral serenity of the valley below:

I rode along the top of Red Mountain, and looked over that beautiful valley where the city of Birmingham lies to-day. It was one vast garden as far as the eye could reach, northeast and southwest. It was on the first day of June, in the year 1858. Jones Valley was well cultivated then. I had before traveled all over the United States. I had seen the great and rich valleys of the Pacific Coast, but nowhere had I seen an agricultural people so perfectly provided for, and so completely happy. They raised everything they required to eat, and sold thousands of bushels of wheat. Their settlements were around these beautiful, clear running streams found gushing out everywhere in this valley. Cotton was raised here also, but on account of the difficulty of transportation, only in small quantities. It was, on the whole, a quiet easy-going, well farmed, well framed, and well regulated civilization.[24]

After several months of devoted effort, Milner announced that he had successfully completed his survey. He introduced his report by declaring that the Alabama Central Railroad was the most important enterprise to ever come before the people of Alabama. "They have thought and talked over the connection of South and North Alabama, and the development of their mineral wealth for forty years or more," Milner wrote, "but until the recent survey was made, it has always been considered impracticable to build a railroad through these mountains at a reasonable cost. For the first two months I had nothing to encourage me; but becoming better acquainted with the topography of the country, one difficulty was avoided here, and another there, until I have succeeded in obtaining a line for the Central Railroad that will compare favorably in costs, grades, alignment, and every thing else, with the railroads in the neighboring States, and far better than any other route across the Allegheny Range, except perhaps, the Georgia State Road."[25]

Milner's report to the governor was more than a recital of the salient features and specifications for the proposed railroad. He knew that detractors would demand strong justification for building the Alabama Central, and he took time to develop compelling arguments supporting the entire concept. Declaring that "Alabama is to the Gulf what Pennsylvania is to the Atlantic," Milner presented statistical comparisons proving that the road would be an economic boon to the state. Coal was projected to constitute a large portion of the railroad's traffic, and the report suggested that coal usage was bound to increase as it replaced wood as a locomotive fuel. Milner also predicted that a thriving iron industry would arise in Jefferson County at the point where the Alabama Central crossed the North East & South West Alabama Railroad, and that Alabama's railroad industry would reap great cost savings when iron rails could be produced locally.[26]

Although the potential benefits of the Alabama Central Railroad were enormous, Milner knew that the project faced an uphill battle in gaining public acceptance. In an attempt to assuage the "deep and widespread suspicion and want of confidence in such investments" that Milner sensed in Alabama, he carefully explained how the iron horse had dramatically changed the lives of rural Georgians:

> When I was engaged on the Georgia State road, I became acquainted with the people along that road—their habits, and their means. Beyond their actual wants for food, they raised nothing at all. The men moped around and shot at a mark. The women seemed to do but little, whilst their children, poorly cared for, sauntered about from place to place, as if their highest thoughts were bent on catching rabbits, opossums, or some such small game. What was the use of working, when it would cost them two dollars per bushel to get their wheat to market, and then only get one?
>
> In 1857 I went back again, and what a change! The rivers were the same, the Kennesaw Mountain had not changed, the "Crooked Spoon" still rolled along, the men and women that once I knew were there, the boys had grown

to men, and the girls to women; but their mien was changed. The old men stood erect, as with conscious pride they looked upon the waving fields of grain. The matrons busied themselves about their dairies and their looms; whilst the sturdy boys were grappling with the plow. What had brought this change about? Listen for a while, and soon you will hear the iron horse storming along. He stops at a station for fuel and water—a man gets off the train. He is a Charleston man, or perhaps the agent of the Montgomery Mills. The cars go on, and he goes to the house. He meets the farmer—they have met before. His business is to buy his grain. Strange but true, that the demand for wheat should be so great as to induce the merchant to buy at the farmer's door. He offers $1.50 per bushel, cash, for his crop and furnishes the sacks to put it in. "That won't do. Savannah was here yesterday, and Columbus the day before, and they offered more." Here is the key to this change. This solves the mystery. The great State road—the iron horse—the dollar and a half per bushel, cash, tells the tale.[27]

"Until recently, the merits of the railway have not been fully tested," Milner admitted, but he went on to note that neighboring states were "using every exertion to build them," and exhorted Alabamians to acknowledge the great usefulness of railroads, which was being proven with every passing day. Pointing to a land grant of 400,000 acres for the proposed Alabama Central Railroad, Milner also warned that provisions of the grant required that the Alabama Central be completed by 1866 or the land would revert to the U.S. government. He also asserted that the Alabama Central would accomplish the dreamed-of unification of the state by bringing all Alabamians together in a common community of commercial, social, and political interest. And he envisioned so much trade between the Tennessee Valley and Mobile that "an emporium second to none in the South" would be established at the Port City. In short, Milner unequivocally assured readers of his report that the Alabama Central Railroad was "the most important road in the State for the interest of the people."[28] Milner's report was submitted for the legislature's approval in 1859.[29] The survey had consumed every fiber of Milner's being, but now his report was in the hands of politicians—politicians with a propensity to kill railroad measures.

The legislature was divided into two camps: champions of the Alabama Central and supporters of the Alabama & Tennessee River Railroad. With an exclusive mandate already in hand to extend their line to the Tennessee Valley, backers of the Alabama & Tennessee River Railroad considered the Alabama Central Railroad to be a threat to their franchise and were determined to wage political war against Milner in order to protect their vested interests.[30] A&TRRR sponsors promptly went on the offensive when Judge Thomas Walker, senator from Calhoun County, attacked the report and made a motion to table it. "That country up there is so poor that a buzzard would have to carry provisions on his back or starve to death on his passage," Walker proclaimed, referring to Milner's projected route.

Milner reacted with dismay. "I felt that I was on trial, and every word of that speech was burned into my soul. The judge began by remarking that the State had already pledged her faith to build a road via Guntersville, and that if the two roads were begun they would both fall by the wayside, and if completed, they would never pay on account of their competition with each other." No sooner had Walker finished than Sen. J. M. Calhoun of Dallas County joined in maligning Milner's work. "When Calhoun got through I felt like a convicted felon!" Milner exclaimed.

When it appeared that all of Milner's work was in vain, Senator Burnett of Butler County recommended that the report be printed. The motion was seconded by Governor Robert M. Patton, and it appeared that Milner's survey stood a slim chance of being sanctioned by the state. Finally, George S. Houston stepped forward. Houston, from Limestone County, had made David Hubbard a three-time loser in congressional races. Nonetheless, Congressman Houston shared Hubbard's enthusiasm for railroads and was convinced that the Alabama Central was good for Alabama. Through Houston's generous efforts enough votes were secured to have the report printed. "I have never ceased to thank him," Milner declared. "That was the turning point of my life, and then and there was the beginning of the city of Birmingham."[31]

John Turner Milner, ca. 1870s. (Courtesy of the Alabama Department of Archives and History, Montgomery, Alabama)

5

THE
CIVIL
WAR

WHEN JEFFERSON DAVIS stepped from a train in Montgomery to assume the Confederate presidency, Alabama's infant rail system was ill equipped to handle the demands of war. In the Tennessee Valley, the South's only continuous rail route from the Atlantic to the Mississippi River remained precariously isolated and exposed to the threat of seizure by Union forces. The only other viable trans-Confederate route was the unfinished line from Montgomery to Meridian. Critical gaps in the state's rail system also loomed outside Mobile and Pensacola. The Civil War was the first conflict in which railroads played a vital role, and at the beginning of hostilities war planners did not fully appreciate its importance. Therefore, steps to prepare Alabama's railroads for action were painfully slow and ultimately inadequate.

Although most railroad promoters and managers in the state had voted against secession, once the ordinance of secession was adopted, they threw all their energy into the war effort.[1] For the duration of the war, they would work diligently under extremely adverse circumstances to satisfy military officials who had little idea how to properly run a railroad. Despite the unquestioned allegiance of most of Alabama's railroad men, the General Assembly chose to legislate their cooperation. In February 1861 legislators passed an act requiring Alabama railroads to haul troops and munitions without charge in exchange for a state tax exemption.[2] The legislature found the task of welding together a viable and efficient rail system to be much more challenging, however.

Gaps in Alabama's trackage caused bottlenecks from the start. When Confederate troops were dispatched to Pensacola in March 1861 to attack nearby Fort Pickens, severe delays occurred as some of this force had to get off the cars and march across the unconnected roadbed. The situation was so bad that the state legislature made an emergency loan of $30,000 to the Alabama & Florida Railroad of Alabama to complete the work. The trackwork was finished by May 3, and on May 6 a regular ten-hour passenger schedule was established between Montgomery and Pensacola.[3]

Alabama took another step to improve the efficiency of her rail communications when the state granted the Alabama & Florida the right to extend its line through Montgomery to the Montgomery & West Point depot. Until this connection was made, freight interchange between the narrow gauge M&WPRR and the A&F was made by wagon at a cost to the Confederate Government of $2,000 per month. Extension of the A&F saved this expense and, more importantly, reduced the time required to transfer a regiment from one line to the other from five hours to only one hour.[4]

The unfinished Mobile & Great Northern Railroad, which was projected to run from a point on the Tensas River twenty-two miles north of Mobile to connect with the Alabama & Florida Railroad at Pollard, was another pressing problem. Although tracklaying did not begin until March 28, 1861, the line was expected to be in operation by autumn. But by fall it was only half finished and all available construction money had been exhausted. A $15,000 emergency loan from the state of Alabama finally got the iron out of Mobile warehouses and onto the roadbed. By November 15 the line was complete to Pollard and a fourteen-hour schedule from the Tensas River landing to Montgomery was in effect. General Braxton Bragg, who understood the value of the iron horse better than most, proclaimed the road to be worth three thousand men at each end.[5]

All these improvements would greatly benefit the Confederate cause, but no flaw in Alabama's rail system screamed for remedy more than the trackless region between Montgomery and Meridian. With the Memphis & Charleston in jeopardy, it was becoming increasingly apparent to Confederate leaders that they had to close this gap to provide an alternate route from the seaboard to the Mississippi River. This work took on added urgency as events unfolded in the Tennessee Valley in the spring of 1862.

As the Confederate army concentrated its forces at Corinth in preparation for the Battle of Shiloh, the Memphis & Charleston served the Confederacy well by transporting thousands of men and countless sup-

Army of the Cumberland at Stevenson, Alabama, in 1863. The Union Army secured control of the routes leading to this important railroad junction and used them to deliver thousands of tons of vital supplies to General Sherman's forces during the decisive Atlanta campaign. Four groups of trains, consisting of four trains per group, left Nashville each day and headed for Stevenson over the Nashville & Chattanooga Railroad. This route was kept open for continuous southbound traffic by rerouting the returning trains to Nashville over the Memphis & Charleston and Tennessee & Alabama Central railroads. (From an engraving by Theodore R. Davis, Harper's Weekly, *December 12, 1863)*

plies from east Tennessee to northern Mississippi. Cars were appropriated from Georgia's Western & Atlantic Railroad for this task, and troops were packed so tightly into them that they were forced to cut holes in the car sides and tops for ventilation. The call for troops was so great that Pensacola was practically abandoned as her defenders were hurried to Corinth over the Mobile & Ohio Railroad. The M&O joined the Memphis & Charleston in transferring nearly forty thousand men to Corinth in less than two months.[6]

Despite this concentration of soldiers, the rebel army could not claim victory in the butchery at Shiloh and eventually withdrew to Tupelo, Mississippi. The Shiloh stalemate was followed immediately by the Confederacy's devastating loss of the Memphis & Charleston Railroad. This railroad had been called the "Vertebrae of the Confederacy" by the Union's secretary of war. Secretary Judah Benjamin of the Confederacy had once wired Robert E. Lee imploring that "The railroad line from Memphis to Richmond must be defended at all hazards."[7]

But on April 11, General O. M. Mitchell invaded the Tennessee Valley and captured the key rail facilities at Huntsville, including eighteen locomotives, one hundred freight cars and six passenger cars. Considerable Union sympathy existed in the Tennessee Valley, due in no small measure to its physical isolation from the rest of the state, and many believed that some Memphis & Charleston employees collaborated with the invaders to insure the success of the attack. Regardless of why the Memphis & Charleston fell into Federal hands, the line was lost for the better part of the war, thus cutting off continuous rail communication between the eastern and western Confederate armies.[8] Of even greater significance was the fact that the Union now controlled trackage that stretched from the Ohio River to Chattanooga—a vital supply route that ultimately assured the success of General William T. Sherman's Atlanta campaign.

The government in Richmond had addressed the need for an alternate trans-Confederate route on February 15, 1862, when it loaned the Alabama & Mississippi Rivers Railroad $150,000 to complete the line from Selma to Meridian. Difficulties ensued, however, because the Alabama & Mississippi Rivers Railroad only planned to build to Reagan, Alabama, where it was to connect with the North East & South West Alabama Railroad. The NE&SW was to construct the remainder of the road to Meridian. Following weeks of critical delay, a final agreement was negotiated providing for the Alabama & Mississippi Rivers Railroad and the NE&SW Alabama Railroad to share the loan. The Confederate government sought to expedite the project by appointing a special agent to press the work forward. The Confederates chose A. S. Gaines, a civil engineer from Demopolis, for the job.

Gaines was faced with a problem that would plague the South throughout the war—a shortage of iron. The problem was exacerbated when New Orleans fell to the Federals, denying the rebels access to iron in her warehouses and through her port facilities. Undaunted, Gaines set out to appropriate any iron he could find for the desperately needed project. On the bankrupt Cahaba, Marion & Greensboro Railroad he found four hundred tons of new iron and four hundred kegs of spikes. Other material was scavenged from the Montgomery & Eufaula Railroad, including a new locomotive. But despite these successes in finding construction supplies, the enterprise still fell woefully short of material.

General Bragg had just been appointed commander of the Army of the Mississippi and was growing extremely impatient of what he considered an intolerably slow pace for such a strategically important project. "I cannot present in too strong language the mischief that must result from further reliance on this company," he vigorously complained as he threatened to take over the road. Inevitably, Gaines was replaced, and Sam Tate, the well-known president of the Memphis & Charleston Railroad, took over. Tate and the remnant of his M&C Railroad had taken refuge in Tupelo with Bragg's beleaguered army and he was all too happy to requite his losses by engaging in this work. Gaines was actually grateful for having Tate assume the burden and continued to offer both amiable and able assistance.

Tate scoured the South for supplies in what was sometimes perceived as a highhanded or even illegal manner. In addition to the shortages, Tate encountered other difficulties. In the fall, for instance, the government allowed planters to pull their slaves off the work to bring in the harvest, leaving Tate short of labor. Bureaucratic bungling and deprivations notwithstanding, work proceeded slowly until December 10, 1862, when workers finally completed the line between Selma and Meridian. At Meridian, the cars were turned over to another company for the final leg to the Mississippi River. Therefore, the Alabama line assumed the name of its terminal towns to become known as the Selma & Meridian Railroad. But there was still no bridge over the Tombigbee River, and cars had to be unloaded at Demopolis for the steamboat trip to McDowell's Bluff. East of the river, there was a car shortage, and another steamboat trip was required between Selma and Montgomery. The new trans-Alabama route left much to be desired, indeed.[9]

The Confederate woes of 1862 multiplied when the Federals overpowered the depleted defenses of Pensacola. A shortage of iron rail continued to be a consummate problem, and the retreating rebels sought to relieve this affliction by tearing up the iron of the Alabama & Florida Railroad of Florida and using it to extend the Selma & Meridian Railroad. What was left was used to build sidings on the Mobile & Great Northern Railroad. In April 1863 more A&F track was pulled up to make repairs on the Montgomery & West Point Railroad. This tactic would be repeated many times as the conflict wore on, to the great detriment of the victimized lines. Whenever a section of track was in danger of falling under enemy control, the rails were ripped up to deny their use to the other side. This strategy visited complete ruin on the Memphis & Charleston Railroad, since it was frequently raided by both sides during the course of the war.[10]

The Confederate government eventually created an Iron Commission to manage the critical iron problem. This commission exerted great power and decided which railroads would live and which would die. Its growing authority soon extended beyond the impressment of rail. Even locomotives were impressed, and by August 1863 the Commission had seized all of the motive power of the A&F of Florida.[11]

The loss of the M&C coupled with slow progress on the Selma & Meridian Railroad meant that troop movements across Alabama had to be made over the circuitous route connecting Mobile with West Point, and Columbus, Georgia. Inevitable delays occurred as personnel detrained for the ferry ride across Mobile Bay and transferred between cars of different gauges at Montgomery, West Point, and Columbus. In the face of these impediments, the largest troop movement over a single route ever attempted by the Confederate army occurred along this line through Alabama in the summer of 1862.

After capturing Corinth, the Union army under General Don Carlos Buell marched for east Tennessee and Chattanooga. Confederate defenders in this region needed all the firepower they could muster, and Bragg considered transferring his Army of the Mississippi from Tupelo to Chattanooga by rail. Having little experience at moving a large army by train, Bragg sent a trial unit of three thousand men to Chattanooga via the Mobile–Montgomery–West Point route. The trial run was eminently successful and Bragg's men arrived in Chattanooga just six days after their departure from Tupelo. As the Federal army slowly advanced on east Tennessee, Bragg became convinced that the iron horse was of more value than he had previously thought, and he decided to confront the bluecoats by moving his entire infantry to Chattanooga by rail. Cavalry, artillery, and wagon trains would make the trip overland through northern Alabama.

Bragg issued his orders on July 21, 1862, and on July 23 the first southbound train embarked from Tupelo over the Mobile & Ohio Railroad. Elements from Mobile, Pollard, and other places along the line left in advance of Bragg's men to avoid bottlenecks. The troops were given seven days' rations before leaving, which proved to be plenty for the trip. Altogether, approximately twenty-five thousand of Bragg's men were transported to Chattanooga by rail, allowing the Confederates to concentrate their forces effectively to meet the Federal threat. Although Bragg ultimately failed to take advantage of the initiative the iron horse had brought him, the railroad had proven its worth in war.[12]

As the war progressed, increasing demand for raw material at the Selma arsenal stimulated development of the mineral resources advertised by Michael Tuomey. Frank Gilmer and John T. Milner went to Richmond and convinced Secretary of War Seddon to employ them to construct a railroad leading from Calera to the iron and coal fields of Red Mountain where they were to establish furnaces and rolling mills. Contract in hand, the pair returned to Jefferson County, where they joined with Daniel Pratt and other prominent Alabama businessmen to organize the Red Mountain Iron and Coal Company.

The railroad to Red Mountain would follow the route Milner had surveyed for the proposed Alabama Central Railroad. The name "Alabama Central" was not descriptive enough, however, and was dropped in favor of the "South & North Alabama Railroad." This name was thought to reflect more accurately the long-term vision of unifying the southern and northern ends of the state by building a railroad through the mineral fields. Yet the name was ironic, since the immediate purpose of this road was to supply war material aimed at severing the union of southern and northern states.

Daniel Pratt was imbued with the infectious enthusiasm of Gilmer and Milner, and would not rest until the South & North Alabama Railroad reached the Tennessee Valley. In normal times Pratt's riches would have assured rapid success, but wartime shortages restrained progress. Iron was requisitioned wherever it could be spared, and the South & North Alabama Railroad was born of an amalgamation of various types of pieced-together rail. Everything from strap to assorted sizes of T rail were used to push the South & North from its junction with the Alabama & Tennessee River Railroad at Calera to the charcoal furnace location near the foot of Shades Mountain. Motive power was provided by the Iron Commission, which had appropriated a little wood burner from a northwest Florida lumber mill during the evacuation of Pensacola. In another unusual twist, this Florida sawmill was owned by John T. Milner's father, and the locomotive bore the elder man's name. Fittingly, the *Willis J. Milner* was the only engine to see duty on the South & North Alabama Railroad during the Civil War. The *Willis J. Milner* faithfully rendered invaluable service as it hauled enormous quantities of indispensable minerals to the Confederate arsenal at Selma.

In the winter of 1863 another furnace was put in blast at nearby Oxmoor, and Frank Gilmer opened coal mines at Helena. Gilmer's management of these facilities drew high praise from John T. Milner. "He sent thousands of tons of coal all over the South," Milner averred, "and thousands of tons of Red Mountain pig iron were shot away in shot and shell at Charleston and Mobile."[13] Although little more than a flimsy branch line of the Alabama & Tennessee River Railroad, the South & North Alabama Railroad was a palpable inspiration to Gilmer, Milner, and Pratt as they relentlessly campaigned to connect south Alabama and the mineral district with the Tennessee Valley by rail.

The Alabama & Tennessee River Railroad was the main artery feeding minerals to the great arsenal at Selma.[14] But the northern end of this important road terminated inconsequently at Blue Mountain, so plans were made to change its route to make connection with other lines at Rome, Georgia. In order to finance this extension, 300,000 acres of property secured through an antebellum land grant were put up for sale, with Confederate veterans eligible to purchase the land at $1.25 per acre. Little was accomplished during the war years to extend the railroad from Blue Mountain to Rome, however.[15] Yet, in 1863 a costly branch of the Alabama & Tennessee River Railroad, using expensive rock-arched culverts, was constructed between Ashby and Four-Mile Creek to reach the Cahaba coal fields as well as a nearby forge and nailery.[16]

For the most part, daily operation of the railroads within the state remained the responsibility of railroad men. But conflicts and disputes with military authorities were common, as Daniel H. Cram, engineer and superintendent of the Montgomery & West Point Railroad, points out in this excerpt from the Company's annual report for 1864–65:

Every year that passes but intensifies my idea, that a manager of railway transportation should be, so far as the discharge of his duties are concerned, the most absolute of autocrats. The very service itself seems to me to necessitate such a course of action, at least, it is to my mind the only principle of Management that can save the railroads from destruction, when they are, as now, so constantly in contact with military authorities, whose agents, generally ignorant of railway management, frequently interfere with and obstruct transportation. Over and often have I been called on to do impossible things, at impossible hours. Well do I remember when a Second Lieutenant threatened to report me because I would not transport by passenger train a carload of spittoons, under his charge, not worth the transportation, but preferred to carry a car load of buckshot cartridges, which I knew General John H. Morgan was waiting for; and my memory passing over many similar instances recalls another case in which a Brigadier General, of no mean repute, threatened to arrest me because I refused to move out a train of his troops, when there was an actual certainty that his train would come in collision with a downward passenger train.[17]

Triumphant whistle blasts of U.S. Military Railroad locomotives at the roundhouse and shops of the Memphis & Charleston Railroad proclaim the occupation of Huntsville in 1864. (Courtesy of the Heritage Room, Huntsville-Madison County Public Library, Huntsville, Alabama)

At first glance, Alabama's railroads appear to have enjoyed a previously unseen profitability during the war years. The Montgomery & West Point, for example, reported net income of $91,745 in 1861, $143,995 in 1862, $628,529 in 1863 and $353,283 in 1864. It must be remembered, however, that many of these perceived gains were the phantom profits of inflation. Real gains in profits were much more modest, and accrued at the expense of physical plant. A chronic shortage of maintenance materials together with the extraordinary traffic demands of the war caused Alabama's railroads to suffer extremely excessive wear.[18] Nevertheless, the iron horse became a more and more important component of the military machine. As Superintendent Cram avowed, "The time has passed when Railroads can be considered as the property of soulless corporations worked alone for the benefit of the stockholders. The exigencies of war has made them a part of the great military system of the country."[19]

With the exception of the Memphis & Charleston, Alabama's railroads were remarkably insulated from hostilities during the early years of the war. But this abruptly changed in the summer of 1864 when the commander of the District of Tennessee, Maj. Gen. Lovell H. Rousseau, formulated plans for a daring raid deep into Alabama. Originally, Rousseau intended to attack the arsenal at Selma, but was overruled by Gen. William T. Sherman. Sherman thought that a strike at the vital rail facilities of the Montgomery & West Point Railroad would be of greater strategic importance than the proposed raid upon Selma. In July 1864 Sherman authorized Rousseau to carry out this bold plan.[20]

Rousseau gathered twenty-five hundred well-equipped troops at Decatur and, after considerable delay, moved south on July 10, intent upon interrupting the flow of food and munitions from Alabama to besieged Atlanta. As Rousseau rode deeper into rebel territory, Maj. Gen. Andrew J. Smith, with nine thousand infantry and three thousand cavalry, left Memphis to engage Nathan Bedford Forrest in northern Mississippi. This diversionary action worked beautifully as Confederate attention was drawn to Smith. Most of the command of Gen. Gideon J. Pillow that had been defending northeast Alabama was ordered to assist General Forrest, leaving only about three hundred regulars under Gen. J. H. Clanton to defend the entire region. Rousseau traveled fast, and Clanton did not learn of his advance until the Yankees were crossing the Coosa River near Greensport. Clanton raced to engage Rousseau at Ten-Islands Ford, but was pushed back by the overwhelming Union force. After breaking through the rebel defenses, Rousseau's troops marched for Talladega, destroying an iron furnace along the way. Reaching Talladega, the bluecoats systematically destroyed the depot, two gun factories, and several boxcars. Ironically, one of these boxcars contained Calhoun County records that had been transported to Talladega to avoid an anticipated attack by Rousseau on the county seat at Jacksonville. The Federals also seized a great quantity of salt, sugar, flour, and bacon. What they could not use was distributed among the town's citizens. Rousseau kept a tight rein on his troops and tolerated little destruction of private property.[21] The raiders lost no time in pressing toward their ultimate objective. Feigning a move to destroy the railroad bridge across the Coosa, Rousseau turned south, and by the evening of July 17 his cavalry swept down upon the Montgomery & West Point Railroad at Loachapoka.

The Yankees had ridden forty miles that day and a short rest was in order; but soon the work of destruction began in earnest. Following a trademark Yankee procedure, the rails were ripped up and heated over a fire fueled by cross-ties and fence rails. The iron rails were then bent around trees and discarded in useless, twisted heaps. The light rail and highly combustible pitch pine ties that were used on this part of the road only served to make the fires hotter and the bending easier. After destroying several miles of track, the raiders torched the depot at Loachapoka, but as the station became engulfed in flames, sparks threatened to bring conflagration to the whole town. With great effort, the Union troops all fell to the task of saving the town. The soldiers finally brought the fire under control and, exhausted, brought their day's activities to an end. Had Rousseau arrived at Loachapoka a few hours earlier, he might have captured a valuable prize: Braxton Bragg had just come through en route to Montgomery from Atlanta on an inspection tour of the western armies.[22]

As the sun rose on July 18, Rousseau sent detachments east and west along the track. The line was to be destroyed as far west as Chehaw Station and Notasulga, while another wrecking crew proceeded to Opelika. At Montgomery, Bragg had received word of the raid at Talladega and immediately took steps to defend the Montgomery & West Point Railroad. Earlier, elements of Pillow's forces had been dispatched to Selma, and Bragg ordered them to Montgomery, where they would board trains to pursue Rousseau. Meanwhile, the only force available in Montgomery consisted of raw recruits who had enlisted at the age of seventeen and whose main service experience was guard duty. They were augmented by a few cadets from the University of Alabama. These poorly equipped young soldiers, armed only with old, rebored rifles, were loaded hurriedly onto a train and rushed into battle.

At Auburn, Capt. Thomas H. Francis, who had assumed command just two days earlier, could only muster a few shotgun-armed militia to resist the railroad wreckers. This band gallantly confronted the Yankees a few miles west of town, but when Francis saw the strength of the force he faced, he prudently ordered his men to flee. The bluecoats then entered Auburn and torched the depot as well as a large stack of lumber. As the Yankees departed eastward, slaves broke into stores and looted them. The raid had been such a surprise that a westbound locomotive chugged straight into the hands of the approaching Federals, and the bluecoats capped their day by destroying the engine.

At Chehaw Station, the Union raiders encountered the detachment from Montgomery. The young Confederates bravely fought the Federals for the better part of the morning until Rousseau sent reinforcements. The Confederate guns could not match the range of the Yankee Spencers and the defenders were soon overwhelmed by the larger and more experienced cavalry group. As the butternuts retreated into the surrounding swamp, the raiders renewed their assault on the railroad. After thoroughly wreaking havoc on their assigned portions of the road, the Notasulga and Chehaw contingents returned to Loachapoka. Rousseau immediately ordered a march to Opelika but stopped to encamp for the night at Auburn, giving his men a much-needed rest.[23] Down the line, the valiant Confederates buried their dead and bandaged their wounds. Although reports of Confederate losses varied considerably, they were unquestionably substantial.

At dawn on the 19th, Rousseau's forces stormed into Opelika. They burned the depot, destroyed the turntable and the wye,[24] and demolished six cars. They also located large stores of bacon, sugar, and flour. After taking as many provisions as possible, they destroyed the remainder. Rousseau then took his men one mile north of Opelika, where he rested them in anticipation of the strenuous sprint for friendly territory that lay ahead of them.

Rousseau wasted no time in beating a path for Marietta, Georgia, and the protection of Sherman's army. He encountered no resistance whatever in this dash and entered Georgia on July 21. At Villa Rica, the raiders were joined by escaping slaves, who brought about seven hundred horses and mules with them that they had appropriated from their former masters.

The Confederate regulars from Selma arrived at Chehaw Station on July 19 to find thirty miles of ruin stretching before them. Pillow's men marched for a short distance along the smoldering roadbed before they realized the futility of pursuit and encamped for the night.

So thorough was the destruction that it would be six weeks before the railroad could be restored to service. Bragg attempted to shore up this vital supply route by calling for two hundred wagons and teams to haul desperately needed supplies to Atlanta. But Black Belt grain and Selma munitions ceased to flow freely to Atlanta, and Sherman's breakthrough was greatly assisted by Rousseau's raid.[25] The August 10, 1864, edition of the Montgomery *Weekly Advertiser* acknowledged the success of the Federal operation: "We doubt whether any other raiding party since the commencement of hostilities, comprising no more men has penetrated as far into the country, done as much damage, and succeeded in escaping with so little loss."[26]

This was the beginning of the end for Alabama's railroads. In the spring of 1865 a mighty Federal cavalry under the command of Gen. James Harrison Wilson invaded the mineral district and the Black Belt. On March 29 Wilson's forces reached the Alabama & Tennessee River Railroad facilities at Montevallo and Calera, where they began a rampage that within a few short days would decimate rail operations in Alabama. When news of Wilson's approach reached the Alabama & Tennessee River Railroad headquarters at Selma, most of the serviceable locomotives and rolling stock were rushed westward over Selma & Meridian tracks in search of a hiding place.[27]

Nathan Bedford Forest's outmanned Confederate cavalry desperately resisted Wilson's advance, but the Federal army soon swarmed over the Selma & Meridian tracks, burned the Valley Creek and Cahaba River bridges and reduced all railroad equipment in its path to rubble and cinders. As Wilson bore down on Selma, Forrest retreated to the arsenal and prepared to fight to the death. Wilson's attack on the arsenal commenced on April 2 and the battle raged all day. Late in the evening the bluecoat hordes broke through the breastworks and engaged the defenders in mortal hand-to-hand combat. As fearful detonations rocked the arsenal, ordnance-laden wagons slipped into the darkness in a pitiful attempt to salvage something for the dying cause. Ethel Armes vividly captures the mood of that fateful night at Selma when raging fires lighted the sky: "Over across Valley Creek, quick along the Cahaba road, and under cover of the dark, a long wagon train retreated, loaded with quartermaster's and ordnance supplies—all that was saved for the Confederacy out of Selma. As the teams under lead of Captain Huey of old Jonesboro were whipped up and rumbled along in the darkness, the stubble fields and clumps of woods in that vast level stretch of country began to glow with a savage light. Hour after hour, mile after mile, the red glow sped like screaming shells after them. At midnight they halted at the Cahaba ferry, and even then—ten miles away—every bush and tree stood etched in sharp black lines against the flaming sky that told the fall of Selma. The very links in the trace chains and the buckles on the mules' harness glittered like wild eyes."[28]

The destruction of the railroad at Selma matched that of the arsenal. All the shops and depots of the Selma & Meridian Railroad were laid waste, and much of the rolling stock was ravaged. The roundhouse, depot, and shops of the Alabama & Tennessee River Railroad were consumed by fire, and the ruins of the road's foundry and storehouse lay heaped upon broken machinery and tools. The burned-out hulks of five locomotives and 169 cars were strewn along severely damaged A&TRRR track. When Wilson turned toward Montgomery, the railroad as well as the arsenal boiled with flames.[29]

Meanwhile, north of Talladega, General John Thomas Croxton was busy destroying three bridges and all the depots on the Alabama & Tennessee River Railroad. Ethel Armes interviewed an eyewitness and described the dramatic spectacle at Blue Mountain: "There they destroyed the railroad station, the quartermaster stores, and a number of cars, some of which contained loaded shells and other mixed ammunition. It was an awe-inspiring sight he witnessed from the top of the mountain, the flames shooting up a hundred feet or more and illuminating the heavens. He could hear the terrible explosions too, from the shells in the burning cars. Much of this ordnance and ammunition had just previously arrived from Selma, having been shipped to prevent its falling into the hands of General Wilson."[30]

This sad circumstance was destined to be repeated on the Montgomery & West Point Railroad, but on a much larger scale. In anticipation of Wilson's advance upon Montgomery, Charles Pollard decided to send the entire outfit of the M&WP as well as the Alabama & Florida Railroad eastward. Since the A&F equipment was broad gauge and matched the track of the Georgia roads, some of its rolling stock found refuge in Georgia. The M&WP was narrow gauge, however, and the cars could retreat no further than West Point and Columbus.[31]

On April 11, terrified Montgomerians watched as Wilson's juggernaut menacingly approached the outskirts of the city. The Federal troops seemed to be in no hurry to enter defenseless Montgomery, however, as column upon column of bluecoats rode to the edge of the city and pitched tents. The sight of this great army at the city gates excited further apprehension and rumor. Fearing the worst, the Confederates contemplated scorched-earth tactics and intentionally burned a large quantity of cotton. But capital city citizens had few reasons to fear for life or property. Wilson showed no malice toward the people of Montgomery; it was the railroad he was after.[32]

When the Federal army finally entered Montgomery on April 12 and 13, Wilson's troops concentrated all of their destructive power upon the rail facilities. Following the Selma blueprint, the Federals obliterated the roundhouse, machine shop, car factory, blacksmith shop, freight depots, oil house, and passenger depot. All that was left was the

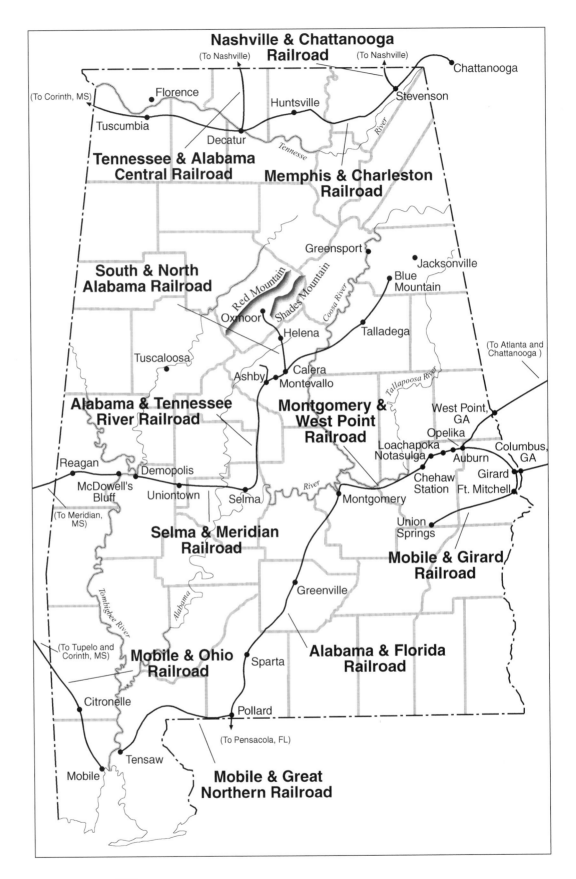

Nashville & Chattanooga Railroad

(To Nashville)   (To Nashville)

Chattanooga

(To Corinth, MS)

Florence

Huntsville

Stevenson

Tuscumbia

Decatur

Tennessee *River*

Tennessee & Alabama Central Railroad

Memphis & Charleston Railroad

Greensport

Jacksonville

South & North Alabama Railroad

Blue Mountain

Red Mountain

Shades Mountain

Coosa River

Oxmoor

Helena

Talladega

(To Atlanta and Chattanooga)

Tuscaloosa

Ashby

Calera
Montevallo

Tallapoosa River

Alabama & Tennessee River Railroad

Montgomery & West Point Railroad

West Point, GA

Opelika

Loachapoka
Notasulga

Columbus, GA

Reagan

Demopolis

Auburn

Girard

McDowell's Bluff

Uniontown

Selma

River

Chehaw Station

Ft. Mitchell

(To Meridian, MS)

Montgomery

Selma & Meridian Railroad

Union Springs

Mobile & Girard Railroad

Greenville

(To Tupelo and Corinth, MS)

Mobile & Ohio Railroad

Sparta

Alabama & Florida Railroad

Tombigbee River

Alabama

Citronelle

Pollard

(To Pensacola, FL)

Tensaw

Mobile

Mobile & Great Northern Railroad

Alabama's Civil War Railway System, 1865

foundry and paint shop. Not content with the destruction of the railroad physical plant, Wilson's cavalry turned eastward and relentlessly stalked the engines and rolling stock. They caught up with the fleeing locomotives, cars, and equipment at West Point and Columbus on April 16.[33] As Superintendent Cram explained, this property "had been equally divided between these points under the vain hope of saving one half of it." But the retreat turned out to be a tragic trap, and almost nothing was left of the Montgomery & West Point Railroad when the Federals were finished. "All the effective locomotives, 19 in number, owned by the company at the beginning of the year, were as nearly destroyed as fire and a liberal use of the sledge hammer could accomplish it," Cram lamented.[34]

Samuel G. Jones of the Alabama & Florida Railroad related a similar sad tale concerning the equipment under his charge. Like the Montgomery & West Point, the A&F had also divided its locomotives and cars between Columbus and West Point. Unfortunately, the Yankee attack at Columbus was swift and sure, and everything at that location was utterly destroyed. At West Point, Jones was successfully transporting engines and cars into Georgia until the Confederate commander inexplicably placed the remaining property under guard with strict orders that it was not to be moved. Thus, its certain destruction was assured. "The forces under Colonel LaGrange very soon attacked the town," Jones recalled, "and capturing Fort Tyler, the sole dependence for successful resistance, immediately crossed the river, captured and destroyed three engines and seven cars, with their contents, among them our entire stock of patterns. This loss left us with only four effective engines and about forty cars of every description, all more than one hundred miles from home, and all communication with Montgomery completely destroyed. The armistice between Generals Johnston and Sherman alone prevented the total destruction of all the property we took to Georgia."[35]

Mobile fared much better than Montgomery and Selma. General Canby's siege lasted long enough to allow an effective evacuation of machinery, locomotives, and rolling stock to unmolested areas of Mississippi. The Mobile & Great Northern gradually transferred all of its operating equipment to the west side of Mobile Bay, and on April 11, one day before the Federals entered the city, successfully moved the equipment to safety at Shubuta, Mississippi. The company's steam ferryboat *Senator* was taken up the Tombigbee River to Columbus, Mississippi.[36]

Nevertheless, the Mobile roads bore their full share of the scars of war. In 1866 the Mobile & Ohio Railroad toted up damages and found that the company was owed $5,228,562.23 in Confederate currency for services it was compelled to provide for the rebel army. In addition, three fourths of the M&O rolling stock had been destroyed, and the remainder was in terrible condition. Even worse, few means were left for a new beginning. Regrettably, the M&O's litany of losses typified those sustained by all the other railroads in Alabama.[37]

The universal destruction of railroad properties within the state presented a woeful picture to those who would pick up the pieces. President Pollard's description of his road's state of affairs could summarize the mood of all the state's railroad men: "The severe losses sustained by the Company in the destruction of depot buildings and work shops, of every bridge on the road, of nearly the entire outfit of cars, locomotives and machinery, and a treasury left without one dollar of available means, presented on the first day of June, 1865, a very gloomy and discouraging future."[38]

6

AFTERMATH

Even though the Civil War exhausted Alabama's resources and left the state's blighted railway system at the mercy of the United States Provisional Military Government, railroad managers wasted no time in wresting their roads from the army's grip and beginning the work of reconstruction. Within a few months after the fighting ended, the basic skeleton of Alabama's railway system was tenuously restored.

Charles T. Pollard went right to work to renew his Montgomery & West Point Railroad and extend the Western Rail Road of Alabama across the center of the state. The Provisional Military Government also wanted to get the trains running as soon as possible, and Pollard commended Gen. A. J. Smith, commander of the occupying army at Montgomery, for supplying the first effective aid to get the Montgomery & West Point back in operation. Smith gave Pollard the authority to issue up to fifty thousand dollars in scrip to pay for vital equipment and services, but Pollard frugally used only thirty thousand dollars of these bills. "They were received without hesitation on the line of the road," Pollard acknowledged, "in payment of labor, material, and supplies, and we were enabled to make rapid progress in rebuilding bridges and in repairs of cars and locomotives."

Pollard also reached out to northern financiers for help—a noble expedient in this case, but the first step on a treacherous and ultimately tragic road. "As soon as I saw that forces were properly organized and at work," Pollard said, "I deemed it advisable to go north, and provide, if possible, additional means. I succeeded in obtaining from the Southern Express Company, upon favorable terms, a loan of fifty thousand dollars, for which I consider the company under obligations ever to be recognized and acknowledged by its stockholders, for without the aid thus timely given, and upon most liberal terms, I could not have accomplished what has been done."[1]

But neither could the rehabilitative work have been accomplished without the characteristic perseverance and ingenuity of devoted Montgomery & West Point employees. As soon as the federal troops withdrew, Daniel Cram went to West Point to preserve what was left of the company's property and restore railroad operations:

> It was no easy task, surrounded by the blackened walls of buildings, and amid the smoking debris of a hundred loaded cars, to select or even distinguish what belonged to the company; but out of this confused mass, fragments of cars and locomotives, parts of rolling mills and printing presses, arsenals and arms, the most valuable portions of our property were cared for, and my attention was next directed to rebuilding bridges and repairing such engines as could most quickly be put in running order. Fortunately the engine *John Caldwell,* with five flat cars attached, which had formed the train last in service on the morning of the 16th of April, and was more remote from the depot than any other train, had sustained but comparatively slight injury, and was soon put in condition to work down to Osenappa creek, seven miles from West Point.

> From this stream to the Ufoupee, a distance of 39 miles, there was a continuous and unbroken line of road, with sufficient timber scattered here and there to rebuild the Osenappa; the question was to transport it.

> It was with great doubt, and only as a last resort, that I could entertain the belief that the engine *Abner McGehee,* which was on this portion of the road, could help us in our distress. Purchased 27 years ago, it was an engine which had already served nearly three times the period allotted to such machines; no longer reckoned among our living engines, it had long since been laid in the grave of our reports, and, abandoned by my orders at Steam Mill, it had been passed by the federals as of too little value to merit even destruction.

> In this emergency, however, after a week's repairs, it was brought into service and seemed to recover some of the power of former years. Like its honored namesake, though going forward with great facility, it went backward with as much reluctance; still, like him, it was equal to all the requirements demanded, and—attached to a couple of cars, hastily repaired, which had run off the track at Loachapoka, and had escaped destruction—it was our sole reliance for furnishing material and supplies for the work at Osenappa, and it continued in service until the day of the completion of the bridge at that point, when, as if its work were done, by the bursting of a tire it became utterly useless, and was laid up, never again probably to be called into action.

In this extraordinary manner the Osenappa bridge was rebuilt, and after twelve freight cars were patched together, regular trains were running over forty-six miles of repaired trackage by June 16—though none too profitably. "Although many passengers had been carried," Pollard explained, "there were none but returning soldiers without money or transportation, or citizens who, claiming to be soldiers, demanded the same immunity, and no receipts were obtained; but from memoranda kept, there were not less than 16,000 passengers transported, for which the company did not receive one dollar."[2] Still, with "a limited supply of tools, no machinery, and no more shelter than the passenger shed at West Point afforded," Pollard was gratified to report that a small work force under the direction of master machinist J. H. Graff continued to make repairs until the road was completely reopened from Montgomery to West Point.[3]

In the summer of 1865 president Sam Tate of the Memphis & Charleston Railroad traveled to Washington and persuaded President Johnson to approve his plan of organization. By September, the Memphis & Charleston was back in the hands of its former owners, but Tate's inspection of the right-of-way revealed that the 114-mile stretch between Pocahontas and Decatur was in terrible shape. Almost forty miles of track had been burned, and nothing was left but charred cross-ties and twisted rail. The remainder of this section was almost totally destroyed, including all the trestles, bridges, buildings, and water tanks. Ditches were filled up and cross-ties rotted along a roadbed that was now choked with weeds and bushes. A monumental rebuilding task was at hand, and the machinery to accomplish it was strewn across the South in neglected disrepair.

The Provisional Military Government cooperated with Tate by authorizing credit for the purchase of desperately needed locomotives, rolling stock, tools and material. Tate used almost $500,000 of this credit to purchase ten engines, 226 freight cars, fourteen passenger cars, and a considerable quantity of construction equipment. Terms of the loan were harsh, however. Tate and the other officials of the M&C pledged their personal bonds to secure the loan and promised repayment within two years. Although the government agreed to accept transportation credits as part of repayment, the impoverished condition of the war-ravaged country through which the line ran made it highly doubtful that the loan could be repaid out of earnings.

Within a few months after the close of hostilities, eighteen M&C locomotives that had been seized by the U.S. Military Railroad were returned, and the work of rebuilding the track commenced. By the winter of 1865 the entire line, with the exception of the Tennessee River crossing at Decatur, was open for traffic. By the summer of 1866, the bridge at Decatur was finally completed as well.[4]

The government advanced similar credits to the Selma & Meridian Railroad, which had also been under Tate's wartime management. At first, Selma & Meridian executives went to New York hoping to secure commercial loans, but the money-center bankers saw little hope that the penniless people served by this road could sustain sufficient earnings to assure repayment of a loan. Therefore, the company was forced to apply to the Quartermaster Department of the U.S. government for assistance and obtained $142,000 of aggregate credit, which was used to purchase six locomotives and fifty freight cars, as well as materials, supplies, and tools. A board of appraisers fixed the cost of this equipment at about 60 percent more than prewar prices, but less than currently prevailing prices. Loan provisions were only somewhat better than those required of the Memphis & Charleston. Although Selma & Meridian bonds were accepted in lieu of individual security, the principal still had to be repaid within two years.

The highest priority project on the Selma & Meridian was the reconstruction of the bridges over Valley Creek and the Cahaba River. Until these bridges were repaired, not only was the Selma & Meridian shut down, but stranded Ala-

Top: *Selma & Meridian Railroad annual pass for 1871. Bottom: Memphis & Charleston Railroad annual pass for 1881. During the Civil War, both railroads were managed by Sam Tate. (From the author's collection)*

bama & Tennessee River Railroad equipment remained cut off and could not be returned to Selma. Temporary trestle bridges were erected immediately at these sites and three thousand feet of permanent trestles were put in place throughout the road. Plans were even made to span

the Tombigbee River, something the Confederate government had found impossible to accomplish. A machine shop and freight depot were also constructed at Selma in 1865.[5]

When the Selma & Meridian was put back in operation on May 28, the Alabama & Tennessee River Railroad retrieved its salvaged locomotives and rolling stock. Until that time, reconstruction work was carried on by the durable little engine *Willis J. Milner* of the South & North Alabama Railroad, which had miraculously escaped the strikes of both General Wilson and General Croxton. Trains were running over temporary trestles to Talladega on May 29, and the whole road was opened to Blue Mountain on July 10.[6]

The Mobile & Great Northern was able to save most of its locomotives and cars, but they were in bad condition. Only one of their four engines was in good order and its two passenger coaches were sorely dilapidated. Within a month of the armistice, the U.S. engineer forces had accomplished makeshift repairs and the road was back in operation. By May 19 regular train service was available five days per week.[7]

Circumstances were quite different on the Alabama & Florida Railroad, however. Although some of its locomotives and rolling stock had found a safe haven in Georgia, they could not be returned until the Montgomery & West Point was rehabilitated. In the meantime, the

Freedmen rebuild the roadway of the Alabama & Tennessee River Railroad amid the ruins of Selma Arsenal in 1866. (From the Oxford Scrapbook, William H. Brantley, Jr., Collection, Samford University Library, Birmingham, Alabama)

A&F had only seven freight cars, not a single locomotive, and—needless to say—not a dollar in its bank account. Therefore, the Alabama & Florida was also forced to partake of a two-year government loan of over $50,000, which the road used to buy two new locomotives and twenty-one boxcars.

Although Samuel Jones arranged to borrow enough Mobile & Great Northern equipment to run a tri-weekly mixed train between Montgomery and the Tensas River landing, irritated riders of this combination freight, passenger, and work train pelted Superintendent Jones with ceaseless complaints. "Many a blessing did both the road and its manager receive," Jones grumbled in exasperation, "from impatient passengers when . . . the train was obliged to stop, sometimes for an hour, to receive lumber and other material needed in repairs for our own company, and for rebuilding the bridges on the Montgomery and West Point railroad, the speedy reconstruction of which was of paramount importance to us as affording the only means by which our rolling stock could be restored to us." Most of the Alabama & Florida's scanty resources were expended helping Pollard rebuild bridges on the Montgomery & West Point Railroad, leaving material and money in such short supply on the A&F that Jones considered any thought of work proceeding on this line to be "ridiculous." Nonetheless, complaints continued to roll in from the impatient occupying army. "Overlooking the difficulties by which the road was surrounded," Jones reacted, "the military were often loud in their complaints of the want of promptness in compliance with requisitions for transportation, and seemed to think that because there was a railroad, any failure to meet all of their wants was due to bad management, notwithstanding the company had not within its own control and could not command a single engine, and but half a dozen freight cars." The Alabama & Florida roadbed was also in wretched condition, and drainage problems were so severe on the main line that essential ditching work had to go on despite a lack of locomotive power. Extra hands were added to the ditching crews and they were transported to the work sites on hand cars in order to carry out this top-priority task.

In September 1865 the bridge over the Chattahoochee River at West Point was rebuilt and the A&F anticipated the return of its engines and rolling stock. The property did not arrive in time for the cotton harvest, however, and the railroad lost this all-important revenue. Although daily service was restored between Montgomery and Mobile, the company was, in Jones's words, "forced by the scarcity of engines to run freight and passengers together, and furnishing but poor facilities to either." Jones also admitted that the trips were seldom profitable. "The whole people were as much impoverished as the railroad company," he said, "and so scarce was money that in a round trip to Mobile our total cash receipts footed up only thirteen dollars."[8] Jones's complaints could just have easily been uttered by any other railroad official in the state. Short-term loans and ingenuity had allowed Alabama's railway system to stagger to its feet, but full recovery would be years away.

A bright hope in this dark landscape glimmered at Mobile, where able men of the Mobile & Ohio Railroad took substantial steps on the road to recovery. In 1870, a reporter for the *Mobile Register* paid a visit to the M&O shops at the Port City suburb of Whistler and found four hundred highly skilled mechanics and artisans of many nationalities hard at work in refurbished facilities. The large engine house contained a dozen locomotive stalls that were serviced by a wide variety of power tools. The reporter's attention was drawn to one particularly large lathe that he said "takes a pair of driving wheels of a locomotive in without their being removed from the axle, and turns them both off at the same moment by almost automatic machinery, requiring the attention of only one man, and executing the job in incredibly short time." In an adjoining shop the newsman gazed in awe at an immense steam hammer. "It was made under the direction of General McCallum, Superintendent of military railroads for the United States Government, without any regard to expense, but simply to perfection of work," the visitor noted. "The war closing just as it was completed, it was offered for sale with the other vast quantities of railroad machinery accumulated by the government, and was purchased at a very low price by Major Fleming for his shops. It is a remarkable hammer, so ponderous as to crush to a wafer a heavy bar of iron, yet so nicely adjusted that the man who manages it says he can crack the crystal of a watch under its face without injury to the mechanism." In addition to the locomotive shops, an extensive car-building shop was also producing two first-class freight cars each day. The reporter surmised that the public, "who are in the habit of looking to the North for every manufactured article," would be surprised to learn that "every article of use on the road—down to the stoves and water coolers of the cars—except new locomotives, car wheels and axles" were being made in these shops. "And the work turned out in every department is in no way inferior to that of Northern shops," he said. "Even locomotives can be constructed at Whistler entire, and a *reconstruction* of the old wrecks which travelers have noticed ranged along the side track at Whistler, the debris of war, is now going on; and we were surprised when told that a beautiful locomotive we saw about ready to come out, was one of those wrecks rejuvenated."[9]

Dependable labor was required to build the Mobile shops. Indeed, reliable laborers were indispensable for all maintenance and operating activities, and railway managers throughout the South fretted that, with the end of slavery, it would be impossible to find an adequate supply of reliable labor. But their fears were unfounded. Ex-slaves were employed on all Alabama railroads after the war and their work was almost uniformly considered acceptable. A lone exception occurred on the Selma & Meridian Railroad, which claimed to have "had great difficulty controlling the labor of the freedmen."[10] But other Alabama roads were almost unanimous in their approving assessment of the freedmen's performance. Chief Engineer G. Jordan of the Mobile & Great Northern put it best: "The change in the labor system of the country, brought about by the war, was a source of much anxiety for some time, as it was believed the negroes would not labor. Our experience, so far, has been favorable, and, under all the circumstances, very satisfactory. Many of the old and expert track men that belonged to the company have wandered off and engaged in other pursuits, while quite a number have remained in their old homes, as faithful and cheerful as under the old system. Their management has been just and humane, and shall continue so. We have had no difficulty in securing all the labor required on the road and steamers."[11]

Although unskilled labor was in abundant supply, skilled and resourceful managers were harder to find. Thomas Walker, president of the Alabama & Tennessee River Railroad, found an exceptional one in the person of Milton Hannibal Smith. Smith, born in New York and raised there and in Illinois, had served as superintendent of transportation for the U.S. Military Railroad at various places, including Stevenson and Huntsville, Alabama. His "genius for organization" earned him rapid promotions and he remained with the USMRR for four months after the war ended. Smith then went to work for the Eclipse Fast Freight Service in Louisville, Kentucky. But business fell off at Eclipse in the spring of 1866 and Smith was asked to take a pay cut. Smith, with a caustic temperament, chafed at this suggestion and dropped the following blunt message to his supervisor: "I beg leave to resign the position of Agent of Eclipse Line at this place to take effect June 5th. When I inform you that Mr. Bradly Asst Supt has reduced my salary to $150 per month and that I have been tendered the position of General Freight and Ticket Agent of the Alabama and Tennessee River Railroad with salary of $200 per month my reasons I presume will be satisfactory."

Smith went to Selma and was disappointed to find that he had little to do in his new position with the Alabama & Tennessee River Railroad. The destruction inflicted by war had been compounded by devastating spring floods, and no trains ran over the line. Smith soon became intolerably bored as he idled the time away at Selma, and he decided to move on. After only two months he resigned to accept a job offer from Albert Fink of the Louisville & Nashville Railroad as local freight agent in Louisville. Smith made a wise decision. His talents were being wasted at Selma, and he was destined to earn fame with the L&N. But he had made some important acquaintances during his brief stay in Selma, and the state of Alabama would hear more of Milton H. Smith—much more.[12]

Meanwhile, another newcomer was also exerting his influence in Alabama. Charles Pollard's Montgomery & West Point Railroad, like others in the state, reeled under heavy indebtedness and suffered from a dearth of traffic along its impoverished route. As the debts fell due, Pollard desperately turned to the renowned president of the Central Railroad & Banking Company of Georgia, William Wadley. In 1870, with financial assistance from Wadley, the long-wished-for trackage from Montgomery to Selma was finished, and the entire 161 miles of railroad between Selma and West Point was consolidated under the Western Rail Road of Alabama's corporate name.[13] As early as the mid-1840s another Georgia enterprise, the Georgia Railroad & Banking Company, had secured an interest in the Montgomery & West Point Railroad. Now, with the Central's investment, an ambitious regional railroad system had penetrated the state by acquisition, and Alabama's railroad resources slipped even further from local control. The floodgates of exploitation were opening, and the *Mobile Register* immediately expressed its concern in an editorial:

> Fully one-third of Mobile's cotton crop comes from the territory or basin having Selma for its centre. Until recently there was no possible outlet for all the products of that region save via Mobile and the trade consequent was rich and of real value to our city. The smart city of Savannah and her vigor-

ous railroad king, Wadley, observed this Alabama river and canebrake region trade with longing eyes, and determined to "go for it." To secure the cotton of the Selma region and the return trade to Savannah, Wadley and his Savannah backers have constructed the Montgomery and Selma road, and recently have purchased and obtained full control of the Montgomery & West Point Road so that now the Georgia Central road virtually extends to Selma from Savannah direct. In other words, Savannah has thrust a large tap into our barrel, and during the coming season will make great effort to draw the larger share of our hitherto tributary trade of Selma.[14]

Wadley's Central Railroad & Banking Company gained an additional foothold in Alabama by supplying an influx of capital that kept the Mobile & Girard railroad out of bankruptcy. The Mobile & Girard was repaired and extended from Union Springs to Troy in 1870.

The Montgomery & West Point and Mobile & Girard were not the only railroads that were forced to apply to outsiders for assistance. The Alabama & Tennessee River Railroad had originally been projected to Gadsden, where the proposed Tennessee & Coosa Railroad was to connect it with the Tennessee River. But the Tennessee & Coosa Railroad had never been built, and the Alabama & Tennessee River Railroad essentially led nowhere. Company officials characterized Gadsden, the road's ultimate destination, as a "point of no importance." In 1868, therefore, the route was redirected to Rome, Georgia, where important connections to the east were effected via Dalton, Georgia. After an appropriate name change, the Selma, Rome & Dalton Railroad became a link in a chain of railways that joined the nation's capitol with New Orleans. Selma, Rome & Dalton managers emphasized that construction of this 101-mile extension, as well as repair of the original trackage, was deliberately contracted to a northern firm with the hope that this patronage could help in "securing the co-operation of capitalists in the northern states." In order to pay these Northerners, as well as to repay the federal government and other creditors, the company issued five million dollars in bonds. Significantly, the company published a communiqué apprising the politicians in Washington that "three million of these bonds were taken by citizens of Ohio and New York."[15]

With no means or credit, other insolvent Alabama roads fought for survival through consolidation. The end-to-end Mobile & Great Northern and Alabama & Florida Railroads were merged in 1868 to form the Mobile & Montgomery Railroad. But the consolidation did little to relieve the critical shortage of capital, and the Mobile & Montgomery Railroad teetered on the brink of failure for more than a decade.[16]

In the decade following the Civil War, Alabama railways increasingly came under the sway of northern capitalists who brought with them the black clouds of financial and social calamity. As receipts ran low and bills came due, Alabama railroad men searched everywhere for money or credit—and neither was available except through the federal government or northern bankers. Therefore, Alabama railroad managers felt compelled to curry favor with northern interests while carefully avoiding conflicts in Washington. Intimidating bills introduced in the U.S. Congress elicited responses from Alabama railroad executives that clearly manifested these attitudes. In 1869 Congress was threatening to totally withdraw land grants that had been issued to the states of Florida, Alabama, Mississippi, and Louisiana, and executives of the Selma, Rome & Dalton Railroad tried to thwart this action by repeatedly offering assurances that Northerners and Europeans were in control. One of their appeals poignantly illustrated the measures that had to be taken by all of Alabama's railroad companies in order to ensure survival. The company assured Congress that "a majority of the stock . . . and nearly all its bonds are held by loyal citizens of the United States, residing in the cities of New York and Cincinnati, and by residents of Europe; that the president of the company and a majority of the board of directors reside in the State of New York; and that the means for the repairing and completion of the road have been subscribed and furnished by northern capitalists since the close of the war." The petition further emphasized "that the construction of said railroad has been vigorously prosecuted by the contractor, who has employed a thousand laborers, a greater part of whom are freedmen, and many of whom but for this employment would have been a charge upon the government for their support."[17]

The plight of the Selma, Rome & Dalton Railroad was typical. The credit extended by the U.S. government to get southern roads back in operation was coming due, and more money was also needed for improvements and maintenance. Where would the money come from?

Memphis & Charleston passenger cars at Huntsville Depot in 1870. (Courtesy of the Heritage Room, Huntsville-Madison County Public Library, Huntsville, Alabama)

Memphis & Charleston mixed train, crossing the Tennessee River at Florence around 1890. (Courtesy of the Alabama Department of Archives and History, Montgomery, Alabama)

The formula for rehabilitating Alabama's railroads now called for a transfer of financial and administrative control to Northerners and Europeans. Unfortunately, the intrusion of northern capitalists soon gave way to an invasion by mercenary financiers who aspired to emulate the notorious "robber barons" of the day. Many of them were abetted by equally unprincipled Southerners who aimed to loot the state of the few remaining resources available for renewing her prostrate railroad industry. Most of these rascals were allied with the "Radicals," the more extreme elements of the Republican party. The Radicals vied with conservative politicians for control of the state, and for several years the Radicals held the upper hand. Throughout this period Radical votes were for sale, and one of their most eager patrons was the Boston financier, John C. Stanton.

7

RADICALS
AND
RASCALS

JOHN C. STANTON embarked upon his Alabama railroad adventures in 1867, when Robert Jemison, president of the North East & South West Alabama Railroad Company was frantically searching for means to finish building his railway line. When all attempts to secure local financing failed, Jemison turned simultaneously to the state legislature and to northern entrepreneurs for help. Jemison dispatched two representatives northward, Captain Bozeman and ex-Governor Robert M. Patton. Bozeman and Patton were soon introduced to J. C. Stanton, who represented himself as an investor with pockets deep enough to assure successful prosecution of the railroad work. In reality, Stanton had little money of his own but saw a chance to become a real man of means by posing as a legitimate railroad developer. Stanton's keen interest in Alabama railroads had been aroused in no small measure by Jemison's coincident activities at the state capitol.[1]

The desire for state aid for railroad construction had been growing steadily before the war and was now considered a necessity, since Alabama could never expect to recover economically until her infrastructure was adequately developed. Robert Jemison and other railroad promoters vigorously pursued state aid, and in early 1867 found sympathy with provisional legislators. Unfortunately, many of these politicians looked upon such aid as a way to enrich themselves and their associates; and any incidental benefits that might accrue to the state through the development of railroad properties were of secondary importance. On February 19, 1867, the Second Provisional Legislature of the State of Alabama passed the infamous Internal Improvement Act that opened the door for "financial buccaneers" such as Stanton to plunder the state treasury.

In its original form, however, the act gave the appearance of providing desperately needed capital to aid in building railroads, while safeguarding the state in extending her credit. The law guaranteed the principal and interest on bonds issued by railroad companies that were legally incorporated by the state. Specifically, the state provided $12,000 in loan guarantees for each mile of track that these companies opened for traffic within Alabama. The initial guarantees went into effect as soon as the railroad company completed twenty miles of construction at either end of its road. Then, further endorsements would accrue at the same rate for each additional twenty-mile section that was fully equipped for operation. The guaranteed bonds were to be used solely for building and equipping the designated line within the state.

The act stipulated that the president and a majority of the directors of any railroad company receiving an endorsement must reside within the state, and that the corporate offices of the company must be located in Alabama. At least two of the directors of the company were to be appointed by the governor. Further, the endorsed bonds could not be sold for less than ninety cents on the dollar. The bonds were to include covenants insuring the prompt payment of interest and principal, and semiannual reports on the condition of the road were to be made to the governor. Minimum standards of construction were also specified. The track had to be five feet in width and the rail was required to have a minimum weight of fifty pounds per yard. The first twenty miles of track were to be completed within three years of the first endorsement and the entire railroad was to be completely finished within seven years. In addition, roads receiving an endorsement were to transport all state freight without charge. If the railroad company failed to meet these loan provisions, the state was authorized to seize its property.[2]

Ignoring the safeguards built into this act, J. C. Stanton and his brother Daniel found its provisions to be so generous that they immediately took steps to establish themselves as Alabama railroad promoters. The Stantons came to Alabama and toured both the Wills Valley Railroad and the North East & South West Alabama Railroad. The Wills Valley Railroad, running from Chattanooga to Trenton, Georgia, had emerged from the Civil War relatively unscathed. After examining these properties, the Stanton brothers were convinced that the antebellum plans to consolidate the two roads should be carried out. The consolidated line would link New Orleans with Chattanooga and also provide access to the potentially valuable mineral deposits of north

Alabama. The Stantons proceeded to rent the Wills Valley Railroad, and instructed Jemison to liquidate the North East & South West Alabama Railroad's debts and transfer the company to them and their associates. Eventually, Jemison called in all of the North East & South West Alabama Railroad securities, extinguished the company's obligation to the state for a loan from the Three Percent Fund, and effected the merger with the Wills Valley Railroad. The merged line was called the Alabama & Chattanooga Railroad, and J. C. Stanton was its president.[3]

Stanton's first action as president of the Alabama & Chattanooga Railroad was to secure more legislation favoring railroads. Stanton's agents lobbied the legislature to liberalize terms of the endorsement act, and on August 7, 1868, the act was amended to allow endorsement for consecutive five-mile sections of completed track after the initial twenty miles of qualifying tracklaying had been done. Less than two months later, the act was further amended to increase the amount of the endorsement to $16,000 per mile. Provisions requiring home rule of railroad companies were also dropped. Stanton even succeeded in having clauses included in the amended act pertaining exclusively to his rented Wills Valley Railroad, which had not yet been extended into the state, that enabled it to receive endorsements. These clauses effectively allowed Stanton to partake of the munificence of the state by avoiding the inconvenience of actually building track in Alabama.[4]

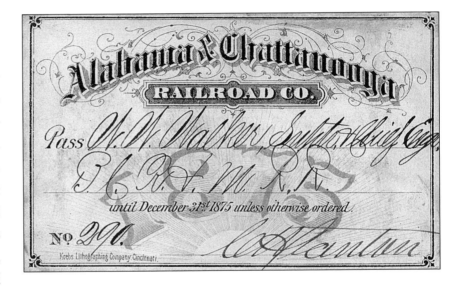

Alabama & Chattanooga Railroad annual pass for 1875. (From the author's collection)

The Internal Improvement Act was passed during the administration of Governor William H. Smith, who was initially opposed to it. In his message of November 15, 1869, Smith warned of the problems the act potentially could promulgate. "An entire road might be built upon public credit, and without the contribution of any individual capital," Smith cautioned, "and it might be done through parts of the State, and between points where there is not sufficient business to justify the expenditure of so much money, raised upon credit alone. It is possible, indeed, to construct a road in this way that would not pay running expenses after it was put in operation." Predicting that the "law will probably so operate as to embarrass the State's credit," Smith called for its repeal.[5] Governor Smith was correct, of course, but the Reconstruction legislature refused to heed his remonstrations and passed laws that basically reaffirmed the original statutes.[6] Smith then decided to adopt the old adage "if you can't beat 'em, join 'em," and went on to become one of the principal abusers of this law.

On December 31, 1868, the state legislature also authorized towns, cities, and counties to subscribe to the stock of railroad enterprises operating in Alabama. This law compelled local government officials to order a vote on such stock subscriptions if the promoters of any of these railroad ventures merely requested a referendum. If the proposal were rejected, another vote could be similarly ordered within twelve months. If voted down a second time, the referendum was finished; but if the proposal were approved, the local government was legally bound to purchase stock in the railway company. The law further stipulated that the governmental body had to pay for the stock with a bond issue, which was to be funded by a special tax levy. Once the railroad promoters gained possession of these bonds, the door was opened wide for abuse. When the promoters took the bonds in payment for stock, they could sell them in the open market for cash, pocket the proceeds, and forget about constructing the railroad. This left the local government with nothing more than worthless railroad stock and desperate creditors clamoring for redemption of its bonds.

All these state, county, and municipal aid laws invited an avalanche of railroad speculation, and the state was soon besieged by a bevy of financial adventurers seeking to pilfer her financial coffers. In most cases, the only ones to benefit from the railroad aid acts were the promoters. All of the roads that received state, county, and municipal aid would eventually default, saddling their benefactors with staggering losses.

Demographics caused the county and municipal aid law to be especially onerous in Black Belt counties. The newly enfranchised but landless black population greatly outnumbered the white landowners in this region; and corrupt promoters of varying political stripes used any means possible, including bribery and intimidating threats, to win this large block of votes. Thus, railroad referendums continued to force impossible debts upon the taxpayers. Many counties were left in such poor financial condition that they were unable to continue governing themselves, and became known as "strangulated counties." Among these were Randolph, Lee, and Chambers counties, which were victims of the East Alabama & Cincinnati Railroad Company.[7]

The East Alabama & Cincinnati Railroad Company, organized in 1868, was projected to connect Eufaula with Guntersville. The only capital this line ever had consisted of state, county, and city aid. Even though the first twenty miles of track from Opelika to Buffalo Wallow were not completed before 1871, Governor Smith nonetheless immediately endorsed $400,000 of the company's bonds. No public books of subscription were ever opened for this road, and everything was done with borrowed money. The company even counted its common laborers as creditors.

The president of this road fraudulently certified that the prescribed twenty miles of track had been built solely with the company's resources, but the few miles of track that were finished certainly did not meet the standards set down by the endorsement law. Rail was light, trestles were flimsy and wood was substituted for stone in culverts. Samuel G. Jones had signed on as engineer for this company and knew an endorsement could not legally be obtained. When he found that the company expected him to lie to the legislature concerning the road's construction, he refused to have a part in the conspiracy and tendered his resignation. The line was sold under foreclosure in 1880 and reorganized as the East Alabama Railway Company. No more construction was accomplished until 1887.[8]

Opelika squandered a substantial sum on the East Alabama & Cincinnati Railroad and, together with Mobile and Selma, suffered grievously in supporting various railroad schemes. These and other Alabama cities encumbered so much railroad debt that they fell into bankruptcy and eventually became wards of the state, functioning only as districts under the governor's supervision.[9]

Referendums on railroad aid came frequently in Selma. Various promoters aspired to make Selma the railroad hub of the state by projecting lines north to Nashville, northwest to Memphis, and south to New Orleans and Pensacola. The line to Pensacola was called the Selma & Gulf Railroad. The only capital the road ever put together consisted of $40,000 paid in by private capitalists, $60,000 loaned by the city of Selma, and $36,000 loaned by the state from the Three Percent Fund. Nevertheless, Republican Governor Smith endorsed this road for $480,000 and Democratic Governor Lindsay followed with an endorsement of $160,000, proving that neither political party monopolized extravagance and mismanagement during the Reconstruction era.[10]

Another Selma project that was enthusiastically promoted on Wall Street and in the military legislature was the New Orleans & Selma Railroad, which was to be part of a proposed rail system connecting New York with Mazatlán, Mexico. After laying the requisite twenty miles of track from Selma to Martin, Alabama, organizers secured a state endorsement of $320,000. The road was then "permitted to slumber," a lull that inevitably led to insolvency.[11]

Other Black Belt pikes got their share of state aid. The Montgomery & Eufaula Railroad Company received loan guarantees totaling $1,280,000. This road started auspiciously in 1860 when an engine named the *John H. Murphy* chugged along a few miles of track. Those tracks were unceremoniously ripped from beneath the *Murphy* during the Civil War, and the engine was soon found shuttling munitions between Selma and Meridian. The old roadbed lay dormant until city and state governments came to its aid after the war. But the state endorsements were not enough to tide the company over, and the legislature decided that the Montgomery & Eufaula deserved a direct loan of $300,000. When charges of bribery were leveled against the promoters of this road, its former president refused to testify before an Alabama house investigating committee. The entire eighty miles of track were in operation by 1871, but the road's assets were worth only about $842,000, even after the company had obtained $1,580,000 in state credit. It would eventually have to be pulled out of receivership by William Wadley of the Central Railroad & Banking Company of Georgia.[12]

The movement for state aid behooved promoters of the Mobile & Alabama Grand Trunk Railroad to accept $800,000 in state endorsements. When this amount was added to the $1,500,000 in county and city subscriptions already under its belt, the road was able to progress sixty miles along a proposed 270-mile route that was to connect Mobile "with any other roads which are now or may hereafter be constructed in the State of Alabama." Doubtless the long-suffering subscribers thought it would be the "hereafter" before this line was finished, and wondered where their money went. The entire company was valued at only $704,225. When the inevitable default occurred, the railroad completely ceased operations for a number of years while awaiting a well-heeled buyer.[13]

Although conservative Southerners revered their Civil War heroes and reviled the Radicals, the railroad aid programs seemed to blur the distinction between the two. The best example of this phenomenon occurred on December 31, 1868, when the Alabama legislature amended the acts incorporating the Cahaba, Marion & Greensboro Railroad Company, changed the line's name to the Selma, Marion & Memphis Railroad, and welcomed Civil War hero Nathan Bedford Forrest as president of the new company. The road was intended to connect Selma with Memphis, and construction began on June 1, 1869. Later that month, the city of Greensboro voted to subscribe to $15,000 in the railroad's stock. In July, Hale County voted in favor of a $60,000 subscription. On October 9, 1869, the Selma, Marion & Memphis received a state endorsement. Even though the endorsement law only authorized $16,000 for each mile of track, Nathan Bedford Forrest was able to secure an endorsement for $18,000 per mile. The state granted this endorsement despite the fact that there was no documentation to show what had been accomplished on this line. If records had been kept, they would have revealed that the qualifying twenty miles of trackwork had not been completed. In fact, only two and three fourths miles of track had been laid by September, and the road had progressed no more than eight miles west of Marion by November 19, 1869. Nathan Bedford Forrest later sold $400,000 of the bonds in New York at a rate of 92.5 cents on the dollar. Finally, on January 1, 1870, the first engine, the *Porter King,* named after a judge in Perry County and a member of the board of directors, was put in operation.[14]

Clashes between conservative government officials and railroad endorsees sometimes precipitated rather unorthodox courtroom antics. A celebrated case in point occurred when a special session of the Commissioners Court convened to issue the bonds that Hale County voters approved to pay for the Selma, Marion & Memphis stock subscription. General Forrest appeared with the bonds, ready for the signature of the probate judge, W. T. Blackford. But Judge Blackford had a rigorously conservative temperament, and stubbornly refused to sign the securities. General Forrest, confident that Blackford could be persuaded to change his mind and endorse the certificates, consulted with his lawyer and instructed him to schedule a hearing before the judge.

At the hearing, Forrest's lawyer used many proper Latin phrases as he earnestly argued the railroad's case. But the judge was unimpressed and curtly told the lawyer: "Sir, I don't give a damn about your nunc pro tuncs, your nolens volens or your amicus curis. I am not going to sign them bonds." The indignant attorney couldn't hold his temper, exploded in a rage, and went for the judge's throat. But Judge Blackford was well prepared and quickly reached for his six-shooter to defend himself. Impulsively, Forrest intervened. The general threw himself upon the judge, disarmed him, and in a measured voice said, "Wal, Judge, I don't care a damn whether you sign them bonds nunc pro tunc, nolens volens or amicus curi; you are going to sign 'em. Come along with me." Forrest took Blackford to an anteroom, and after some time, a smiling judge emerged with Forrest to silently sign the bonds. It is unknown what transpired between Judge Blackford and General Forrest in the anteroom.[15]

In a later incident, Forrest heard that one of his contractors, Col. A. K. Shepherd, was not getting his work done properly. Although Shepherd was a man of good reputation, Forrest acrimoniously confronted him with abusive accusations. Forrest's charges made Shepherd so angry that he challenged the general to a duel. Forrest accepted and chose to settle the matter by firing "navy sixes" starting at ten paces until one or the other of them was killed.

Col. Charles E. Waller spent the night preceding the duel with Forrest and recorded what happened. "I noticed that General Forrest was restless throughout the night, for with the knowledge of the impending duel I was unable to sleep. About day-light, I looked across the room and saw the General sitting upon the side of his bed, and inquired of him why he was restless."

"I haven't slept for thinking about the trouble with Shepherd," Forrest replied. "I feel sure I can kill him, and if I do I will never forgive myself. I am convinced that he was right in resenting the way I talked to him. I am in the wrong, and do not feel satisfied about it."

"General Forrest, your courage has never been questioned," Colonel Waller responded. "I have no reputation of being a brave man, but under the circumstances I should feel it to be my duty to apologize to Colonel Shepherd and openly tell him that I was wrong."

Forrest agreed, "You are right, I will do it." The men then arose, and at the appointed time Forrest approached Shepherd and admitted, "Colonel, I am in the wrong in this affair and I have come to say so." Shepherd stated that he was glad and the two men parted peacefully.[16]

The line was finally completed to Greensboro on November 3, 1870, and passenger and freight trains began running the next day, but poor construction contributed to several accidents during the ensuing months. On October 11, 1871, an engine ran off the track about two miles from Marion, scalding the engineer and fireman, though not severely. On December 20, 1872, the shoddily laid track buckled under the weight of a train and the engine ran off the roadbed, killing the fireman, George Evans. The engineer, George King of Marion, broke both legs and died two days afterward. On April 23, 1874, a trestle near Greensboro collapsed while a train was crossing, and the engine fell thirty feet, injuring the engineer, mail agent, and brakeman. Meanwhile, Gen. E. W. Rucker, superintendent of the railroad, took advantage of a long-standing Alabama custom and leased prisoners to work on the road between Eutaw and the Warrior River as well as on the Warrior River bridge. Presumably, the convicts' work was no better than that done on the rest of the line.[17]

Although this company had received an abundance of aid, Forrest warned that work on the railroad would have to stop unless more money could be obtained. The general allowed that northern investors didn't want to invest in southern businesses. The company adopted a resolution expressing confidence in General Forrest, but the road was to meet the same fate as its contemporaries and become a victim of the panic of 1873. Forrest went to New York in September 1873 and was there when the panic struck Wall Street. He said that in all of his military and civilian life he had seen nothing like the demoralization produced by the panic. He did not believe that his or any other railroad could get money under the current circumstances, and he was right. Forrest eventually lost his personal fortune when the Selma, Marion & Memphis Railroad failed—with no more than forty-five miles of the line finished.[18]

General Forrest was a picturesque figure, but his impact on Alabama's railroads paled when compared to that of J. C. Stanton. Stanton's manipulative hand could be found in almost all of Alabama's Reconstruction railroads. Stanton had moved to Montgomery and rented four rooms at the Exchange Hotel, where he set up a command post to personally supervise the administration of Alabama's railroad endorsement law.[19] Corrupt legislators paraded between the state house and Stanton's hotel rooms to receive their bribes, and by November 1869 Stanton had obtained $1,800,000 in state endorsements for his Alabama & Chattanooga Railroad. He used the portion of this railroad already completed between Meridian and York as a basis for claiming endorsement of the company's bonds. Although the other end of the road was rented, Stanton also secured $320,000 in endorsements for the old Wills Valley segment, despite the fact that this part of the A&C had already been endorsed by the State of Georgia at a rate of $3,000 per mile. Stanton used proceeds from the endorsed bonds to pay the rent on this part of the line instead of building new track as the law required.[20]

Stanton also secured a renewal of the land grant to the Alabama & Chattanooga Railroad. The renewal agreement stipulated that the railroad had to be completed within three years in order to retain the land. The land was also to be sold to settlers in small tracts at a price of not more than $2.25 per acre. Stanton did not abide by these provisions and sold large tracts of valuable mineral land to speculators.[21]

Stanton's influence in the legislature was so powerful that in 1870 he was able to obtain a direct loan from the state when Alabama lawmakers issued $2,000,000 in state bonds that were secured by the A&C land grant properties. In return, Stanton promised to complete the Alabama & Chattanooga as a first-class railroad by June 1, 1871. A common legislative practice of the time, blatant bribery, was used to get this loan. The bill failed at first, but after Stanton and his associates conferred privately with some key representatives, it was sent back to the committee with instructions to report back in fifteen minutes. Suddenly enlightened, the representatives promptly approved the measure.[22]

In a later investigation, a representative named Jesse Harrellson shed some light on the manner in which this legislation was handled. Harrellson initially refused to vote for the "Stanton Bill," as it was called, because he felt he had been underpaid for previous votes. Harrellson then heard that money was to be had and went to the Exchange Hotel, where he patiently waited with other representatives in one of Stanton's rooms. One by one, the other delegates were called into the hallway to receive their bribes. One of these statesmen proudly boasted to Harrellson that he had held out for no less than five hundred dollars. Harrellson was never called into the hallway, however, and went home disappointed. Learning the next day from other representatives that Stanton was still distributing money, Jesse returned to the hotel and finally got an audience with the railroad magnate. Questioning the representative's reliability, Stanton sternly denounced Harrellson for being a Democrat. Intimidated, and anxious to pacify Stanton, Jesse pleaded that he had "left that party." After being assured of Harrellson's vote, Stanton proceeded to "loan" him fifty dollars.[23]

Collusion with Stanton often brought benefits to other railroad promoters. When the Stanton Bill was introduced, it was reported that Frank Gilmer, president of the South & North Alabama Railroad, went to his bankers asking for $25,000 to be "used at the capitol." Gilmer was rebuffed at first, but later the bankers got the money for him. The money was requested by committee chairman John Hardy to "oil the bearings" of government. In order to get the Stanton Bill passed, Hardy later determined that he would need another $10,000. When Gilmer handed over the additional $10,000, the chairman was able to get enough votes to secure passage of the measure.[24] Executives of the South & North Alabama Railroad Company evidently became quite adept at securing state aid. In a coup that would have made General Forrest blush, they eventually obtained an endorsement for the S&N at the exorbitant rate of $22,000 per mile.[25]

The state bonds aiding the Alabama & Chattanooga Railroad were to be issued to Stanton's company from time to time, as required, to build the railroad. But Governor Smith issued them all at once, and Stanton immediately sold the bonds in Europe and used part of the money to build a hotel and an opera house in Chattanooga. Meanwhile, Smith continued to affix the state's endorsement seal to even more Alabama & Chattanooga Railroad Company bonds.

In the gubernatorial election of 1870, incumbent Smith was opposed by Democrat Robert B. Lindsay, who denounced the corruption that led to the Stanton loan. Stanton liberally contributed to Smith's campaign, and on election day he ordered nine hundred Alabama & Chattanooga Railroad employees to the polls to cast their vote for Smith.[26] Lindsay was elected, however, and he immediately began an investigation of Smith's endorsements. It was evident that the Alabama & Chattanooga Railroad had received more endorsements than legally entitled: 250 miles had already been endorsed even though only 154 miles of track had been finished in the state. But Smith had kept few records, and Lindsay was unable to determine accurately the total extent of the state's obligations.

All of the money from the state bond issue had disappeared in less than a year, and in January 1871 the Alabama & Chattanooga defaulted in all its interest payments.[27] Work continued on the line, however, and on March 6, 1871, the first train rolled into Tuscaloosa. The *Tuscaloosa Observer* marked the exciting occasion with an editorial gratefully lauding Stanton and admonishing the newly elected governor to make good the state's guarantee of interest on the railroad bonds. The article predicted that the Alabama & Chattanooga Railroad would make the Tuscaloosa region "not only the Lowell, but the Pittsburgh of the South," thanks to the enterprise of men "like Mr. J. C. Stanton and his brothers, the millionaires of the rejuvenated South."[28]

Employees of the Alabama & Chattanooga Railroad found it hard to praise Stanton, however. In an all-out effort to complete the road by the June 1 deadline, Stanton had hired one thousand Chinese laborers to work on the eastern end of the line. On March 6, 1871, the coolies engaged the black gandy dancers in a game of dice. The black men became indignant after being stripped of all their money, and an altercation broke out. The blacks were losing this contest also and had to be rescued by a group of ex-soldiers. It can be readily understood why these workers were so distraught over losing their money. A steady paycheck could not be counted on when working for Stanton. Destitute farmers along the route who had been persuaded to quit their farms and work on the road would certainly attest to this fact.[29]

With the default, it was now imperative that Smith's sloppy handling of the railroad bonds should be pieced together. Governor Lindsay headed for New York in March to try to assess the state's liabilities, and published the results of his investigation the following month. "My first step in the investigation," Lindsay reported, "was to ascertain what had become of these bonds, whether they had been sold to innocent purchasers or remained in the hands of the Alabama and Chattanooga Railroad Company, or any of the corporators or agents thereof . . . or held by parties cognizant of fraud in their issuance or endorsement. To accomplish my objective I availed myself of every accessible avenue of information." One of these avenues was Soutter & Company, the original financial agents for the Alabama & Chattanooga Railroad Company. From Soutter & Company, Lindsay obtained a sworn statement certifying that four thousand state-endorsed bonds, as well as the two thousand straight bonds issued on behalf of the railroad, had been sold to Americans and Europeans who were portrayed as being ignorant of any scheme to defraud the state of Alabama. Lindsay then walked down the street to the offices of German banker August Goettel, where he procured another sworn assurance that the two thousand straight bonds had been purchased in good faith by the firm's Parisian client, Emile Erlanger. "From other sources which I considered perfectly reliable," Lindsay disclosed, "I obtained corroborating information, all of which satisfied me that four thousand endorsed bonds, and two thousand direct bonds of the State, were purchased by, and were on the 1st day of January, 1871, the property of innocent and *bona fide* holders, who had never participated in any fraud upon the State or cognizant of such."[30]

Lindsay's investigation led him to conclude that at least thirteen hundred more Alabama & Chattanooga bonds had been issued than were authorized by the endorsement law. In fact, this was five hundred more bonds than the road would ever be entitled to when totally complete and equipped. Still, Governor Lindsay maintained that the state was legally bound to pay the interest on four thousand endorsed bonds and two thousand straight bonds.[31] To him and other conscientious citizens, it was unthinkable that Alabama could ever endanger its credit rating by defaulting on legal obligations. But had Lindsay uncovered the truth of the matter? Were these bonds indeed legally purchased by innocent parties? The following editorial comment in a Jacksonville daily expressed great skepticism:

> Facts . . . strongly show that the House of Erlanger & Co. were "participe criminis" in with the Directors of the Road and Soutter & Co., their financial agents, in the fraudulent issue and sale of these bonds.
>
> It is a little strange that Governor Lindsay should have examined no other witnesses than the very parties implicated in the fraud. He first called on Soutter & Co. and was so overpowered by their wonderful condescension, in furnishing him with a sworn statement, from their books, that he at once jumped to the conclusion: "It is all right." How these bankers must have chuckled over their politeness and blandishments, as well as the easy credulity of the Governor. They probably sat down and wrote to Stanton . . . "We are now in a very snug condition. The State will pay all or nearly all of the interest on the bonds."
>
> The next witness called upon by Governor Lindsay is a German Banker by the name of August Goettel, an agent as he represents himself to be, of Erlanger & Co. . . . Goettel comes right up to the scratch and swears the two million bonds straight through, and the interest into the coffers of his house.[32]

Despite these suspicions, the state paid interest on the bonds that Lindsay deemed to be legally purchased. The excess bonds were declared fraudulent and the state refused to pay interest on them. Legal proceedings were then commenced against the Alabama & Chattanooga Railroad as the state sought to indemnify herself. On June 8, 1871, the company was adjudged bankrupt and the state of Alabama moved to seize its assets.[33]

The wily Stanton was often a step ahead of the authorities, however. On June 17 a news flash appeared in a Volunteer State newspaper proclaiming "The Stantons in Hot Water":

A great deal of commotion was created in Chattanooga Friday, by a general levy upon all the rolling stock and other property connected with the Alabama and Chattanooga Railroad by creditors who claim to have been kept out of their money by J. C. Stanton, Superintendent of that road: They attempted to levy on the $7,500 silver tea set presented to Stanton by the employees of the road but he was too sharp for them. On the approach of the officer, it is said that Stanton had the set taken out of the box in which it was kept and then relocked it. The officer seizing the box, it was subsequently opened among a large number of spectators and, found to be empty.

All the trains on the road have been stopped. It is stated that Stanton has $2,000,000 at his command but will not cash any of his liabilities unless absolutely forced to do it, that he owes six months wages to his employees; that he is indebted to the people of Chattanooga to the amount of one million of dollars and also indebted largely to the merchants of Nashville.

There is a good deal of excitement at Chattanooga about the affairs of the road and serious trouble is apprehended.[34]

Angry employees at the southern end of the line, demanding their wages, commandeered a large amount of equipment and rolling stock and hustled it to Meridian, Mississippi. On July 20, 1871, Governor Lindsay appointed Col. John H. Gindrat as the company's receiver and instructed him to go to Meridian to gain possession of the property being held by the strikers. Hoping to get their pay from the state of Alabama, the A&C hands willingly negotiated with Gindrat and relinquished the property to him. Lindsay then ordered Gindrat to go northward and seize all the assets along the line.

The employees ensconced at Meridian supplied Gindrat with a locomotive and passenger cars and he proceeded to follow Lindsay's orders. Gindrat encountered no opposition as the agents along the line surrendered all property to him and promised to hold it in the name of the state. When Gindrat returned to Meridian, he found that A&C lawyers had obtained an injunction preventing him from removing equipment from Mississippi, but after a short legal battle, U.S. marshals seized the property and arranged to have it returned to Alabama.[35]

Meantime, the bankrupt Selma & Meridian Railroad had been purchased by its bondholders, who changed its corporate name to the Alabama Central Railroad. The Alabama Central Railroad depended upon the Alabama & Chattanooga for its connection between Meridian and York and, because of the default, had been prohibited for several weeks from using this route. The U.S. mail was routed over the Alabama Central, and now its movement was virtually stopped. The Alabama

Central was desperate to get the mail moving again, and joined with Gindrat in trying to restore service over the whole length of the Alabama & Chattanooga Railroad. Managers of the Alabama Central agreed to pay $1,000 per month for trackage rights between Meridian and York for the next year and put up $10,000 of this amount immediately. With this money, Gindrat could assure A&C employees that they would be paid, and by August 10, 1871, trains were running from Tuscaloosa to Attalla.[36]

But the road was in bad shape when Gindrat renewed operations. The roadbed was poorly drained and covered with weeds, and landslides blocked the right-of-way at many places. With cautious deliberation, Gindrat made the most urgently needed repairs while he carefully estimated the revenues that he could reasonably expect to receive from the railroad. After concluding that the railroad could generate enough profits to pay for the necessary repairs to ensure its safe operation through the winter, he stepped up the pace of rehabilitation.

No turntables existed between Tuscaloosa and Attalla, and trains had to be run straight through this lightly settled region, even though it provided no business of any consequence. Nevertheless, Gindrat was confident the road would soon be opened to Chattanooga, and continued to run the trains between Tuscaloosa and Attalla. The two ends of the line finally met in November 1871, and regular schedules were established between Chattanooga and Meridian. Still, much work was left to be done. Several temporary trestles would have to be replaced later with permanent structures, at considerable cost, but the line was complete despite all the scandal.

In 1872 the road passed into the hands of its bondholders, and in 1876 Alabama's Debt Commission paid $1,000,000 to extinguish its claims against the Alabama & Chattanooga and rid itself of the "disgusting business."[37] In 1877, Emile Erlanger and Company purchased the road outright for a little less than $1,500,000.[38]

The Alabama & Chattanooga case was just the tip of Alabama's railroad endorsement iceberg. The state ultimately shouldered $30,000,000 in aggregate railroad debt, which caused her credit rating to severely sag.[39] Some state bonds traded as low as twenty cents on the dollar before confidence in Alabama's credit could be restored.[40] Although the cost was heavy, the endorsements were by no means completely wasted, and much critically needed mileage was added to the state's railway system during the Reconstruction years. Included in

Alabama Great Southern Passenger Depot, Tuscaloosa, Ala.

This rare view shows the charming little Alabama Great Southern depot, which served Tuscaloosa until it was replaced by a substantial brick building around 1910. (Postcard ca. 1905, from the author's collection)

this mileage was the Mobile & Montgomery Railroad's long-awaited entrance into Mobile. With the help of endorsements, the enormously expensive tracklaying across the marshes, swamps, and watercourses leading into Mobile was accomplished in 1872, and the tedious twenty-two-mile Tensas River ferry trip between Mobile and the pier at Hurricane, Alabama, became a thing of the past.[41] From 1865 to 1875, thanks largely to the endorsements, Alabama tallied an increase of 115 percent in railroad mileage, and bounded from seventh to second place in total trackage among the southeastern states.[42] And Emile Erlanger's investment in the Alabama & Chattanooga Railroad proved to be very wise indeed. In 1877 the Alabama & Chattanooga Railroad was renamed the Alabama Great Southern Railroad; and in 1881 Erlanger led a European syndicate that put together a giant combination of southern lines, anchored by the Alabama Great Southern Railroad, that extended from the Ohio River to New Orleans. The great integrated system of Erlanger roads became known as the Queen & Crescent Route.[43]

Even though Alabamians lost millions to conniving railroad promoters and politicians, the Alabama experience was far from unique. In the North as well as the South, postwar corruption was rampant. Reckless manipulators plundered great national systems like the Erie

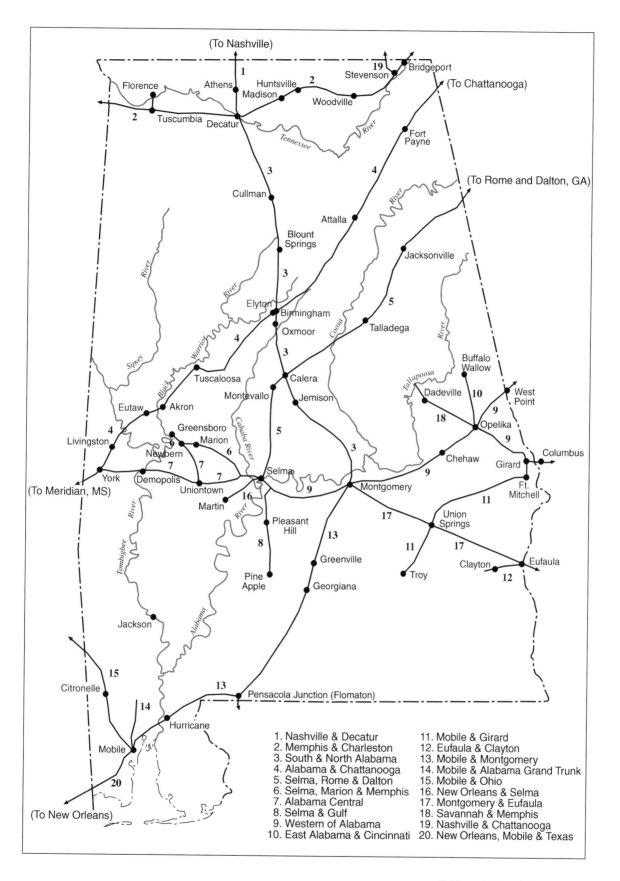

(To Nashville)

1

Florence
Athens
Huntsville
Madison
Decatur
Tuscumbia
2
2
Woodville
19 Stevenson
Bridgeport

(To Chattanooga)

Tennessee River

3

4

Fort Payne

(To Rome and Dalton, GA)

Cullman

Attalla

River

Blount Springs

3

Jacksonville

Elyton
Birmingham
Oxmoor

5

Talladega

Coosa

River

4

3

Calera

Buffalo Wallow

West Point

Sipsey River

Warrior

Black

Warrior

Tuscaloosa
Montevallo

Jemison

Tallapoosa

Dadeville

10

9

18

Opelika

9

Eutaw
Akron

Cahaba River

5

Columbus

Livingston

4

Greensboro
Marion

6

6

Chehaw

Girard

9

Ft. Mitchell

Newbern

7

7

6

9

Demopolis

7

Selma

Montgomery

11

York

Uniontown

16

Union Springs

(To Meridian, MS)

Martin

River

9

17

17

Pleasant Hill

13

11

Clayton

Eufaula

Tombigbee River

8

Greenville

Troy

12

Pine Apple

Georgiana

Jackson

Alabama

15

Citronelle

14

13

Pensacola Junction (Flomaton)

Hurricane

R.

Mobile

20

(To New Orleans)

1. Nashville & Decatur
2. Memphis & Charleston
3. South & North Alabama
4. Alabama & Chattanooga
5. Selma, Rome & Dalton
6. Selma, Marion & Memphis
7. Alabama Central
8. Selma & Gulf
9. Western of Alabama
10. East Alabama & Cincinnati

11. Mobile & Girard
12. Eufaula & Clayton
13. Mobile & Montgomery
14. Mobile & Alabama Grand Trunk
15. Mobile & Ohio
16. New Orleans & Selma
17. Montgomery & Eufaula
18. Savannah & Memphis
19. Nashville & Chattanooga
20. New Orleans, Mobile & Texas

Alabama's Reconstruction-Era Railway System, 1873

RADICALS AND RASCALS   95

and the Union Pacific, and in the nation's capital, legislators were only slightly less corrupt than those occupying the state houses.[44] Among the southern states, the Carolinas and Georgia were exploited just as liberally as Alabama.

Still, the trauma of Reconstruction in Alabama was especially excruciating due to the extreme poverty of her citizens. Those who had had wealth before the war were mercilessly stripped of it and were left with worthless Confederate currency and bank deposits; pitifully undeveloped industries that had been destroyed, seized or sold; and vastly depreciated property. The agricultural economy that had been their lifeblood was in complete disarray, and the labor system had been totally transformed. For planter and freedman alike, little was left to begin anew. Long years of war and blockade had taken a heavy toll, and the impoverished populace could find only worn-out tools with which to begin rebuilding. And these were the lucky ones; tens of thousands of Alabamians never returned from the battlefields.[45]

Noted historian Albert B. Moore concluded that the tactics used to promote Alabama's Reconstruction railroads were "neither better nor worse than those generally practiced throughout the country. They have seemed to be worse only because of the impoverished conditions of the people and because they were foisted upon the people by alien hands upheld by the military power of the Nation."[46] Not everyone could accept corruption as philosophically as Moore, however, especially those who dreamed of the great state railroad connecting north and south Alabama through the mineral region—the South & North Alabama Railroad. They had a much less charitable opinion of the scandalous schemes employed by men like J. C. Stanton—and justifiably so. Stanton was not satisfied with the fraud he perpetrated through the Alabama & Chattanooga Railroad Company, and his greedy hand reached for John T. Milner's prized mineral district.

8

L&N
TO THE
RESCUE

As JOHN C. STANTON rose to power in Alabama, he was acutely aware that Frank Gilmer's cherished South & North Alabama Railroad was vulnerable to his opportunistic schemes. Gilmer had not only committed himself to the Confederate cause through his efforts on the South & North Alabama Railroad, but he had also served as president of the Central Bank of Alabama and the war had left him a broken man.[1] Although dispossessed of resources, Gilmer and his associates continued to cling to their dream of building iron furnaces and a great workshop town in Alabama's mineral heartland, with railroad lines extending in all directions to distribute the mineral wealth to the world. As the specter of J. C. Stanton threatened this grand plan, John T. Milner contemplated the predicament of Frank Gilmer and his colleagues: "His millions were gone, and Frank Gilmer was a poor man, but before the hot embers of his grand conception in Jefferson County had cooled, men were at work securing and saving what was left. Collecting his scattered forces and unfurling his standard with his watchword 'On to Nashville,' Frank again began the work of resurrection. Though our strong men had gone to the wall, and our stockholders could not pay, a few of us kept our chartered interest alive."[2]

Stanton intended to deprive the Alabamians of their great workshop town by terminating the South & North Alabama Railroad at its junction with his Alabama & Chattanooga Railroad, thus diverting the coal and iron over the A&C to Chattanooga, where Stanton had substantial financial interests. Stanton wielded great power in Montgomery and soon had Gilmer replaced as president of the South & North Alabama Railroad by a prominent cotton factor, John Whiting. Stanton contrived to gain Whiting's support by disguising his scheme so that it appeared to benefit the cotton business. Whiting was "favorably impressed" with Stanton.[3]

Although Milner was extremely suspicious of Stanton, he feared that all he had so fervently worked for was in extreme jeopardy unless he cooperated with the Montgomery establishment. "I soon saw that Stanton, by a single wave of his hand could do away with that . . . which we were the beneficiaries, under the Act of 1859–60," Milner asserted. "I told Mr. Whiting he had better watch these matters of legislation. He spurned the idea of getting among these Yankees at all, much less of paying them for their votes, but he said I might do so if I felt like it. I had then been engaged in the work of building this railroad for over ten years, and my heart and soul were in it. So I went."[4]

Stanton wasted no time in presenting his plan to Whiting. Construction of the South & North Alabama Railroad was to end at Elyton, where it joined with the Alabama & Chattanooga Railroad, thus making it only a feeder line to Chattanooga. As Stanton anticipated, Whiting liked the idea. It would give Montgomery another connection directly with New York and facilitate the transport of cotton, which was Whiting's principal concern. Whiting declared that "Alabama was a cotton state" and the prospect for mineral development was "mainly talk after all." But Milner quickly realized that this was a plot designed to strip Alabama of her mineral heritage. "I saw at once, that this meant the ruin of our great railroad enterprise forever," he later recalled, "and the transfer of everything to Chattanooga, an irretrievable loss to Alabama. . . . The matter went far enough to require me to turn over all the profiles and maps I had made to Stanton's chief engineer, Major R. C. McCalla."[5]

Whiting was pondering the proposal to shorten the line when he went to Washington to confer on another matter related to cotton. While there, Whiting suddenly died, without making a firm decision to truncate the route. The following week the board of the South & North Alabama Railroad Company met in Montgomery to elect a new president, and everyone at that meeting was shocked when Frank Gilmer appeared. John Milner was as astonished as anyone: "Suddenly and without premonition, Frank Gilmer—this ghost of a man who was thought to be forever lost—appeared at the board in November, 1869, with proxies for a majority of the stock in his hand! The scenes at the feast of Belshazzar most fitly describe what happened in that room when this revelation was made. Gilmer was again elected president."[6] With Gilmer once again at the helm, the South & North Railroad might effectively resist Stanton. But Gilmer inherited little more than a weed-infested roadbed, with a lone locomotive, the trusty *Willis J. Milner,* forlornly rusting on a side track. The task of rehabilitation would be colossal.

On April 12, 1869, the railroad had executed a contract with Sam Tate and Associates to complete the line from Montgomery to Decatur, following Milner's route. For $5,014,220, Tate agreed to finish construction from Calera to Elyton by April 1, 1871, and to Decatur by December 1871.[7] At Decatur, James Sloss had already accomplished part of the grand plan by connecting his Tennessee & Alabama Central Railroad with the two Tennessee lines leading to Nashville, the Central Southern and the Tennessee & Alabama Railroad. Sloss had consolidated these three roads to form the Nashville & Decatur Railroad in 1866. If the South & North could make it to Decatur, Alabama minerals would have a direct route to the North through Nashville.[8]

Seeking to finish the road as rapidly and cheaply as possible, Gilmer instructed Tate to substitute long grades and curves for costly tunneling and bridgework. And long grades with winding curves he got! Milner recoiled at the thought of such a jerry-rigged route but reluctantly consented to the plan because he knew the company was critically short of money. The young engineer swallowed his pride and kept repeating, "More curves, more curves, more stiff grade," as the road snaked tortuously through the Alabama hills.[9]

Tate started at Montgomery and had the sixty-three miles of road to Calera in place by November 1870. A year later, the line reached Elyton, thirty-three miles away. As the road approached Elyton, Milner proposed that he and Stanton form a partnership to buy land near the junction with Stanton's Alabama & Chattanooga Railroad, where an industrial center could be built. Just as Gilmer had envisioned the development of the mineral region for years, Milner had dreamed of establishing a great workshop town where the two railroads would cross. He and Tate had discussed such a dream as they sat around construction site campfires at night. The A&C directors initially favored establishing the town near the pioneer blast furnace at Oxmoor. The Oxmoor furnace was the kernel of the budding mineral region that Milner hoped to nurture into an industrial giant. But Milner had selected a perfect site ten years earlier when he gazed down on beautiful Jones Valley from atop Red Mountain. His iron and coal metropolis would be in

Jones Valley, near the little brook known as Village Creek. This place had everything his town would need: dozens of springs for drinking water, adequate drainage, and plenty of room for expansion.

Milner eventually convinced Stanton that the Village Creek site was best and the two men procured options on seven thousand acres of Jones Valley farmland. But the ever-scheming Stanton only catered to Milner's wishes in order to cheat him. Stanton immediately ordered a change in the route of the Alabama & Chattanooga Railroad so that it crossed the South & North Alabama Railroad nearer to Elyton. He then proceeded to take up options on 4,150 acres of land around Elyton and backed out of his deal with Milner. Milner and the stockholders of the South & North Alabama Railroad Company were now in danger of losing their share in the proposed great workshop town.

The road had been surveyed to the crossing point originally agreed upon, and Milner was already busy laying out the streets of the new town when he received the news. Milner seethed in angry silence when he heard of Stanton's villainy and was unable to utter a word. Years later Milner remembered that "the infamy of the thing paralyzed me for a moment." After some time, the engineer gathered his composure, cabled his protest to Chattanooga, and resumed his work.[10]

Milner's wire was never answered. He had fallen into Stanton's web, and Milner's associates in Montgomery thought the South & North Alabama Railroad was irretrievably lost. But Milner was a man who kept his own counsel, and he quietly formulated a plan to save the railroad and his beloved but unborn city. He knew that Stanton's options would expire in sixty days, and decided to use delaying tactics while working behind the scenes to block Stanton's move. For weeks Milner acted as if he were uninterested in the options, while deliberately changing the route of the South & North Alabama Railroad so that the exact intersection of the two roads remained in doubt. Stanton saw no reason to exercise his options until the exact intersection was fixed, and continued to wait impatiently while Milner procrastinated. Meanwhile, supporters of the South & North Alabama Railroad feverishly searched for money to rescue the railroad and the proposed Jones Valley city. One of these men, Maj. Alburto Martin, managed to obtain the deeds to the land upon which Stanton held options. He was to safeguard them until money to exercise the options was deposited in Josiah Morris's bank in Montgomery.

Everyone wanted to know where the lines would cross, but Milner remained silent, making a new crossing each day. Finally, the sixty days expired. Stanton, by Alabama law, now had only a three-day grace period in which to exercise his options. Two days came and went and Stanton took no action. On the third day, the Jones Valley landowners and Alburto Martin, deeds in hand, anxiously gathered at the Morris bank. Still no word came from Stanton. Milner entered the bank at noon and waited to see his secret plan of salvation unfold. Exactly at the moment the grace period expired, Josiah Morris triumphantly stepped forward and paid Martin $100,000—enough money to purchase each of the 4,150 acres of land surrounding the S&N and A&C railroads. As a personal favor to Milner, Morris had acted on behalf of the South & North Alabama Railroad men and unobtrusively raised enough capital to take possession of all the land near Elyton. Milner's plan had worked to perfection, and the great workshop town was saved. Twelve supporters of the South & North Railroad then gathered at the bank and established the Elyton Land Company, which was incorporated to develop the great workshop town. Morris chose to call this town Birmingham in honor of the great English iron center. The company approved the name and Alabama's Birmingham was born.[11]

A new contract was put into force with Tate to finish the road, and trains were soon running between Montgomery and Birmingham—which was not much more than a stubble field inhabited in the main by rabbits. A few dedicated men, including Milner, Morris, Bolling Hall, and J. R. Powell—Robert Jemison's competitor in the mail coach business—began to clear this field and lay out the town. They were especially careful to reserve land for railroad expansion. The first buildings they constructed were Alabama & Chattanooga Railroad construction shacks. A little later the A&C built the first depot in Birmingham. Then, a two-story frame hotel called the Relay House was erected near the railroad; it served as headquarters for Birmingham's mineral men for many years. Colonel Powell sought as much publicity as possible for the infant city and invited northern journalists to personally investigate. Many came, and, thanks to Powell's hospitality, many were impressed. As they looked at Red Mountain they were amazed at the resources they saw for making iron. One enthusiastic scribe was moved to write, "The fact is plain. Alabama is to be the manufacturing center of the habitable globe." Little did the writer know that Birmingham's greatness would be long in coming. If J. C. Stanton could prevent it, it would never come.[12]

Stanton remained determined to execute his plan of building up Chattanooga at Birmingham's expense. He knew that the South & North men had expended all their means at Birmingham and would soon need an infusion of money to complete the sixty-six miles of unfinished road between Blount Springs and Decatur. The S&N would also need funds to pay interest due on $2,200,000 of state-endorsed bonds that had been hypothecated to Russell Sage and Vernon K. Stevenson. Stevenson had been president of the Nashville & Chattanooga Railroad and, having extensive financial interests in Chattanooga, was an ally of Stanton's. When the interest payment on the bonds controlled by Sage and Stevenson fell due in April 1871, the Chattanooga men convened a South & North directors meeting at the Exchange Hotel in Montgomery. At that meeting, Sage and Stevenson demanded immediate redemption of the bonds with accrued interest. If this demand was not met, all work on the South & North Alabama Railroad was to cease and all its assets were to be handed over to the Nashville & Chattanooga Railroad.

A weary, hollow-eyed Gilmer responded, "You know I've exhausted every resource in New York. We've raked that city and this state with a fine toothed comb for funds, and it's no use. I don't see but that we've got to accept this proposition as it stands." But the other Birmingham men were not so easily dissuaded. Josiah Morris passionately shouted, "The deuce we do!" and his companions all stood up in unison to voice their objections. Stevenson flew into a rage. Sage waited for the uproar to subside and then calmly and quietly repeated his threats. The stormy confrontation continued until after midnight. As the directors left the hotel, Milner was seized with trepidation and labeled the crisis "the most critical and dangerous period in the history of Birmingham and of the South & North Railroad."[13]

It was common knowledge that the South & North was in a fix, and no one was more distressed than James Sloss. The viability of his own line, the Nashville & Decatur, hinged upon a connection with the South & North Alabama Railroad. But the resourceful Sloss had devised his own plan to deliver the South & North out of Stanton's hands, and he hurried to Nashville to implement it. Sloss knew that the Louisville & Nashville Railroad was seeking a route through to the Gulf, and suggested that the L&N could secure such a route by rescuing the South & North Alabama Railroad. Sloss offered to lease his Nashville & Decatur to the L&N in exchange for a commitment by the L&N to absorb the

South & North, redeem its bonds, and finish the road from Birmingham to Decatur. Such an arrangement would give the L&N a direct connection to the Gulf via Montgomery. The proposal intrigued the expansion-minded Albert Fink, general manager of the Louisville & Nashville Railroad. A German by birth, Fink was trained as an engineer and had immigrated to America to distinguish himself as both a bridge builder and railroad manager. His six-foot seven-inch frame had earned him the title "Teutonic Giant." Under Fink's guidance, the L&N had prospered through the Civil War to become one of the strongest roads in the country.[14] After meeting with Sloss, Fink immediately called a board meeting to present the proposition. The board rendered a split decision: three for and three against. Fink was impatient, and while the board deliberated further, he left for Montgomery to inform Sage and Stevenson of his intentions. While in Montgomery, Fink assembled Gilmer, Milner, and Tate and asked them to accompany him to Louisville. Over breakfast in Louisville, Milner's glowing assessment of the opportunities in the mineral district won Fink's unqualified approval of the plan. Fink then conferred with L&N president H. D. Newcomb and arranged to have the S&N delegates meet with the L&N directors that night in the Blue Parlor of Louisville's Gault House.

The meeting convened as scheduled, but after Gilmer and Milner had presented their case, the board continued to grapple with the dilemma of expansion. The situation was a familiar one. Three of the directors favored a conservative course of action, while the other three were willing to gamble. "Both were right," Milner explained. "A paradox it may seem, but the parties viewed this question from different standpoints. The one party said 'let well enough alone and pay us our accustomed dividends.' The other party saw in the future, by extension, the greatest railroad in the South, and perhaps in the United States."[15]

L&N president Newcomb was uncommitted but seemed to be swayed by Fink's advocacy. Sam Tate had listened silently as the discussion earnestly progressed, but suddenly broke the decorum when he sprang to his feet and demanded a bonus of $100,000 to relinquish his construction contract to the L&N. Newcomb was incensed. Shouting "D'ye think I'll stand for any highway robbery?" he abruptly ended the meeting. Tate drew back his stick and started for Newcomb but arrested himself with a comment that Newcomb was not even worthy of the small end of the stick. Tate then declared that he had already negotiated to deliver the South & North Railroad to Stevenson and Sage, but would bargain with the L&N if he could get a better deal. A harmless struggle ensued between the two old men, which was broken up when the hulking Fink stepped between them. In broken English Fink commanded, "Colonel Tate, you stop this! Colonel Newcomb, you come along with me!" Fink separated the men and led Newcomb out of the room while Gilmer and Milner pleaded with Tate to change his mind.[16]

The only hope for the South & North Alabama Railroad appeared to be certainly lost. But the mood soon changed. As Milner observed, "Whiskey is cheaper in Kentucky than water, and, for some purposes, much better. Mr. Fink rang a bell, and pretty soon every man in the Blue Parlor had his glass." The Kentucky bourbon settled many frayed nerves, and after a semblance of calm was restored, Fink adjourned the meeting and wired for Colonel Sloss to take the next train to Louisville. Sloss arrived at once and assured all parties that Davidson County, which owned most of the Nashville & Decatur stock, would unanimously support the L&N lease. By the next afternoon, Fink had persuaded Newcomb to accept the entire proposal except for Tate's bonus, which was reduced to $75,000. Final agreements were signed in April and May 1871 and approved by L&N shareholders by a four-to-one margin. The South & North was now part of the L&N Railroad.[17]

Fink's decision to plunge into Alabama had been strongly influenced by an exhaustive study compiled by Milton H. Smith, the erstwhile U.S. Military Railroad transportation superintendent at Stevenson and Huntsville, who had risen to the position of general freight agent for the Louisville & Nashville Railroad in 1869.[18] Smith was well aware that interstate traffic between the Ohio River and the Deep South was his company's lifeblood, even though the L&N had to depend exclusively upon the Nashville & Chattanooga Railroad for its connection between the two regions. But the N&C also had a financial interest in a road called the Nashville & Northwestern that led from Nashville to St. Louis and, as much as possible, tried to divert traffic away from the L&N in favor of this subsidiary. "In other words," Smith explained, "it was claimed by the L&N that the N&C Railroad discriminated against it on business delivered to it by the L&N from Louisville and Cincinnati, by exacting higher proportional rates from Nashville to Chattanooga and beyond than it exacted on traffic coming to it over its long line, the Nashville and Northwestern." The L&N considered this an intolerable state of affairs, and was actively seeking an outlet that would render it independent of the N&C and its Chattanooga gateway when the Alabama opportunity arose. Impelled principally by these competitive pressures, Smith had presented Fink with a forty-five-page report that recommended investment in the South & North Alabama Railroad.[19]

After the agreements were ratified, construction began immediately. Blasting through the hills of north Alabama consumed more money than the L&N had ever anticipated, but Fink continued doggedly to pursue his Alabama commitment until the line between Birmingham and Decatur was completed in September 1872. Enormous sums were expended, not only in new construction but in straightening twisting curves and refurbishing portions of existing trackage between Nashville and Montgomery.[20]

Confident that Alabama's promise would soon be fulfilled, Milton H. Smith extended favorable freight rates to many Alabama products as he worked hard to implement a liberal development policy for the region. As part of Smith's comprehensive revision of the railroad's local tariff, a sliding scale was instituted for Alabama minerals so that freight rates for coal and iron varied directly with their market price. Also, fearing that cutthroat competition might undermine the region's development, Smith entered into unprecedented agreements with the Memphis & Charleston, Iron Mountain and other railroads that effectively stabilized these rates. Smith's commitment to Alabama mineral development was total, and coal and iron entrepreneurs would rely on him again and again.[21]

L&N development policy extended beyond offering reliable transportation at favorable rates. The hill country was mostly wilderness, and the L&N offered incentives that encouraged settlement all along its route through Alabama's mountains as well as in Birmingham. In 1872 a group of German immigrants, led by John S. Cullman, accepted the L&N's inducements and established a town fifty-three miles north of Birmingham that eventually grew to become an important source of revenue for the railroad. German immigrants colonized another town thirteen miles south of Cullman, called Garden City, on land donated by the L&N.[22]

The L&N commitment appeared to assure the development of what was now being called the Birmingham District, and optimism abounded in the spring of 1872. "A little more than seven months ago," the *Montgomery Advertiser* boasted, "the site of Birmingham was a cotton-field. There was not a hut upon the place. There are now over 300 buildings, 80 framed storehouses, 20 brick stores and houses two and three stories high, and 40 brick stores under contract. . . . Enterprising men from the North are being daily attracted to Birmingham by the wonderful stories told of its great wealth, now buried in the bowels of the earth. When once on the spot, they find themselves spellbound by the superior quality and quantity of the ores, and they at once resolve to invest." In addition to "rich and fertile agricultural lands" and "the finest mineral country in the world," the paper went on to promise that immigrants to the Birmingham District could expect to find a "paradise of lovely women."[23] The remark concerning a "paradise of lovely women" is attributed to Col. J. R. Powell, who was selling lots for the Elyton Land Company. It is said that this declaration "brought more farmers into town than you could count. While they were looking all over Red Mountain for the ladies, the colonel sold them building lots. Powell was undoubtedly the most astute real estate agent in Alabama history."[24]

President Newcomb viewed the Alabama expansion as an opportunity to gain a vital advantage over competing trunk lines, and presented an equally optimistic assessment of the venture in his 1873 report to shareholders. "The importance of this enterprise can not be overestimated," Newcomb wrote; "without it the Louisville and Nashville Railroad would be entirely dependent for its connections in the Southeast and Southwest upon other railroads, whose interests are not identified with ours, but are directly opposed to them. It would have been in the power of these companies to exclude us at any time from the business of the South, and make the property of this Company comparatively worthless. . . . The location of this line is such that this Company can never be excluded from the business of the Southeast and Southwest, from which it might have been cut off at any time at the pleasure of rival interest."[25]

Despite Colonel Powell's fantasies and Newcomb's rational defense of the L&N expansion, no one could foresee the horrible panic that would strike in 1873. As economic depression paralyzed the Birmingham District, the stock of the Elyton Land Company plummeted to seventeen cents on the dollar, and Powell resigned in despair. The iron furnaces ravaged by the Civil War had scarcely been rebuilt when business dried up, stripping the L&N of its hoped-for revenue. There was hardly enough business on the L&N between Calera and Decatur to warrant one passenger coach a week or one freight car a day.[26] With consternation, Milton Smith was forced to trace the sudden reversal of fortune that befell the Louisville & Nashville Railroad in 1873:

> The L&N railroad carried out its contract, completed the road, and opened it for traffic the last of September, 1872. At that time there was a good deal of business activity. . . . We had more than we could do, and had a great deal of difficulty in operating the new road. The very next spring, the panic of 1873 came along and we had no business.
>
> Now the cost of constructing the South and North Alabama was very great. . . . And with the limited capital, a first-class road was not, and in such a country could not be constructed. The road has heavy grades, one and a quarter per cent, and excessive curvature. . . .
>
> The result was that the first cost of the South and North Alabama Railroad was very great. This was materially increased by the absolute lack of credit of the South and North Alabama Railroad Company, and the then not very good credit of the L&N Railroad.
>
> . . . The transaction was a most unfortunate one for the L&N Railroad Company. It very nearly bankrupted it. It was with the greatest difficulty that the company succeeded in keeping from defaulting on its obligations. The load was heavy. It struggled as best it could, having gotten itself into a trap by entering upon the construction of the South and North Road, and endorsing its bonds. To extricate itself, it had to patiently encourage the development of traffic. In 1873, there was almost none. There was scarcely a sawmill that could operate successfully, and practically no coal and ore.[27]

As the L&N suffered under its Alabama burden, Albert Fink felt betrayed by Milner. Soon after the panic the two men met on the street in Montgomery, and an irate Fink vehemently upbraided Milner. "You have ruined me, you fool!, me and the Louisville and Nashville Railroad. The railroad will not pay for the grease that is used on its car wheels! Where are those coal mines and those iron mines you talked so much about that morning, and write so much about? Where are they? I look, but I see nothing! All lies!—Lies!"[28]

Fink and Milner would meet only once more—but the next encounter would be under entirely different circumstances, and Milner would not be addressed as a fool.

9

"THE FOOLS DOWN IN ALABAMA"

BIRMINGHAM WAS A DISMAL PLACE after the panic, and the adversity was compounded by an outbreak of cholera. It is not surprising that the disease spread among the city's population of 2,500, since the site near Elyton lacked the drinking water, sewerage, or adequate drainage that had prompted Milner to initially prefer the Village Creek location. "Destruction walked roughshod over the morning of its prospects," John W. DuBose wrote of Birmingham's plight. "Hardly had the fearful scourge subsided than the financial revulsion, beginning with Black Friday in Wall Street, prostrated every interest in the Union. Birmingham, feeling the shock, ceased to grow, and practically disappeared from all calculation and influence."[1]

The only viable iron furnaces in the Birmingham District, at Oxmoor and Irondale, were shut down. Gilmer and Milner had established Oxmoor furnace during the war and kept its fires ablaze until General Wilson's onslaught brought destruction. After the war, Daniel Pratt, the distinguished Alabama industrialist and enthusiastic supporter of the Birmingham District, invested heavily to rebuild this furnace. An old man now, Pratt considered this project to be "the last and crowning act of his life." With high expectations, Pratt proudly appointed his son-in-law, Henry DeBardeleben, as manager of Oxmoor. But the inexperienced DeBardeleben, unable to contend with the relentlessly deepening depression, was forced to close the ironworks. DeBardeleben profoundly regretted his inability to reward his father-in-law's confidence and considered himself a complete failure when he extinguished the fires of Oxmoor.[2]

In order to keep the Oxmoor charter alive, several prominent Alabama entrepreneurs—including Charles T. Pollard and members of the Gilmer and Pratt families—organized the Eureka Mining and Transportation Company of Alabama in the fall of 1873. The state acknowledged the importance of these ironworks by granting the Eureka Company powers that were extraordinary for the time; including unprecedented tax exemptions and the abolition of personal stockholder liability. But there were few experienced iron men running the practical operations at Oxmoor, and the furnaces continued to struggle for survival under Eureka management. The widely publicized Birmingham District was becoming a laughingstock. In Pittsburgh it was said, "The fools down in Alabama are shipping us ferruginous sandstone and calling it iron ore!"[3]

The Oxmoor furnaces used the charcoal process, in which timber from the surrounding woods was converted into charcoal and used to reduce the Red Mountain iron ore. But the charcoal process was inefficient and costly and produced a grade of iron that could not compete economically with iron made in the North. If the Birmingham District were to exploit its resources successfully, its ironmaking process had to be improved. Some felt that this could be accomplished by substituting coke for charcoal, as northern ironmasters were doing. Coke was made by burning coal in special ovens, and the surrounding coal fields promised to provide coke in abundance.[4]

Under the direction of Levin S. Goodrich, a pioneer ironmaker who had came to Alabama from Kentucky in 1873, the Oxmoor furnaces were refired by the Eureka company and made more efficient. Goodrich proposed experiments to develop a coke process, but the Eureka board hesitated to make such an effort. As the Oxmoor furnaces kept struggling with the charcoal process, Eureka sank relentlessly into debt and failure. In the face of continuing ridicule, the managers of Eureka finally made a desperate proposal. They would turn the company over to any person who could show ironmaking to be profitable in Alabama. This challenge would soon be accepted by a man well known in Alabama railroad circles. Frank P. O'Brien, a Birmingham contractor and builder, explains:

> Just here, those of us who had invested every dollar we possessed in Birmingham under the impression that the wealth untold that had been described to us by the promoters of the then infant city would, in a few years, make each one of us a millionaire, saw that something must be done to

demonstrate the truth of the many claims made for this region. Who was the man to lead us out of this wilderness of despair? That man came forward in the person of Colonel John T. Milner. Colonel Milner sent out notices to "All those who are interested in the success of Birmingham," calling them to meet in the offices of the Elyton Land Company. . . .

This meeting was pretty well attended. . . . Colonel Milner stated the object of the call to be the formulation of a plan to organize a Cooperative Experimental Company, which would take advantage of the offer of the Eureka Mining and Transportation Company. He, on his part would subscribe one thousand dollars in cash and a good sample of coal from three properties, to test its coking qualities. He called upon all others owning coal lands to take up the matter and do all they could to bring about some practical result which would demonstrate that our mineral deposits were not failures.[5]

Milner's speech was typically eloquent as he rallied support for the Cooperative Experimental Coke and Iron Company. "We have been crying 'natural resources,' and depending on others to come and develop them," Milner chided, "like the man calling on Hercules to come and pull his wagon out of the mud. Hercules will not come until we put our own shoulders to the wheel. . . . We don't know what we can do. Let us find out for ourselves. We have been resting long enough on our natural resources. It is time we should be creating resources."[6]

Milner's appeal succeeded, and Birmingham men stepped forward to invest in the Cooperative Experimental Coke and Iron Company. Goodrich was elected superintendent of the new company and immediately went to work improving the furnaces. Meanwhile, a Belgian named Shantle had heard of Birmingham's dilemma and proposed installation of his patented new invention, the Shantle Reversible Bottom Ovens. Living up to its name, the Experimental company adopted Shantle's process and five of his ovens were built to convert coal to coke.[7]

Only four coal mines were open at the time in the Birmingham District, and after samples from all these mines were tried, coal from the Warrior field proved to be most suitable for making coke. After Goodrich installed some of his own inventions for converting from cold to hot blast, the first pigs were made on February 28, 1876. Birmingham promoters, delighted with the result of the experiment, proclaimed the iron to be of excellent quality and expected it to be universally accepted. Northern iron masters continued to be skeptical, however. Some even described the iron as a "wretched product."[8]

Oblivious to the isolated voices of derision, those individuals who were vitally interested in the experiments, including managers of the Louisville & Nashville Railroad, were highly encouraged. The accomplishment was especially good news to Henry DeBardeleben, who had now inherited the Oxmoor properties as well as a major portion of Red Mountain from his father-in-law. The Cooperative Experimental Coke and Iron Company had proven that Red Mountain ores could be successfully reduced by a coke process; but could enough good quality coking coal be found near the ore beds so that the iron could be profitably made? The answer to this question would determine Birmingham's future, and to a great extent, the future of the L&N Railroad.

Despite the lingering uncertainties, L&N directors knew their company's fortunes were inextricably linked with Alabama's, and were willing to gamble personally on the opportunity to revitalize the Birmingham District. Along with Colonel Sloss and several Cincinnati investors, they joined with DeBardeleben to purchase options on the old Eureka property and formed a new Eureka company dedicated to the profitable development of Red Mountain minerals. The L&N was also induced to make a corporate investment of $125,000 to improve the coke process. But even with this backing, ironmaking in Birmingham continued to flounder, principally because of a power struggle within the new Eureka company. Long-standing rivalries between the Louisville and Cincinnati interests had degenerated into a full-fledged battle for control, and as both sides tried to make deals with DeBardeleben, he stubbornly resisted attempts to buy his stock. "I would not sell," DeBardeleben firmly asserted. "I

Oxmoor Furnaces in 1885. (Woodward Iron Company photograph)

knew if either party got full control the property would go to pieces again. So I stayed umpire to keep the peace."[9]

Umpiring did not consume all of the energetic DeBardeleben's time, however. While others were fighting over the spoils of the Birmingham District, he and Colonel Sloss followed Milner's advice and went out creating resources for the state—by searching for the coal seam that could make the iron furnaces profitable. Until that coal seam was found, however, the Birmingham District would have to depend upon its steam coal production for subsistence.

Even though iron horses were consuming ever growing volumes of steam coal, the efficacy of Alabama coal, like her iron, was yet to be proven. It was not easy to convince the nation that Alabama coal was an acceptable boiler fuel. Along with Milner, Capt. A. C. Danner fought to build the reputation of the state's steam coal. Near the turn of the century Captain Danner recalled these efforts with pride:

Along about 1874 the Alabama mines began to turn out more coal than there was market for. Very low water prevailed for a long time in the Kanawha and Ohio rivers, thus preventing the floating down of Pittsburg coal, and during a storm in New Orleans a great many barges of Pittsburg coal were sunk. I decided that here was an opening in New Orleans for the sale of Alabama coal. An arrangement was made between the Louisville and Nashville Railroad Company and my firm making a rate through from the mines to New Orleans of two dollars and twenty-five cents per ton. A yard and office was established in New Orleans, and we went to work to sell coal from the Alabama mines there. The people of New Orleans had not then been accustomed to use any coal excepting Pittsburg coal. There were many dealers in Pittsburg coal in New Orleans, nearly all the large mines in the Pittsburg district having their local representatives there. They, of course, combined to fight the introduction of Alabama coal into that city. Much prejudice was, in consequence, engendered against it, some of which lasts until this day.

We had a hard time selling Alabama coal there, but the trade grew, nevertheless, year by year. I remember one sale that I, personally, made in New Orleans that was rather startling at that time to the coal trade. The Gas Company of New Orleans then made gas from Pittsburg coal. The Pittsburg people never for a moment thought that there was any danger of their losing their trade.

The president of the gas company was induced to make a test of the Black Creek Alabama coal from a mine that had been opened and was being operated by Colonel John T. Milner. This test in its results surprised the gas company. They made a further test, and then one day closed a contract with me for twenty thousand tons of Black Creek coal. That, so far as I know, was the first large sale of Alabama coal made in New Orleans, and it was a great help to the trade for our coal. We had been trying to sell some of it to the railroads. Of course, the railroads running through the Alabama coal district into New Orleans used it, but the railroads running out of New Orleans to the West or to the North would not have it. Colonel Milner went to New York and succeeded in getting from the president of the Southern

Pacific Railroad Company an order for a large amount of coal, but when it was being delivered to the railroad company there was almost a strike on the part of the engineers. They claimed that they could not run their locomotives with Alabama coal! The management of the railroad company finally put up a notice to the effect that as engineers on the Alabama, Mississippi, and Georgia railroads could use to advantage Alabama coal, any engineers on the Southern Pacific who could not use it and get results from it would be considered incapable and their places filled by more competent engineers. That ended the "kick" against Alabama coal from that source, and from that day until this the Southern Pacific and other roads running out of New Orleans have used more or less Alabama coal, and the use of it in the country adjoining has steadily grown, year by year, to the great advantage of not only the Alabama mines, but of New Orleans as well.[10]

As Captain Danner continued to promote Alabama coal as a boiler fuel, DeBardeleben and Sloss kept searching for a coking coal suitable for use in the Birmingham District iron furnaces. Soon, both men would strike pay dirt with the aid of another prospector, Truman H. Aldrich. Aldrich had the credentials and talent that were needed for this quest. He was a New York mining engineer who had ventured into Alabama in 1872 to enter the banking business at Selma. The next year Aldrich returned to his original vocation as a civil engineer at the Montevallo coal mines. In Aldrich's estimation, coal mining as well as locomotive power in Alabama at that time was not particularly awe inspiring. "Mining operations over the State then were pretty small potatoes," Aldrich said. "Montevallo, mind you, a small potato, too, like the rest of 'em. Why, the average carload of coal from 1873 right up to 1879 . . . was only eight tons. If I ever loaded ten tons on a car by mistake, I had to unload, for it was considered too heavy for a locomotive to pull." Thanks to Aldrich, DeBardeleben, and Sloss, coal mining in Alabama would not stay "small potatoes." Twenty years later, an average of fifty tons of coal would be loaded into each car at Alabama mines.

The well-trained and experienced Aldrich initiated a thorough scientific survey of the vast Warrior coal field. Realizing the importance of infrastructure in profitably exploiting natural resources, he restricted his search to within six miles of the South & North and A&C tracks. Concurrently, Colonel Sloss was looking for exactly the same kind of coal in the Warrior field. Each of these men focused their search on coal that was close to the railroads and suitable for use in both the iron furnaces and locomotive fireboxes. They knew that coal meeting all these specifications was needed to assure profitable operation of the

The coking process was the key to successful mineral development in Alabama. (Postcard ca. 1908, from the author's collection)

Birmingham District mineral industry. Sharing the same goals, Aldrich soon teamed up with Colonel Sloss, and the pair intensified their search for a thick, long-lasting seam of top-grade coking coal. They were soon rewarded by the discovery of the prolific Browne seam.[11]

DeBardeleben had been prospecting with little success in the Tennessee Valley, and when he returned to Birmingham, Sloss and Aldrich revealed their discovery and asked him to join their partnership. DeBardeleben was deeply impressed with the Browne seam, and instinctively realized that the lifeblood of Birmingham could flow from its rich veins. He eagerly accepted the offer, and the company's capital immediately doubled. "He put the whole power of his fortune, his credit, and his tremendous vitality for the advancement of the company," Aldrich said.[12] Much of the money that DeBardeleben invested in the partnership with unrestrained enthusiasm had been inherited from Daniel Pratt, and the Browne seam was renamed in his honor. The partnership continued to buy land until they owned thirty thousand acres in the Warrior basin, and in January 1878 the Pratt Coal and Coke Company was formed to develop the Pratt seam.

As soon as the first slope of the Pratt mine was sunk, a railroad linking the L&N with the mine was started. Coal soon issued forth, and industrial life in Birmingham began to stir from its panic-induced sleep. Aldrich, DeBardeleben, and Sloss were convinced that the red hematite ore could be profitably smelted with Pratt coke and threw all their resources into the endeavor. Six months after the first coke pig iron was produced at Oxmoor, one hundred new coke ovens were placed in operation to supply enlarged and modernized Eureka furnaces.[13] On clear nights, the glow of these great ovens could be seen twenty miles away.[14]

Just as the door to prosperity appeared to be opening, adversity once again stepped in the way. In the summer of 1878 a massive yellow fever epidemic besieged New Orleans, and mosquitoes quickly bore the deadly disease through Mississippi all the way to Memphis and two hundred miles eastward into Alabama. A flood of refugees, with no inkling of what caused the dreaded infirmity, boarded northbound L&N trains to escape infection. The L&N, whose employees were also stricken in large numbers, labored under extraordinarily harsh conditions to provide free transportation to those fleeing the beleaguered towns. Terrified communities along the line tried to insulate themselves from the contagion by refusing to let trains stop that were bearing passengers retreating from distressed areas. The mercy trains were compelled, often at gunpoint, to proceed through town at the maximum speed limit and discharge cargo outside corporate limits. Such a policy was in effect at Montgomery and caused intolerable disruptions to L&N emergency operations.

Milton H. Smith was dispatched to the capital city to urge lifting of the ban on refugees. Smith was not one to mince words, and he soon aroused the ire of determined Montgomerians who threatened violence if the trains attempted to stop. Predictably incensed, the irascible Smith retaliated by halting all freight movements into the city. Montgomery countered by sending a delegation to Louisville, where they convinced E. D. Standiford, president of the L&N since 1875, to countermand Smith's edict. This was more than Smith could take, and he promptly resigned.[15] The yellow fever terror proved to be transient, but Smith's commitment to Alabama was lasting. With Aldrich, DeBardeleben, and Sloss, Smith shared the conviction that Pratt coal was the magic ingredient that insured the success of the Birmingham District. Although Smith had stepped aside, the imprint of his carefully devised and ambitious plans for Alabama could be found in L&N initiatives long after his resignation.

One of these plans called for further southward extension of the L&N main line. Smith foresaw a large export market for Alabama coal that required better connections to the Gulf, and in 1877 a subsidiary of the L&N, the Pensacola Railroad, was formed to purchase the Pensacola & Louisville Railroad, successor of the antebellum Alabama & Florida Railroad of Florida. Acquisition of this forty-five-mile fragment between Flomaton and Pensacola gave the L&N access to Pensacola's wharves, but the connecting roadway between Montgomery and Flomaton was still far from satisfactory.[16] After Pratt mines were opened, coal was transported to the Gulf either via Alabama River barges or over the railroad connecting Montgomery with Mobile, which had been reorganized in 1874 as the Mobile & Montgomery Railway. But the Mobile & Montgomery Railway had become so dilapidated that trains could hardly muster a speed of twenty miles per hour. The marshland route was so inundated at times that work crews had to use long poles to propel boats over the flooded right-of-way to reach their work sites.[17] As early as 1876 president Standiford mused over this situation. "It is of vital importance to our system that we reach the Gulf over roads under our control," he said. "We now reach Montgomery, a thriving city in itself, but remote from the initial points of the traffic we seek. This places us at the mercy of the roads bringing this traffic, and although our relations are now of the most harmonious character, true policy would seem to indicate that we make ourselves independent."[18]

After lengthy negotiations, the L&N finally purchased control of the Mobile & Montgomery Railway on January 21, 1880. Along with the railroad came an additional three hundred thousand acres of land-grant property.[19] A direct line-haul to the Florida Gulf coast was assured on February 27, 1880, when the L&N absorbed its subsidiary, the Pensacola Railroad, through an exchange of bonds. The L&N immediately acted to put Selma in touch with Pensacola by contracting to complete the Pensacola & Selma Railroad, successor of the defunct Selma & Gulf Railroad. By 1871 only thirty-four miles of this line had been finished between the Alabama River and Pine Apple, Alabama. The L&N agreed to complete the seventy-four miles from Pine Apple to Flomaton, and by 1881 had pushed the trackage thirty miles northward from Flomaton to Repton, but the work bogged down and the additional forty-four miles from Repton to Pine Apple would not be in place until 1900. Nevertheless, Selma figured strongly in the L&N's

plans for Alabama. On July 1, 1881, the L&N leased the Western Rail Road of Alabama, gaining entrance into Selma via the Alabama River bridge.[20]

Then, on May 8, 1880, the L&N also secured control of an approach into New Orleans when it leased the New Orleans, Mobile & Texas Railroad. This line was the successor of the New Orleans, Mobile & Chattanooga Railroad Company that had been in operation between Alabama's Port City and Louisiana's Crescent City since 1870 as part of a projected transcontinental route. The New Orleans, Mobile & Texas Railroad bridged numerous bayous leading into New Orleans, and unlike the Mobile & Montgomery Railway, was in relatively good condition at the time of the lease. A little more than a year later, the L&N gained total domination of this route to New Orleans by purchasing the New Orleans, Mobile & Texas Railroad.[21] These acquisitions placed the L&N in the enviable position of having exclusive routes from the Birmingham District to all three of the Gulf's principal ports. Now minerals could be shipped to Pensacola, Mobile & New Orleans with the L&N at the throttle all the way.

Leaving Aldrich to see to the day-to-day operation of the Pratt mines, DeBardeleben set out to attract northern capitalists to Birmingham. He invited a group of Louisville businessmen, including T. T. Hillman, to come to Birmingham and evaluate investment possibilities. As inducements, DeBardeleben offered to send carloads of free coal to Louisville for testing, as well as reduced prices on Pratt coal and special terms on furnace sites. As a result, the Louisville group started the Birmingham rolling mills in 1879.[22]

It was now time to prove to the world what Alabama ironmakers already knew—that the commercial potential of the Birmingham District was boundless. The Elyton Land Company gave DeBardeleben a prime section of land between the South & North and Alabama & Chattanooga railroads, situated near the Pratt mines railroad. DeBardeleben had persuaded T. T. Hillman of the quality of Alabama iron and formed a partnership with him to erect the flagship furnace of the Birmingham District on the donated site. The first furnace within the corporate limits of Birmingham went into blast on November 30, 1880. Named "Alice" in honor of DeBardeleben's oldest daughter, this furnace turned the tide of public opinion in favor of the Birmingham District. Not only was there no doubt that Alice iron was of good quality, but the furnace achieved a record average daily output of fifty-three tons.[23]

The demand for Birmingham District iron steadily increased until it outstripped the capacity of both Oxmoor and Alice. Oxmoor had never reached its potential because of the continuing squabble among its owners, and Colonel Sloss was growing impatient. One day DeBardeleben suggested that Sloss open his own furnace. Always eager to offer encouragement to Birmingham investors, DeBardeleben promised to deliver Pratt coal to the project at 10 percent over cost for five years. Sloss gladly accepted the offer, but he still did not have the resources to go it alone, so he turned to the Louisville & Nashville Railroad for assistance. The L&N and B. F. Guthrie of Louisville furnished the needed capital, and in 1881 construction began on the first of the Sloss City furnaces between the S&N and A&C tracks in north Birmingham.[24]

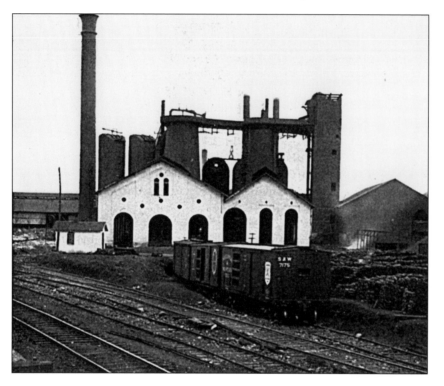

Alice Furnaces in 1885. (Woodward Iron Company photograph)

The good coking coal of the Birmingham District now fed the furnaces of a rapidly developing iron industry. Within three years after the original Alice No. 1 was erected, five more furnaces were put into blast, including Alice No. 2, which would set a daily production record for the South in 1886 with an output of 150 tons.[25] The Cooperative Experimental Company had given hope to the Birmingham District, but the Pratt mines had turned that hope into a reality. "The immediate success of Pratt mines for steam and coking coal fixed as a certainty in the minds of men the enormous value for future development possessed by the Birmingham District," Aldrich acknowledged. "The modern start of industrial development of this entire section dates from the successful test of the Pratt coal."[26]

The L&N had acquired over a half million acres in the mineral region when it took control of the South & North Alabama Railroad, and until the successes at Oxmoor and Pratt mines, there was little demand for this land. In fact, the L&N's Birmingham land office had only executed a total of 231 deeds before 1877.[27] But now demand surged and the L&N had to make a policy decision. Would it develop these extensive coal and iron properties on its own, or would the company refrain from entering the mineral business in favor of a policy designed to generate railroad traffic by helping others develop these resources? The L&N took the latter course. After all, the original purpose of the land grants was to encourage settlement and industrial development so that the value of all the surrounding lands would increase. President Standiford realized that this would indeed happen in the Birmingham District, and it did—more than anyone could have imagined.

Sloss Furnace, Birmingham, Ala.

Pig iron is stacked high at Sloss Furnace(s) ready to be loaded into waiting boxcars. (Postcard ca. 1908, from the author's collection)

The agricultural lands were marketed at prices varying from $1.50 to $5.00 per acre and were sold in large and small tracts to settlers and speculators alike. The mineral lands were treated much differently, however. The L&N was careful to ascertain the value of these lands before drawing up contracts with entrepreneurs who could prove both qualified and determined to develop them. In this manner the L&N avoided selling the land to speculators who would hold large undeveloped tracts, waiting for a higher price, while denying traffic to the railroad.

Standiford also recommended that the road further extend its development policy. Under this policy, special terms were worked out between the L&N and the coal and iron operators for the construction of spur lines to the mines and furnaces. The Warrior Coal Company, for example, sold the L&N steam coal at fifty cents below the market price in exchange for a reciprocal discount and favorable loan terms on iron to build a spur. Sometimes, the railroad would accept coal in lieu of an installment payment on land purchases. The L&N even went so far as to haul cars to and from the mines without charge.

Special low freight rates on agricultural and manufactured goods were also instituted to foster development and settlement of the region. To promote a diversified agricultural economy, sawmills were encouraged on the extensive forest land owned by the L&N.[28]

After stints with the Baltimore & Ohio and Pennsylvania Railroads, Milton H. Smith returned to the L&N in 1882, and within a few months was elevated to vice president of the company. In 1884 a turbulent struggle for control left the L&N presidency vacant and Smith was installed as acting president. The *New York Times* observed that Smith "will probably act until his successor can be chosen." Smith held the presidency until 1886, when he was finally succeeded by Eckstein Norton. Following Norton's tenure, Smith was elected president and would never step down. He would die in office in 1921 after a thirty-two-year reign at the helm of the L&N.[29]

The L&N development policy in Alabama was emphasized all the more under Smith's regime. Mineral development obsessed Smith. He insisted that no coal or iron land could be sold until he was personally assured that the purchaser had the financial resources to open mines or furnaces and would enter into an exclusive transportation arrangement with the L&N.

The timing of Birmingham's rebirth was wonderful. As the nation recovered from the depression, railroads expanded across the country, and coal and iron became growth industries. Iron was needed to build everything from locomotives to car wheels and myriad other appliances. The reputation of Alabama coal and iron continued its dramatic ascent, and it was time for the Birmingham District venture capitalists to reap their rewards. DeBardeleben feared he was contracting tuberculosis and decided to head west for his health; Sloss was occupied with his new furnace; and Aldrich was busy cultivating new coal enterprises. Thus, the Pratt Coal and Coke Company was for sale, and a buyer was found when Enoch Ensley of Memphis arrived at the Relay House.

Ensley was looking for a major coal property and had been rebuffed when he approached the Tennessee Coal, Iron & Railroad Company of Nashville regarding an investment in their Cumberland operation. The resentful Ensley hastened to Birmingham at the invitation of Tom Peters, one of Birmingham's most influential promoters, bent on securing coal properties that would knock the Cumberland coal mines into "a cocked hat." Ensley and his Memphis supporters were prepared to pay as much as necessary to outdo their Tennessee competitors and found Peters and DeBardeleben to be irresistible salesmen. After being assured that Pratt coal was second to none, Ensley purchased the Pratt mines and closed the first million dollar deal in the South. This deal reflected the country's growing confidence in Alabama minerals and was the first great infusion of capital in what would soon become a great boom. Ensley's investment created quite a sensation in the cash-poor Birmingham District. When he placed his initial deposit of $600,000 in the Berney Bank, the assistant cashier, W. P. G. Harding, stated, "That check of Colonel Ensley's was about the biggest check I had ever seen; it was exactly six times the capital stock of the bank!"[30]

Meanwhile, DeBardeleben had taken up sheep ranching in Mexico and was relieved to find that he was not afflicted with tuberculosis as suspected. With rejuvenated spirit, he associated himself with businessmen in San Antonio, including a former Kentucky lawyer named William Thompson Underwood. DeBardeleben formed a partnership with Underwood and returned to Birmingham to open the Mary Pratt furnace, using ore from mines adjoining the Alabama Great Southern Railroad at McCalla. In 1884 DeBardeleben and Underwood expanded these operations by leasing Red Mountain ore properties near the town of Redding. Continuing to pursue its development policy, the L&N built a branch to the Redding mines. The three-and-one-half-mile segment of track branched from the South & North Alabama Railroad four miles south of Birmingham and hugged the southern base of Red Mountain. This small spur would prove to be the progenitor of a great L&N subdivision appropriately called the Birmingham Mineral Railroad. A short time later, another branch was built on the other side of Red Mountain, and as these branches extended and connected, over a hundred miles of L&N track would eventually be concentrated in the heart of the rapidly growing Birmingham District.[31]

A writer for the *Birmingham Age* made an inspection tour of the Birmingham Mineral Railroad in 1886 and issued the following enthusiastic report:

> There is perhaps no more potent proof of the stability of the enterprises upon which this city rests its claims than a ride over the Birmingham Mineral [R]ailroad affords. At 2 o'clock in the afternoon a mixed train . . . pulls out from the Nineteenth-street crossing of the Louisville and Nashville road. For a short distance there is a network of tracks, and then the road separates and, pursuing a generally southwest direction, penetrates for a distance of twelve miles into the heart of a magnificent mineral district. . . . The road terminates in a narrow valley, with high ridges on each side almost shutting it in. The ridges, densely wooded, are of a uniform red color, and the commanding elevation on the left is the well-known Red Mountain. To the top of this ridge runs a switch over high trestling which leads to the mouth of the mine. The ore crops out on the top of the ridge and a tunnel follows the vein, which dips at an inclination of about 35 degrees. From this entry lateral headings branch off for great distances and through them the ore on

Ore Mines, Birmingham District.

Trams brought iron ore to tipples, where it was loaded into railroad cars. (Postcard ca. 1908, from the author's collection)

tramways is brought to the mouth of the tunnel and dumped into the cars on the railroad. . . . The laborers live in neat cottages scattered up and down the valley, and are a peaceful and industrious set of men. . . .

There is a general red hue pervading every thing in the neighborhood. The hills are red and most of the buildings and trestle work are of the same color; the clothes and hats of the operatives exhibit the same sanguinary tint, and even the animals, the hogs and the poultry have adopted the fashion, and display that hue which has ever been associated with revolution and the sansculotte. It means revolution, but it is the revolution of peace and prosperity. . . .

. . . All along the line of this road is one continued scene of activity, and a dozen new industries partially developed or projected will still further add to the enormous volume of business, considering the length, which this road does. Two trains each way per day cannot answer the demands of the traffic, although loaded to their utmost capacity.

It is impossible in the short time at his disposal for the *Age* representative to examine all the various industries along the line of this road, but enough is here given to indicate the solidity and permanence of the various enterprises inaugurated and to fully establish the fact that the Birmingham boom rests not upon the wild assertions of speculators, but upon the assured basis of a permanent and ever-increasing prosperity, as solid as Red Mountain itself.[32]

SOUVENIR FROM BIRMINGHAM, ALA.

Birmingham District coke ovens. (Postcard ca. 1908, from the author's collection)

The Birmingham Mineral initiative proved yet again that the L&N could be relied upon whenever the coal and iron industries needed aid. The Louisville & Nashville Railroad Company came to Birmingham's rescue during the city's darkest days, and without its solid support none of the coal and iron achievements could have come to fruition. R. M. Rawls, editor of the Athens *Courier*, saluted the L&N's cooperative spirit when he bestowed the title "Old Reliable" upon the railroad in an 1884 editorial. The name stuck and would forever identify the Louisville & Nashville Railroad.[33] The L&N continued to nurture Birmingham District coal and iron industries and saw its profits spiral upward as the mines prospered. No one was happier than Albert Fink. Blamed by many for bringing the L&N to the brink of disaster through his endorsement of the Alabama expansion, Fink had resigned from the railroad in 1875. But now he felt vindicated in supporting the Alabama initiative. In the midst of Birmingham's renewal, Fink chanced upon John T. Milner one day in Montgomery. A joyous Fink ran to Milner, clasped his hands, and cried out in his German accent: "Mr. Milner! Mr. Milner! I haf been only too anxious lately to meet you vonce more! I want to take back all that cussing I vas giving you once. The Louisfille and Nashfille Railroad has become von grand success!"[34] Fink then boarded the train for New York, never to see Milner again.

Milner, Sloss, DeBardeleben, and all those who had been so roundly

HARPER'S WEEKLY.
JOURNAL OF CIVILIZATION.

Vol. XXX.—No. 1530.   NEW YORK, SATURDAY, APRIL 17, 1886.   TEN CENTS A COPY.
Copyright, 1886, by Harper & Brothers. $4.00 PER YEAR, IN ADVANCE.

Unprecedented floods in April 1886 brought great destruction and loss of life in Alabama and made front-page headlines in national publications. Thousands were left homeless, and the railroads suffered greatly. The Memphis & Charleston's track was under six feet of water at Decatur; and at Wetumpka, four feet of water covered the public square as the Coosa River rose six feet above its previous high-water mark. Braxton Bragg Comer, who would later become governor of Alabama, became a hero when he traveled from Calera to Montgomery rescuing desperate victims. (From an engraving by Charles Graham, Harper's Weekly, *April 17, 1886)*

derided for their persistent support of the Birmingham District could now bask in the glory of victory. But Milner knew that success would have been impossible without the patronage of the L&N Railroad. In 1889, as Milner's career was drawing to a close, he acknowledged this fact: "The work of development went on, and as the country grew so did the city of Birmingham. The Louisville and Nashville Railroad did not stop. She extended her branches and our markets in every direction. She went to New Orleans. She went to Pensacola. She began trading with the West Indies. She has placed her branches all over our country; other railroads cut but little figure. The Louisville and Nashville is now not only Birmingham, but Alabama. . . . As day after day

SOUVENIR FROM BIRMINGHAM, ALA.

Entrance to Mary Lee Coal Mine, Birmingham, Ala.

Birmingham District coal mines. Top: *Coal mine at Brookside.* Bottom: *Slope of the Mary Lee coal mine. (Postcards ca. 1908, from the author's collection)*

the leaves from the sealed book of Nature are turned over . . . it can be seen in letters imprinted on the sky all over the world that the Birmingham District has no parallel on earth."[35]

Thanks to the "Old Reliable" and the dedication of those characterized as "the fools down in Alabama," the Birmingham District had risen to become Pittsburgh's major rival in the coal and iron business. The merciless ridicule was silenced, and the foundation was in place for hard-won prosperity.

10

THE
IRON
BOOM

ENOCH ENSLEY AND THE MONEYED MEN OF MEMPHIS had just started to invest in Birmingham. After settling down in the Magic City, Ensley acquired control of T. T. Hillman's Alice furnace, as well as an adjacent property, the Linn Iron Works. Ensley consolidated these Birmingham holdings, together with the Pratt Coal and Coke Company, under the corporate banner of the Pratt Coal and Iron Company.

The blood feud with the Tennessee Coal, Iron & Railroad Company followed Ensley to Alabama. Vowing to "do up the Tennessee Company or bust," he used his newly acquired Birmingham properties as competitive instruments, and managed them with a single-minded purpose—to outproduce the mines and furnaces of his adversary. Ensley sunk more coal slopes, threw up more coke ovens, and blew in more furnaces in his obsessive drive to embarrass the Tennessee Company. He encouraged competition between his furnaces, and pitted one against another in spirited contests aimed at increasing production. All these actions further stimulated the growth of diversified supporting industries and contributed heavily to the developing iron boom in Alabama. Ensley pressed his Birmingham operations so hard that they not only bettered those of his archrival but set the standard for the entire southern United States as well. Although Ensley accomplished his objective, his autocratic methods alienated his colleague, T. T. Hillman—a fact that Ensley would live to regret.[1]

Ensley's purchase of the Pratt mines had by no means put Jay Aldrich out of the coal business. Aldrich had been reinvesting his profits in more coal land and by 1881 had amassed thousands of acres of prime coal properties throughout the Cahaba River Valley, south of Birmingham. Using these properties as a nucleus, he organized the Cahaba Coal Mining Company and opened a gigantic mining operation in Bibb County. These mines were so productive that single blocks of coal weighing over a ton each were removed from them. Aldrich dubbed these enormous lumps of coal "bloctons," and the settlement surrounding the mines thus came to be known as the town of Blocton. In 1883 Aldrich began building a railroad to feed his Blocton coal to a recently completed furnace at Woodstock. His Woodstock & Blocton Railway was then extended to connect with the nearby Alabama Great Southern Railroad. Via this link with the Alabama Great Southern main line, Aldrich's company shipped millions of tons of Cahaba coal to a multitude of railroad and industrial companies throughout the country, in addition to a growing number of Birmingham District furnaces. The Cahaba Company supplied steam coal to all but one of the railroads operating out of New Orleans, with the Southern Pacific consuming five hundred tons a day in its New Orleans–San Antonio run. Under Aldrich's expert guidance, the Cahaba Coal Mining Company opened more mines, expanded into Tuscaloosa County, and became the dominant producer in the state.[2]

The patience of some West Virginia investors was also paying off. Since 1869 the Woodward family had been carefully and systematically accumulating choice mineral properties some twelve miles southwest of Birmingham. Reluctant to commit large sums of development capital until the profitability of Alabama iron was proven, they followed the progress of the Birmingham District closely until the success of the Alice furnace prompted them to make their move. In the spring of 1882 they began construction on the first Woodward furnace. The family opened coal and iron ore mines close to the furnace site and laid eight miles of railroad track to move the raw material. The furnace went into blast in 1883 and became part of an enormously efficient integrated ironmaking facility. By hauling all its coal, iron ore, and limestone over its own tracks, the Woodward Iron Company drastically reduced transportation costs and became one of the lowest-cost producers in the Birmingham District. The importance of the railroad was fully appreciated by management, and the dimensions of the Woodward rail operations steadily increased over the years.[3]

Meanwhile, DeBardeleben grew restless and again left Alabama for the Lone Star State. But he quickly realized that the Birmingham District was his dominion, and returned in 1885 to prosecute its development with megalomaniacal verve. Needing more capital, the irrepressible promoter collaborated with South Carolinian David Roberts and a group of British investors to incorporate a two-million-dollar firm, the DeBardeleben Coal and Iron Company. Under the auspices of this new organization, DeBardeleben planned his most ambitious project yet. Steel was rapidly displacing iron for most applications, and DeBardeleben, wanting Birmingham to be on the leading edge of this technology, proposed to build another great Jefferson County industrial center from the ground up—a complex driven not only by iron furnaces, but steel mills as well. The new town was to be erected thirteen miles southwest of Birmingham in the heart of some of DeBardeleben's best mineral property. At this site, officers of the DeBardeleben Coal and Iron Company met in a pine-board shack to organize the new town. "We all cast about for a name that might suggest the steel idea," David Roberts recalled. "I remember we had quite a discussion in the office, and then DeBardeleben, who was always very happy about things of that sort, you know, said 'Bessemer—call it Bessemer'—and we did." Thus, the city projected to produce Alabama's first steel was named in honor of Henry Bessemer, the inventor of the world's premier steelmaking system.

DeBardeleben went to work with zeal. He projected all kinds of diversified industries: iron furnaces, a dummy railroad, a steel mill, pipe works, rolling mills, mines, and quarries that he confidently asserted would "throw in the shade any other operations so far done in Alabama." Impatient for buildings, he went to New Orleans and bought structures remaining from the Cotton Exposition, hauled them back to Bessemer, and integrated them into a potpourri of industrial and civic facilities. The Jamaica building was used as part of the rolling mills, and the Montezuma building was pressed into service as a hotel. DeBardeleben could not hold back. "I was the eagle," he boasted, "and I wanted to eat all the craw-fish I could,—swallow up all the little fellows, and I did it!"

Bearing such magnificent names as King David, Queen Anne, and Little Miss Anne, the DeBardeleben Coal and Iron Company furnaces overshadowed their sisters at Birmingham, and although the steel mill was never built, Bessemer was overtaking the Magic City as the hub of the iron boom in the Birmingham District. As Bessemer grew, these hungry furnaces demanded more ore, and DeBardeleben turned to a familiar source of the raw material. With the assistance of Milton H.

Smith, he repurchased the old Oxmoor property and ousted the feuding Louisville and Cincinnati interests under which the property had languished for so many years. Forty thousand acres of Oxmoor property were added to his holdings, giving him 150,000 acres of mineral land in the Birmingham District—an expanse that required more railroad service.

Removing pig iron from furnace at Bessemer. (Postcard ca. 1910, from the author's collection)

As DeBardeleben opened a plethora of mines, furnaces, and diversified industries, Smith kept pace by ordering more and more L&N spurs. When a seven-and-one-half-mile main branch was opened along the northern base of Red Mountain to connect Bessemer with the South & North Alabama Railroad at a point three miles south of Birmingham known as Magella, the north branch of the Old Reliable's growing Birmingham Mineral Railroad subsidiary was in place.

Bessemer's diversified industries gave impetus to even more frenetic development in the Birmingham District, inspiring DeBardeleben to exclaim, "Break a young mustang into a fox-trotting gait,—that's what we did to the Birmingham District. There's nothing like taking a wild piece of land, all rock and woods, ground not fit to feed a goat on, and turning it into a settlement of men and women, making pay rolls, bringing the railroads in and starting things going. There's nothing like boring a hillside through and turning over a mountain. That's what money's for. I like to use money as I use a horse,—to ride!"[4]

As the burgeoning Birmingham District boomed, more railroads were built to connect the industrial sprawl, as well as to link Birmingham with other regions of the state. Among these was another Aldrich line, the Briarfield, Blocton & Birmingham Railroad, which ran from Bessemer to Gurnee Junction, twenty-five miles south of Birmingham, on a spur of the Selma, Rome & Dalton Railroad.[5] Gurnee Junction was named for one of the Cahaba Company's directors, W. S. Gurnee, a New Yorker who had affiliated himself with two other celebrated Cahaba Company board members, Samuel Noble and Alfred L. Tyler, to perform monumental work in developing mines, furnaces, and railroads in another section of the state's rich mineral regions, the Anniston District.

Samuel Noble was the son of James Noble, an itinerant English ironmaster who brought his family to Pennsylvania in 1837. After a period of employment with the Reading Railroad, where he developed a locomotive brake that the Reading was to use for decades, James resumed his craft as an ironmaker. In 1855 the Noble family relocated to Rome, Georgia, where James and his six sons established the largest ironworks south of the Tredegar Works in Virginia. At these ironworks the Nobles manufactured a wide variety of iron products, including water pipe, bridges, mining machinery, and steam engines. The Noble brothers shared their father's innovative nature, and in 1857 the first railroad locomotive manufactured in the Deep South, called the *Alfred Shorter,* rolled from their production floor. General Sherman's troops destroyed the ironworks in 1864, but it was reconstructed after the war under Samuel's leadership. With Samuel Noble installed as superintendent and his brothers cast in prominent roles, the Rome Steam Engine and Machine Works manufactured steam engines, rolling-mill machinery, and railroad-car wheels using iron ore that was mined and smelted a few miles across the state line in Cherokee County, Alabama. But Samuel Noble knew that he needed a better grade of ore to build high-quality car wheels and was drawn to the brown hematite ore beds that were nestled in the yellow pine–covered mountains a few miles south of Cherokee County. With the help of northern capitalists, Noble accumulated thirteen hundred acres of rich mineral and timber property on either side of the Selma, Rome & Dalton right-of-way near Oxford. Noble now had all the raw materials and transportation facilities needed to provide high-grade iron for the car wheel plant at Rome, but still lacked development capital. Hoping to find backing in Charleston, he arranged to visit the acting vice president of the South Carolina Railroad, Alfred L. Tyler. Fortunately for Noble, Tyler's father, Daniel Tyler, was in the younger Tyler's office when Noble arrived. Following a distinguished military career, Daniel Tyler was now serving as president of the Mobile & Montgomery Railroad. General Tyler had supervised ironworks in Pennsylvania before the war, and those ironmaking ventures had been frustrating, but Noble's description of east Alabama's iron potential stirred the old man's emotions. After patiently hearing Noble's pleas for assistance, the elder Tyler provided this assurance: "I have had the iron business burned into me, and have not forgotten my first experience, but if I can find a property that has on it everything for making iron, without buying any raw material, or bringing any to it, I might be tempted to go into the business again."

According to Noble, it wasn't long before the seventy year old general's words were translated into action: "I had but little idea that a man of his age would, on a second thought, take such a long and uncomfortable journey, and was surprised at his coming to Rome some ten days after our meeting for a visit of inspection. . . . He rode with me over the country, exploring every hill and valley, gathering information from everybody he met about the timber lands, limestone and rock quarries, their location and extent, and then going to the places indicated, and examining them himself. . . . Nothing escaped his observation. . . . I was surprised at his knowledge and practical ideas concerning the requisites of iron manufacture. We rode for three days in succession."

Tyler liked what he saw. After his son also looked over the property, a deal was struck and Alfred L. Tyler became president of the Woodstock Iron Company, with Samuel Noble serving as general superintendent. The first Woodstock furnace, built near Oxford in 1872, produced forty tons of railroad car wheel iron per day using the charcoal process. Woodstock iron achieved a good reputation, and through a combination of hard work and sound management, Tyler and Noble piloted the business through the panic of 1873 with no interruption of production.[6]

Throughout the recovery, Noble continued to apply his exceptional sales skills successfully in promoting Woodstock iron. He made sure that a Woodstock exhibit was placed among those of leading U.S. iron companies at the widely acclaimed Philadelphia Centennial Exhibition in 1876. The prominent display contained "a remarkably comprehensive and instructive exhibit of ores of great variety" as well as a unique iron called Speigleisen and examples of car wheels manufactured at the Noble brothers' plant in Rome. The Philadelphia Centennial exhibit earned Woodstock iron the title "Best Southern" and greatly enhanced its reputation. While other charcoal furnaces failed and closed, Woodstock prospered, and by 1878 was the only one of its type left operating in Alabama. Alfred L. Tyler's wife was called Annie, and in 1873 the name of the company town was changed from Woodstock to Anniston in her honor. Henceforth, this iron-making region would be referred to as the Anniston District.[7]

Business was so good in Anniston that in 1882 the Noble brothers moved all of their Rome, Georgia, manufacturing operations, including their car wheel works, to Alabama. By consolidating manufacturing and raw material operations at one location, the firm realized all the benefits of a fully integrated manufacturing facility, and the Anniston Car Wheel Works enjoyed a brisk and highly profitable business. Two hundred skilled workmen turned out many varieties of car wheels, including tank, Pullman, spoke, English tender plate, and a special thirty-three-inch wheel proudly called "Woodstock." Production started at Anniston in July 1883, and in September the company cast 1,322 car wheels. In 1883 and 1884, twenty-nine railroads, primarily in the South, purchased car wheels from the Anniston Car Wheel Works.

In 1883 Anniston also became the home of a railroad car manufacturing facility when Georgia

Selma, Rome & Dalton Railroad section crew at Blue Mountain, ca. 1880. (Courtesy of the Alabama Room, Public Library of Anniston-Calhoun County)

entrepreneurs established the Anniston Car Company. This company was soon building twenty railroad cars a day using lumber hewn from the region's lush forests and car wheels cast with Woodstock iron. Among the major customers of the Anniston Car Company were the East Tennessee, Virginia & Georgia and the Georgia Pacific railways—lines that were having a major impact on railroading in Alabama.[8]

The East Tennessee, Virginia & Georgia Railroad was rapidly becoming a dominant southern system. As part of an ambitious expansion policy, the ETV&G Railroad had absorbed several Alabama roads that had failed to recover from the postwar depression. Among these were the Memphis & Charleston which was leased in 1877, as well as the Alabama Central Railroad and the Selma, Rome & Dalton Railroad, both of which were taken over in 1881. The East Tennessee, Virginia & Georgia Railroad and all its Alabama holdings were consolidated in 1886 as part of a new organization known as the East Tennessee, Virginia & Georgia Railway System. In 1887 the ETV&G Railway System saw an opportunity to extend its territory further by acquiring the distressed property of the Mobile & Alabama Grand Trunk Railroad. Sixty-two miles of this line had been constructed from Mobile to the Tombigbee River before its owners ran out of money in 1873. In receivership since then, the Mobile & Alabama Grand Trunk was absorbed by the ETV&G Railway, renamed the Mobile & Birmingham Railway, and extended from Jackson to Marion Junction, where it joined the fifty-three-mile long Cincinnati, Selma & Mobile Railway that led through Marion and Greensboro to Akron, Alabama. The Cincinnati, Selma & Mobile Railway, successor to General Forrest's Selma, Marion & Memphis Railroad, was also acquired by the ETV&G in 1890. The ETV&G Railway was growing through acquisitions in Alabama, but its reach proved to exceed its grasp, and the conglomerate eventually followed the all-too-familiar path to receivership.

About this time, the Georgia Pacific Railway was also born when Confederate general John B. Gordon conceived an airline route between Atlanta and Greenville, Mississippi. The proposed line, penetrating directly through Alabama's mineral region via Anniston and Birmingham, had sound prospects for success and had obtained financial backing from the powerful Richmond & Danville Railroad. As part of the right-of-way, Gordon bought a floundering Mississippi line that had been projected to the Birmingham District coal fields. Only twenty-three miles of this narrow-gauge road had been completed from Greenville to Indianola, Mississippi, when Gordon acquired it in 1881. A year later the Georgia Pacific began construction at Atlanta and tunneled through the mountains of east-central Alabama to reach Birmingham in 1883. From there, the gandy dancers slowly worked their way westward toward their ultimate objective in Mississippi.[9]

On September 22, 1886, the westbound Georgia Pacific construction crews were accompanied by a *Birmingham Age* newsman who reported on their activities. After winding its way through high mountains, the work train abruptly clattered to a stop, and the laborers filed off the cars to unload some construction material. "In genuine negro style," the reporter observed, "they began to lift and heave at the heavy timbers, which were to be used on the trestling further up the road. After a few vigorous phrases from their 'caps'—the universal title for the boss among them—a goodly pile of beams were thrown upon the flats."

As the work train continued on, the writer noted an inviting crystal-clear spring that gushed forth from a rocky ledge. Such springs

were numerous throughout Alabama, and offered cool refreshment on hot summer days, but they sometimes flooded tunnels such as the five-hundred-foot-long Fish-Trap tunnel through which the tracklaying train soon threaded. At day's end, the *Age* reporter got a firsthand view of a typical Alabama railroad construction camp.

> The sight of a railroad camp to a person who has never seen one is not likely to inspire one with special regard for its architectural beauty. This camp was down in a gorge of the mountains. The central attraction was the commissary, which was made of rough pine plank, nailed together without much attention to how it was done. But here the happy darkey goes with alacrity when his pocket is stuffed with checks, and never leaves until they are all gone. In front of the commissary stands the stable which is a long shed and underneath the eaves of which slabs are nailed to keep the sleek, fat mules within bounds. The blacksmith shop is at one end, as also the foreman's quarters. The shanty, which resembles an overgrown chicken coop, is made of pine poles. It is a most important structure, for within it, the darkey rests his weary limbs after a day's work.[10]

In typical fashion, the predominately black construction crews heroically persevered under these harsh conditions until a connection with the Mississippi segment was effected in 1887, making the Georgia Pacific Railway part of a first-class through route from the Atlantic coast to the Mississippi River. Thus, the Georgia Pacific became a component of a growing complex of main lines converging on booming Birmingham and provided an important and greatly needed east-west outlet for Anniston District iron.[11]

And there was much more Anniston District iron to haul. In 1879 a second, larger charcoal furnace was put into blast at the Woodstock works, and the following year the original furnace was also enlarged. The car wheel business thrived, as six fully loaded cars of "best standard" car wheels left the Anniston Car Wheel Works every day. Soon, more iron was being produced than could be absorbed by the car wheel plant, and castings were being shipped to many large northern cities as well as the Montana Territory and Canada. Demand was so strong that the Woodstock furnace couldn't obtain enough cars to ship all of its production. But these expanded furnaces still used charcoal and, as local forests became depleted, it was necessary to procure wood from greater and greater distances. For this reason, and as part of a strategy devoted to the total integration of manufacturing and transportation activities, Tyler and Noble concluded in 1880 that the best interests of the Woodstock Company would be served by building a railroad that would tap the mineral and timber resources south of Anniston. The Selma, Rome & Dalton Railroad had served the Woodstock Company well; but on May 24, 1883, the state legislature granted a charter to Noble, Tyler, and their associates that incorporated a competing line, the Anniston & Atlantic Railroad.[12]

The Woodstock Company had already accrued a considerable amount of railroad experience by purchasing two Talladega County furnaces, the Clifton and Jennifer works, and connecting them with a short section of trackage called the Clifton Railroad. The Anniston & Atlantic route was planned to run alongside the Georgia Pacific for six miles west of Anniston, then turn south and follow the Clifton roadbed into Talladega. A versatile hybrid design was to be used in constructing the Anniston & Atlantic. To limit expenses, the A&A was built as a three-foot gauge line; but to make later conversion to standard gauge easier, the roadbed was graded to accommodate five-foot gauge track. As usual, Tyler and Noble made sure their new project was adequately financed, and by August 1883 almost one thousand laborers were ready to lay thirty-pound rail on graded roadbed linking the Woodstock furnace with the Clifton iron mines ten miles south of Anniston.[13] By February 1884 a handsome 4-4-0 locomotive was pulling daily trains of twenty- to twenty-five-ton capacity cars between Anniston and Talladega, a distance of thirty miles, at speeds of up to thirty miles per hour. The curious sight of the narrow-gauge A&A clinging to the broad-gauge Georgia Pacific roadbed provoked the local jocularity, "the Georgia Pacific has got a baby."

The Anniston & Atlantic promised to lower shipping costs for the cotton planters along its route and they enthusiastically welcomed the construction crews that were opening rich agricultural areas of Talladega County. In 1886, as its agricultural and mineral businesses grew, the A&A obtained a piece of machinery called the "Little Giant Excavator," which loaded five cars in eleven minutes, doing the work of fifty laborers. In the same year the Anniston & Atlantic pushed fifty-three miles south of Anniston to reach the quarries at the largest vein of marble in the world near the town of Sylacauga.[14] Riding Anniston & Atlantic cars to distant markets, Alabama marble soon became world famous, and was even shipped to Washington to make the columns of the Supreme Court building.[15]

The Anniston & Atlantic fostered the development of a feeder line

The 4-4-0 American type locomotive, such as this example from the Talladega & Coosa Valley Railroad, was the most commonly used engine in Alabama during the nineteenth century. (Courtesy of Robert A. Scarboro, Scarboro Photo Shop, Gadsden, Alabama)

in 1883 when the Talladega & Coosa Valley Railroad Company was chartered to haul timber to several lumber mills near Talladega. By 1886 this road was in operation for fifteen miles, running from the Coosa River to a station on the Anniston & Atlantic known as Murphy. From this junction, trackage rights were obtained over the A&A for the two-mile run to Talladega. After a bridge was built over the Coosa River at Stemley in 1887, the road was extended to Pell City. In 1890 the 26.9-mile line was rechartered as the Birmingham & Atlantic Railroad.

On October 16, 1894, a Birmingham & Atlantic passenger train was crossing the six-hundred-foot-long bridge across the Coosa River when the 150-foot-long west span collapsed, throwing the engine, cars, and passengers into twenty-two feet of water. One passenger was killed and several more were injured, but the tragedy would have claimed many more victims were it not for the courageous actions of a black porter, Jordan Cranford, and the conductor, Harry Fleetwood. Cranford boldly dived into the water again and again to pull passengers to the safety of Fleetwood's outstretched arms.

Repairs were made, but one of the road's locomotive drivers, Henry Sims, reportedly continued to consider the span unsafe. It is said that Sims would not ride a train across the mended structure for months after the accident. Instead, he built up just enough steam to propel the train slowly across the river. He and the passengers then jumped off and walked across the bridge, leaving the fireman to start the locomotive. After starting the train across the bridge, the fireman would also leap from the engine and wait for Sims to catch it on the other side.

Once, Sims was unable to get aboard to regain control of the train and chased it for miles before it ran out of steam.

By 1899 several B&A spurs probed many of the mines that were opening throughout the area to serve the new Talladega Furnace. The B&A remained in business as long as the lumber mills and Talladega Furnace were operational, but when the ironworks fizzled, this quaint little railroad passed into history.[16]

The concurrent advent of the Georgia Pacific and the Anniston & Atlantic stimulated a passion for railroads in Anniston. Newspapers were filled with speculation concerning new railroads, especially one that was projected to link Anniston with Gadsden. A line to Gadsden would penetrate a particularly rich mineral region north of Anniston and serve several furnaces that had been established in Cherokee and Etowah counties. It would also provide a connection with Coosa River steamers and make possible an important connection with the Alabama Great Southern Railroad at neighboring Attalla. The AGS led to Chattanooga, where the Cincinnati Southern Railroad was opening a new route to Cincinnati that was designed to compete with the L&N for New Orleans–Cincinnati traffic. If a railroad could be built from Anniston to Gadsden, hours could be stripped from travel time to northern markets.

A railroad from Anniston to Gadsden had been attempted during the Reconstruction era when the East Alabama & Cincinnati Railroad surveyed and partially graded a route that led through a mountain pass known as Davis Gap. The route through Davis Gap was the most practical way to breach a formidable mountain barrier between Anniston and Gadsden, and this right-of-way had been purchased subsequently by the Jacksonville, Gadsden & Attalla Railroad Company. In 1884 several Anniston, Louisville, and Chattanooga investors projected a line from Anniston to Gadsden that ran through Davis Gap, and tried to purchase the property. Even though the Jacksonville, Gadsden & Attalla Railroad had little chance of being built, the Jacksonville interests refused to relinquish their rights to the vital gap, and negotiations over the right-of-way dragged on until the promoters ran out of money.

In 1887, as part of the Woodstock Iron Company reorganization plan, the long-anticipated railroad from Anniston to Gadsden became a real possibility when Noble, Tyler, and Gurnee incorporated the Anniston & Cincinnati Railroad Company. With the Woodstock Company backing the project, construction quickly began, but problems immediately arose when two hundred laborers walked off the job to protest the firing of some foremen and the alleged underpayment of wages. Work resumed when replacements were hired, and the road made good progress until the gandy dancers reached Davis Gap and were confronted by armed guards hired by the Jacksonville, Gadsden & Attalla Railroad Company. A standoff ensued until one day the gap was unaccountably left unguarded. The Anniston & Cincinnati Railroad crew hastily commandeered the disputed property and pressed forward until the Jacksonville men went to court and obtained an injunction prohibiting further work. On May 9, the case was heard in Gadsden, where the Annistonians labeled the Jacksonville group obstructionists and pleaded for condemnation of the route. The Jacksonville interests held sway, however, and in a ruling subsequently sustained by the Alabama Supreme Court, the Anniston & Cincinnati was forever forbidden from using the Jacksonville, Gadsden & Attalla right-of-way. The only hope for an easy route through the mountains now lay in negotiations, but the Jacksonville investors would not sell their rights for less than $25,000 plus freight rate concessions. Considering these terms unacceptable, the A&C decided to tunnel through the mountain.

Only six months had been required to lay the thirty miles of track between Anniston and Gadsden, but adversity after adversity delayed completion of the tunnel, and it was not finished for two more years. The area was laced with numerous springs that flooded the tunnel and precipitated landslides; a carload of black powder and dynamite exploded at the north entrance to the tunnel; and to top things off, the bridge over the Coosa River washed out. After reportedly spending one million dollars, an enormous sum for the time, Anniston & Cincinnati Railroad trains finally rolled through the tunnel and across the bridge for the first time in October 1888.[17]

As the first trains ran between Anniston and Gadsden, the great boom of Birmingham was cresting. The DeBardeleben Coal and Iron Company had grown to a thirteen-million-dollar enterprise, and smaller companies were popping up everywhere. This phenomenal industrial growth was accompanied by unprecedented real estate speculation. One Birmingham resident marveled, "Nowhere in the world did things happen as they happened in Birmingham in '86 and '87. Property changed hands as much as four and five times a day. Everybody, everywhere, was talking Birmingham. Men went crazy two hours after getting here; they certainly did."

The record of the Elyton Land Company paints a true picture of the extent reached by the speculative fever:

Such a scene of excitement in real estate speculation as was presented in Birmingham at this time was perhaps never before witnessed in the South. People from all parts of the South flocked to Birmingham, attracted by the reports which had spread all over the country of the wonderful profits being so rapidly realized here by speculation in real estate. Hotels and boarding houses were packed to overflowing by eager fortune hunters. Almost every prominent window facing on the business streets was rented at fabulous prices for real estate offices, while glib-tongued speculators never tired of pouring into listening ears fabulous stories of the enormous profits being so rapidly realized by lucky investors.

Day by day the excitement grew. Upon street corners, in hotel corridors and in private parlors, the one theme of conversation was real estate speculation; young and old, male and female, merchant and clerk, minister and layman—everybody seemed seized with a desire to speculate in town lots. Conservative citizens who in the early stages wisely shook their heads and predicted disaster to purchasers of property, as prices climbed higher and still higher, with scarcely a single exception, ceased to bear the market, and when prices had advanced two or three hundred per cent above what they had thought to be extravagant, entered the market, bought property, and joined the great army of boomers. Wilder and wilder the excitement grew. Stranger and resident alike plunged into the market, hoping to gather

The iron boom attracted thousands of immigrants to the Birmingham District. (Photograph ca. 1880s, courtesy of the Birmingham Public Library Department of Archives and Manuscripts)

in a portion of the golden shower which was now falling in glistening sheets upon the Magic City. Each day the office of the Elyton Land Company was crowded with a throng of eager purchasers, and the president of the company, who alone had charge of the sales of the company, was kept busy at the maps from morning until night, pricing property and making sales. A memorandum of each sale as soon as made was handed over to a clerk, who would receive the cash payment and give a receipt for the same. In many instances the purchaser would seize his receipt and rush out on the street and resell the property at a handsome profit before his bond for title could be executed. . . .

During this phenomenal period of excitement all sorts of corporations were formed and an endless variety of financial schemes were floated. A syndicate would be formed, a tract of land purchased, a land company organized, the land being subscribed for at an immense advance above the purchase price, and the stock put upon the market, to be eagerly taken by a confiding public, with scarcely a question as to the amount of capitalization. Any number of schemes for building suburban towns contiguous to Birmingham were organized, and land five and ten miles from the city, which had never before been considered worth above $10 or $12 per acre, was within a few months valued at from $500 to $1000. Land owners in town and country would, by computing their possessions at the public estimate easily figure themselves rich.[18]

In May 1886 the boom-town cacophony was further exaggerated when the major railroads serving the southeast simultaneously changed their track gauge. These railroads used a five-foot gauge, and in order to facilitate efficient traffic interchange, intended to adopt the standard 4-foot 8½-inch gauge that was prevalent on northern roads. Previously, the problem of unlike gauges had been addressed either by transferring freight from the cars of one railroad to those of another at transfer points, or by using devices such as hoists to physically shift car bodies onto trucks of differing gauge. But such time-consuming devices were rendered impractical as the iron boom contributed to an ever-increasing volume of traffic over southeastern routes, and it became apparent to railroad managers that a change to universal gauge was imperative.

The first Alabama railroad to change to standard gauge was the Mobile & Ohio, which narrowed its track in July 1885. In that same month, Milton Smith conferred in New York with officials from all L&N connecting lines and it was decided that all these roads should make the simultaneous switch to standard gauge on May 31 and June 1, 1886. Accordingly, the work force on Alabama railroads temporarily swelled in May 1886 as preparations were made for the change.

From a practical standpoint, southern roads could opt for a track width that was one-half inch in excess of the standard gauge, since cars could operate satisfactorily over track that was either 4-foot 8½- or 4-foot 9-inch gauge. Therefore, the L&N, which already used a 4-foot 9-inch gauge on some of its divisions, planned to employ four hands per mile to move the west rail of its tracks three inches to the east. For better clearance, the rails would be moved inward by one and one-half inches on each side in Alabama tunnels. On the day of the changeover, which was rescheduled on both the L&N and Alabama Great Southern for May 30, competition was encouraged between section crews as they raced each other to get the job done. Not only was the track to be moved, but the majority of motive power and rolling stock required conversion. This equipment was concentrated in yards at Birmingham and other major traffic centers, and as the sun rose on May 30, swarming workers feverishly labored to effect the transition.[19] Among the massive crowd of spellbound spectators who witnessed the dramatic changeover was a correspondent for a Gadsden newspaper, who sent the following dispatch from Birmingham on June 1, 1886:

> Last Sunday was a day long to be remembered. Such a scene never was and never will be witnessed in this city again. All traffic on the A.G.S. and L.&N. was stopped at 12 o'clock Saturday night, and the work began immediately, and by noon Sunday the entire main lines from Cincinnati to New Orleans, had been narrowed up and were ready for business with the exception of a small portion of the A.G.S. that runs through the state of Georgia. The laws of that state prohibited such work being done on Sunday. Around the shops and yards of the roads there was a scene of bustle and confusion. Many hundred of men, boys and negroes were working with a will. Engines and cars were being "jacked up" and their trucks taken out, the wheels shoved back on the axles by a hydraulic ram. It is astonishing how quick this can be done by men who understand the business. It was a wonderful sight to stand on the 22nd [S]treet bridge and take a bird's-eye view of the railroad yards. As far as the eye could reach on either side the many side tracks were literally covered with engines and cars waiting to be narrowed up. It will take several weeks to get the yards cleared up. The workmen on the L.&N. were furnished with lemonade and refreshments all day at the expense of the company, and 50 per cent added to their wages besides. The G.P. road was changed Monday.[20]

The road from West Point to Selma, called the Western Railway of Alabama since a reorganization in 1883, was unable to change its gauge in only one day. Instead, on May 29 all trains on the Western of Alabama stopped while the wheels and trucks of locomotives and rolling stock were converted to standard gauge. The next day Selma Division track was changed, and on May 31 the main line to West Point was switched to standard gauge. The change must have frustrated W of A officials, since the road had gone to much trouble and expense in 1866 to widen its track to match the 5-foot standard of other southern roads. The reversion to the original 4-foot 8 1/2-inch gauge was accomplished more efficiently this time, however. An operation requiring nine days to execute in 1866 was now done in one third that amount of time.[21]

The accelerating boom continued to attract more railroads to Alabama's mineral fields. The East & West Railroad of Alabama was organized in 1882 to purchase a defunct Georgia narrow gauge line and extend it to the Birmingham District. The derelict road, which ran from Cartersville, Georgia, to the Alabama state line, was immediately rehabilitated, widened to standard gauge, and extended sixty-four miles to Coal City, Alabama. In 1887 a planned connection with the Georgia Pacific Railway was executed when a seven-mile branch was constructed from Coal City to Pell City. Unfortunately, after achieving their construction goals, the East & West Railroad of Alabama failed financially and went into receivership in 1888.[22]

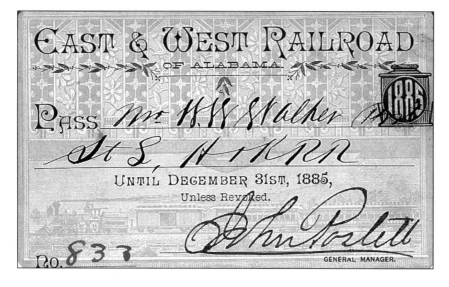

East & West Railroad of Alabama annual pass for 1885. (From the author's collection)

Although good connections were in place for north and eastbound traffic, a direct line to the Midwest from the Birmingham District was needed. This problem was addressed when Boston financiers revived a combination of aborted attempts to connect Memphis with Birmingham and placed the Kansas City, Memphis & Birmingham Railroad in operation on October 17, 1887. The following year a branch was extended from Pratt City to Bessemer. As part of the corporate structure of the Kansas City, Fort Scott & Memphis Railroad, its trains brought midwestern grain and packing-house products to Birmingham and returned loaded with coal. By 1900, coal and coke comprised over 50 percent of the traffic over the Kansas City, Memphis & Birmingham Railroad.[23]

A string band serenades construction workers as they extend the East & West Railroad of Alabama to Pell City in 1887. (Courtesy of Robert A. Scarboro, Scarboro Photo Shop, Gadsden, Alabama)

The new railroads as well as the old enjoyed a steady stream of passenger business as speculators and immigrants surged into the mineral regions. To receive the influx of humanity into Jefferson County, the L&N invested over $134,000 in 1887 to erect a new passenger station at the corner of 20th Street and Morris Avenue, complete with train shed and an expanded coach yard. All railroads serving Birmingham used the new Union Station and shared operating expenses.[24]

By this time, thirty-three major iron and coal enterprises were in operation near Birmingham, including Ensley's Pratt Coal and Iron Company. After Ensley's company acquired T. T. Hillman's Alice furnace, Hillman was virtually excluded from a leadership position with the company he had pioneered. Hillman resented being relegated to a minor role while Ensley basked in the glory of the Alice successes. This resentment fomented a series of intrigues that dramatically influenced the character of industrial development in the Birmingham District. Hillman planned to wrest control of the Pratt Coal and Iron Company from Ensley by enlisting the aid of Ensley's arch competitor, John H. Inman of the Tennessee Coal, Iron & Railroad Company. Inman was also serving as a director of the L&N Railroad and was anxious to expand the Tennessee Company's coal and iron operations into the booming fields of Alabama. Hillman persuaded Inman to join him in a raid on the Pratt Coal and Iron Company, and together they purchased and

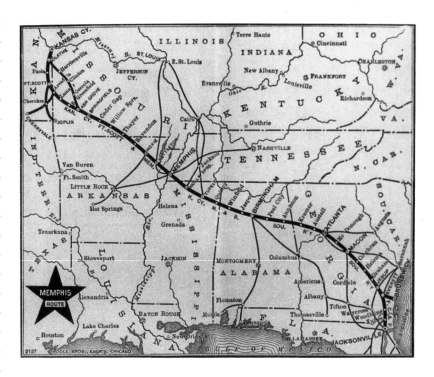

The Kansas City, Memphis & Birmingham Railroad linked Birmingham with the Midwest. (From an 1885 timetable, courtesy of William Stanley Hoole Special Collections Library, The University of Alabama, Tuscaloosa)

exercised enough options to gain a controlling interest in Ensley's company. With an L&N director now in charge of these important enterprises, the Old Reliable was destined to become more committed than ever to the Birmingham District.[25]

Under Inman's ambitious leadership, the Tennessee Coal, Iron & Railroad Company pushed the boom to an even higher pitch. The capital-rich Tennessee Company purchased extensive iron ore tracts throughout Red Mountain, acquired limestone quarries, and erected large-scale furnace operations, including four furnaces of gargantuan proportions near the town that Ensley had established and to which he had proudly given his own name. Inman wanted the L&N to extend its Birmingham Mineral Railroad to serve this far-flung empire and approached Milton H. Smith with a proposal. If the Old Reliable would extend these branches to encircle Red Mountain and construct feeders for his coal and iron enterprises, Inman promised to give the L&N exclusive transportation rights for the Tennessee Company's Birmingham District products. Smith did not hesitate. He immediately drew up a plan to encircle Red Mountain and presented it to Eckstein Norton. The L&N president agreed that this great opportunity was not to be missed. "By encircling the Red Mountain in this manner with a railroad on each side," Norton confidently announced, "the mining and transportation of the immense deposits of iron ore therein contained, will be greatly facilitated and the cost much reduced."

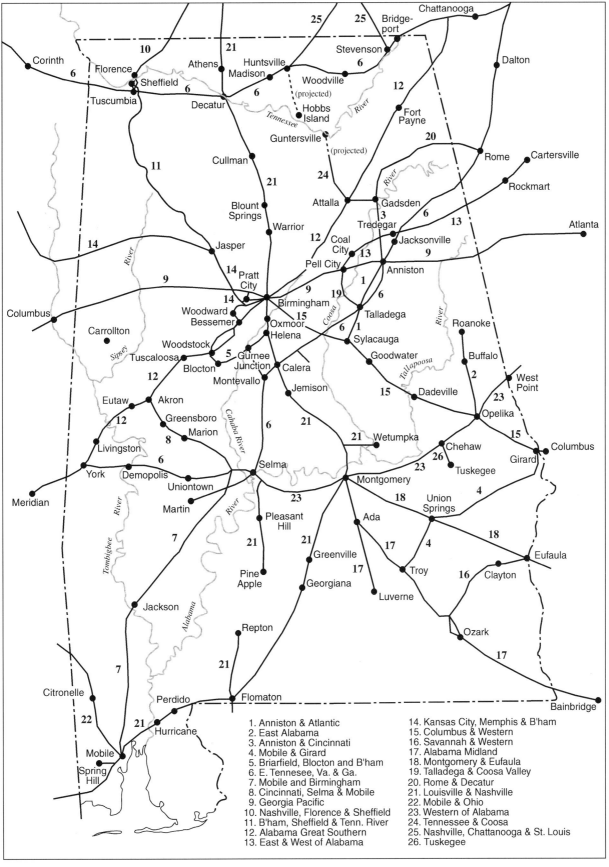

Corinth
6
10
Florence
Sheffield
Tuscumbia
Athens
21
Huntsville
Madison
6
Woodville
(projected)
Hobbs
Island
Decatur
6
Tennessee
River
Guntersville
(projected)
Stevenson
6
Bridge-
port
Chattanooga
25
25
Dalton
12
Fort
Payne
20
Rome
Cartersville
Rockmart
24
Attalla
Gadsden
3
Tredegar
Jacksonville
9
Atlanta
13
6
Cullman
11
Blount
Springs
Warrior
21
12
Coal
City
13
Pell City
1
Anniston
Jasper
14
Pratt
City
14
9
Birmingham
9
19
6
Talladega
Columbus
14
15
Woodward
Bessemer
Oxmoor
Helena
6
1
Sylacauga
6
Roanoke
Carrollton
Sipsey
Woodstock
Tuscaloosa
Blocton
5
Gurnee
Junction
Calera
Montevallo
Goodwater
Buffalo
2
West
Point
23
Dadeville
Tallapoosa
River
Coosa
River
12
Jemison
15
Eutaw
Akron
Greensboro
Marion
8
Wetumpka
21
Opelika
15
Columbus
12
Livingston
6
Chehaw
26
Tuskegee
Girard
23
York
Demopolis
Uniontown
Martin
Selma
6
21
Montgomery
18
Union
Springs
4
Meridian
Tombigbee
River
Cahaba River
Alabama
River
23
Pleasant
Hill
Ada
17
4
Eufaula
18
7
21
Pine
Apple
Greenville
21
Georgiana
17
Troy
Clayton
16
Luverne
Ozark
Jackson
Repton
17
Citronelle
22
Perdido
21
Flomaton
Bainbridge
7
21
Hurricane
Mobile
Spring
Hill

1. Anniston & Atlantic
2. East Alabama
3. Anniston & Cincinnati
4. Mobile & Girard
5. Briarfield, Blocton and B'ham
6. E. Tennessee, Va. & Ga.
7. Mobile and Birmingham
8. Cincinnati, Selma & Mobile
9. Georgia Pacific
10. Nashville, Florence & Sheffield
11. B'ham, Sheffield & Tenn. River
12. Alabama Great Southern
13. East & West of Alabama

14. Kansas City, Memphis & B'ham
15. Columbus & Western
16. Savannah & Western
17. Alabama Midland
18. Montgomery & Eufaula
19. Talladega & Coosa Valley
20. Rome & Decatur
21. Louisville & Nashville
22. Mobile & Ohio
23. Western of Alabama
24. Tennessee & Coosa
25. Nashville, Chattanooga & St. Louis
26. Tuskegee

Alabama Railroads, 1890

L&N 4-4-0 American type locomotive decorated for the 1887 opening of Union Station in downtown Birmingham. (Courtesy of the Birmingham Public Library Department of Archives and Manuscripts)

Ultimately, Smith would not be satisfied with merely encircling Red Mountain. He went much further and developed a plan to build a large-radius belt line around the entire Birmingham District. From the junction of the north and south branches of the original Birmingham Mineral Railroad, he proposed extending a completely new branch that would loop through Bessemer, Woodward, and the new ironworking facilities going up at Ensley, to connect finally with the South & North Railroad at Boyle's Station, north of Birmingham. The belt line was to be tied together by another branch that would extend from Boyle's Station through Red Gap and rejoin the South & North Alabama Railroad at Graces, south of Birmingham. The plan also called for another spur to be built to the Edwards furnace at Woodstock in Bibb County. In all, Smith's proposed Birmingham Mineral Railroad extension would add fifty-four miles of new track to the L&N system.

The extensions were soon built but still proved to be insufficient to serve the phenomenally expanding Birmingham District iron industry adequately. In 1888, the twenty-seven-mile Blue Creek extension was built from the north branch of the Birmingham Mineral Railroad through Valley Creek and Yolande to Brookwood and Blocton Junction. The Birmingham Mineral added sixty more miles of trackage in 1889 and twenty-four more in 1890. Altogether, the Birmingham

Birmingham's Union Station around 1890. (Courtesy of the Birmingham Public Library Department of Archives and Manuscripts)

Mineral Railroad finally encompassed one hundred fifty-six miles of track costing over six million dollars. As the Birmingham Mineral hauled coal from the Warrior and Blue Creek coal fields, limestone from the Gate City quarries, and ore from legions of mines, the output of Birmingham District furnaces doubled from 1886 to 1888. Since each ton of iron production required two tons of ore, one and one-half tons of coke, and a half ton of limestone—all carried over Birmingham Mineral Railroad tracks—the Birmingham Mineral Railroad extensions proved to be wise investments indeed.[26]

As expected, the low transportation rates offered by the L&N produced higher traffic volumes, which translated into a bulging bottom line on the company's income statement. In 1889 President Norton was moved to heartily reaffirm the L&N development policy. "While higher rates would have given a better return on the capital invested," he said, "they would probably have prevented development, or else produced active competition by other roads which would have been built in that section."[27]

The low profit margin policy that served Alabama so well can be credited largely to Milton H. Smith. From the beginning Smith felt that such a rate structure would increase profits for the mine and furnace operators so that production and traffic volume would grow. He knew that low rates and exceptional service were the factors that would keep customers loyal to the L&N and eliminate potential competitors. The strategy worked marvelously as the L&N kept growing along with the mineral industries, and, despite the entrance of other roads into the Birmingham District, the Old Reliable continued to enjoy its highly profitable regional monopoly.

The L&N's most notable challenger was the Central Railroad & Banking Company of Georgia, headed by the savvy William M. Wadley. The mineral frenzy attracted Wadley's eye and he made plans to extend the Central into the Birmingham District. The Central Railroad & Banking Company had already made an incursion into the state by investing in the Western Railway of Alabama. This gave the Central a terminal at Opelika from which a line could be launched into Jefferson County.

Milton Smith worried that competitors could invade L&N territory by absorbing and rehabilitating derelict lines left in the wake of the panic of '73. This is exactly what the Central Railroad & Banking Company did when the Columbus & Western Railway, one of many Central subsidiaries, purchased the Savannah & Memphis Railroad in 1880. The Savannah & Memphis was the latest of many aborted attempts to connect Opelika with Talladega. The line was originally chartered to the antebellum Opelika & Talladega Railroad and 54.9 miles had actually been constructed between Opelika and Goodwater when it was acquired. After also purchasing the Western of Alabama's Opelika-Columbus branch outright in 1882, the Columbus & Western was able to finish the final sixty-eight miles of trackage from Goodwater to Birmingham in 1888. This line, like others in the mineral region, cut through some rugged country, and required a 2,431-foot-long tunnel at Coosa Mountain as well as a 1,198-foot-long penetration of Oak Mountain. Smith watched anxiously as the Columbus & Western, together with the East Alabama & Cincinnati Railroad that linked Opelika with Roanoke, and two other end-to-end roads that connected Eufaula with Ozark were immediately consolidated under the corporate umbrella of the Savannah & Western Railroad, another Central Railroad & Banking Company subsidiary.[28] As the many-lined hand of the Central Railroad & Banking Company challenged the L&N monopoly, Smith became increasingly concerned that other financially troubled roads in his territory might be purchased by well-heeled competitors. With this in mind, Smith warily tracked the fortunes of smaller roads in

L&N territory and considered buying troubled companies before they fell into the wrong hands.

In 1889 Smith saw an opportunity to defend his monopoly and extend it to include almost all of the iron business of the state. The Woodstock Iron Company was in deep financial trouble due to the expensive tunnel project near Gadsden as well as delays in construction of new coke furnaces. Since their old charcoal furnaces had been partially dismantled to make way for the new coke furnaces, the company suffered a temporary loss of cash flow. Initially, Noble and Tyler had intended to use Cahaba coal to fuel these furnaces, and had purchased the old Blocton mines, which covered thirty thousand acres and nine coal seams in Bibb, Shelby, and Jefferson counties. More heavy investment was also required to build four hundred new beehive coke ovens at the Blocton mines. The Anniston men wanted to extend the Anniston & Atlantic Railroad to these mines, but the financial impasse, coupled with the death of Noble in 1888, made this impossible.

In 1888 the L&N entered into negotiations with the Woodstock Company to purchase both the A&A and Anniston & Cincinnati. Smith inspected the A&A in 1890 and concluded that it could be successfully integrated into the Birmingham Mineral Railroad. He saw that the A&A traversed large deposits of brown hematite ore which, when mixed with the red ores found near Birmingham, was known to produce a better quality iron and provide a greater yield as well. Since Birmingham furnaces needed the brown hematite and the Woodstock furnaces needed Cahaba coal, Smith visualized L&N cars perpetually filled with revenue-producing raw materials. If the A&A were connected to the South & North Alabama Railroad, iron ore could be hauled to Birmingham, unloaded, and the same cars reloaded with coke bound for the Anniston furnaces. The fanatically efficiency-minded Smith loved such an arrangement, and in March 1890 the L&N purchased the two Woodstock Company lines. The entrance of the powerful L&N into the Anniston District was hailed in an Anniston newspaper as "of more benefit to Anniston than any other trade ever consummated."

Anticipating large volumes of business, the L&N immediately changed the Anniston & Atlantic Railroad to standard gauge and replaced its thirty-pound rail with fifty-pound rail. Then, in 1891, the A&A was extended thirty-four miles from Sylacauga to join the South & North Alabama Railroad at Calera. Consolidating the two Woodstock company roads with the Birmingham Mineral Railroad produced a

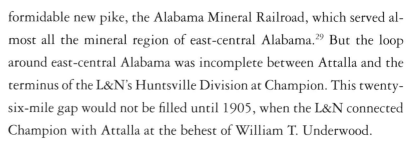

Alabama Mineral Railroad, ca. 1891. (Courtesy of the L&N Collection, University of Louisville Archives and Records Center)

formidable new pike, the Alabama Mineral Railroad, which served almost all the mineral region of east-central Alabama.[29] But the loop around east-central Alabama was incomplete between Attalla and the terminus of the L&N's Huntsville Division at Champion. This twenty-six-mile gap would not be filled until 1905, when the L&N connected Champion with Attalla at the behest of William T. Underwood.

Underwood had acquired a large expanse of coal lands in isolated parts of Etowah and Blount counties in the spring of 1900 and needed rail facilities in order to open mines. Although Alabama Great Southern tracks ran relatively near to his property, AGS officials offered little encouragement when Underwood asked them to extend a branch to the proposed mines. It was a different story when he approached Milton H. Smith, however. Smith told Underwood flatly, "If you have the quality and quantity of coal you think you have, I will build you a road." Smith once again proved to be as good as his word. After test results verified the value of Underwood's coal holdings, the L&N initiated construction of the promised branch in May 1900. By October Underwood was shipping coal over L&N tracks, and by New Year's day the branch was extended to Altoona, ten miles east of Champion. Not only did Smith build the railroad for Underwood, but he also arranged a loan with a Louisville bank for several thousand dollars. These L&N investments proved to be a great boon for Underwood and provided a lasting benefit for the state. "I started this business with but a few thousand dollars of my own," Underwood said gratefully, "and within four years time had paid about $80,000 for the land, paid off the banks, and sold the property for a very large sum, most of which money came from outside the State and remains invested in Alabama." The Old Reliable kept advancing this line, and on May 28, 1905, the final sixteen miles of track leading into Attalla were in place.[30]

The iron boom reached such fabulous heights in 1889 that the L&N hauled over two million more tons of freight than in the previous year, including more coal, coke, iron, and limestone than the total cotton crop for the *entire country.* To handle the increased traffic, the L&N made major capital investments in Alabama. Bridges and trestles were rebuilt to handle heavier loads, more cars and locomotives were acquired, and track was upgraded using relatively heavy sixty-eight-pound steel rail.[31] In order to provide more rolling stock for its growing Alabama needs, the L&N opened modern shops at New Decatur in 1890, where cars of twenty to thirty ton's capacity were turned out to replace obsolete fifteen-ton freight cars. The Old Reliable also laid down four miles of terminal trackage to service these new facilities, and appropriately assigned the name New & Old Decatur Belt & Terminal Railroad Company to the diminutive terminal railroad that connected Decatur with New Decatur.[32]

The mushrooming iron boom soon spread to Gadsden, the "Queen City of the Coosa." Between 1883 and 1904, five iron furnaces were opened in Etowah County, giving rise to demands for better rail connections to the north and east.[33] Two new organizations satisfied these demands: The Tennessee & Coosa Railroad and the Rome & Decatur Railroad. Although the Tennessee & Coosa had originally been char-

By the turn of the century, twenty-five hundred skilled mechanics were producing one hundred new cars a day at the L&N's New Decatur car shops. (Photograph ca. 1890s, courtesy of the L&N Collection, University of Louisville Archives and Records Center)

tered in 1840 to connect Gadsden with Guntersville, it was just beginning to creep toward the base of Sand Mountain, a few miles north of the Coosa River. The recently incorporated Rome & Decatur, on the other hand, was vigorously prosecuting construction between Gadsden and Rome, Georgia. The public anxiously followed the progress of these projects, and on November 19, 1886, was thrilled to learn that the first shipment had been carried over a section of the yet unfinished Tennessee & Coosa Railroad. The inaugural lading, consisting of four bales of cotton, allowed the company to ring up twenty-five cents per bale in revenue as the road continued its glacial trek toward Guntersville.[34]

So much railroad activity was underway at this time that a column entitled "Railroad Racket," written to quench the public's thirst for information regarding the progress of local railroads, was beginning to appear in a number of statewide newspapers. The March 10, 1887, issue of the *Gadsden Times* hit the streets with some upbeat "Railroad Racket" headlines splashed across the front page. "The news in railroad circles is decidedly encouraging and reassuring," the article began. "J. C. Printup, the president of the Rome and Decatur railroad, assures us that the track will be completed ten miles beyond Gadsden by the first of April. The engine has been ordered around to this point, and as fast as the road is graded the steel rails will be laid. Five hundred hands will begin work here at once, while two hundred are on the other end. . . . Our boom begins to materialize and grows each day and hour."[35]

These words sounded mighty good to Gadsden real estate operators. Etowah County land prices escalated in direct proportion to ebullient rumors of impending boom, and speculators hoped that

Side-dumping ore cars were a common sight on Alabama railroads during the iron boom. Several of these cars are shown in this view of the Consolidated Coal & Iron Company blast furnace at Gadsden. (Postcard ca. 1908, from the author's collection)

the Rome & Decatur would achieve what few other fledgling Alabama railroads could—avoid bankruptcy. Unfortunately, this was not to be the case, and the Rome & Decatur soon joined the long list of Alabama railroads that suffered this fate. The crippled company continued to lay track, however, and at ten o'clock on a late July night in 1888 the road's eastbound and westbound construction crews met nine miles east of Gadsden. Even though the hour was late, the occasion warranted a gala ceremony that was attended by a large crowd. One hour after dignitaries drove the final spike home, the first Rome & Decatur train steamed into Gadsden. Rome & Decatur trains ran for two more years before the company became totally insolvent and was taken over by the East Tennessee, Virginia & Georgia Railway System.[36]

Among the beneficiaries of the new railroads to Rome and Guntersville was Gadsden entrepreneur, J. M. Elliott. Elliott's father had been one of the region's earliest settlers and had organized a steamboat business that made Gadsden an important river landing in the upper Coosa River trade. A pioneer iron maker as well, J. M. Elliott, Sr., purchased the Round Mountain Iron Works in 1857 and within fourteen years had increased its output almost four-fold.[37] The younger Elliott succeeded his father as president of the steamboat company and continued the enterprising family tradition by establishing the Elliott Car Works Company in 1887. At various times 250 to 300 men found employment here, building a comprehensive line of cars for major railroads throughout the South. The car wheels were cast using high quality chilling iron from the Round Mountain Iron Works.[38]

Elliott had manufactured freight and passenger cars for a little more than a year when he had an opportunity to further promote his business, as well as the city of Gadsden and Etowah County. The state had recently accepted a donation of two specially built exhibit cars from the L&N Railroad that were to be used to solicit investment and immigration. Called "Alabama on Wheels," these cars publicized Alabama products as they toured the Midwestern states. Elliott donated a similar type of car to Etowah County that was to tout the area's resources at the Alabama State Fair and the Columbus, Georgia, exhibition. "Etowah on Wheels," constructed entirely of Alabama building materials, attracted great interest at these fairs as it exhibited specimens of various Etowah County mineral and agricultural products. The exhibit car must have achieved its purpose, for the *Columbus Sunday Morning Enquirer* wrote the following: "One thing is clearly demonstrated by this exhibit, . . . that profitable employment in mining and manufacturing in all the branches of wood and iron can be found in Etowah County, and that the farms and gardens are capable of producing an abundance of everything needed for the home supply. When this feature is properly considered it is bound to make Etowah the objective point for many who, in more rigorous climate, have not the same advantages offered them."[39]

Steamboats owned by the Nashville, Chattanooga & St. Louis Railway Company ferried passengers and freight between Guntersville and Hobbs Island. This photograph was taken at Guntersville, ca. 1910. (Courtesy of the Heritage Room, Huntsville-Madison County Public Library, Huntsville, Alabama)

In keeping with the spirit of the Columbus fair, the car's curator, Ed Welsh, employed a certain amount of huckstering to embellish the attributes of Etowah County produce. One day he was asked by a lady visitor "What advantage have your pumpkins, Mr. Welsh, over our Georgia pumpkins?" Ed thought for a second, then smiled and said "Why, madam, our pumpkins are seedless and already sweetened and ready for the pie plates."[40]

Many of Elliott's cars found their way northward aboard a ferry across the Tennessee River between Guntersville and Hobbs Island. After about thirty miles of the Tennessee & Coosa Railroad had been completed, the line was taken over by the Nashville, Chattanooga & St. Louis Railway. The NC&StL agreed to finish the remaining 7.6 miles to Guntersville, cross the Tennessee River, and extend the line through Huntsville to its main line in the state of Tennessee. This work commenced in 1890 and was completed three years later, no doubt expedited by the decision to ferry cars across the Tennessee River rather than build an expensive bridge. In 1893 the NC&StL purchased the steamboat *Huntsville* to make the twenty-mile trip between Guntersville and Hobbs Island. In 1903 another steamer, the *Guntersville,* was added to the company's ferry fleet.[41]

Fervid speculation boiled further into the hinterland, and several furnaces started going up in northwest Alabama. To serve the booming Florence-Sheffield area, the Birmingham, Sheffield & Tennessee River

Railway was incorporated in 1886 to construct a line from Sheffield to Birmingham. The following year the Tennessee & Alabama Railroad was chartered to connect with an unfinished L&N line in Tennessee known as the Nashville & Florence Railroad. Milton Smith quickly seized another iron boom opportunity by consolidating the Tennessee & Alabama with the Nashville & Florence to form the Nashville, Florence & Sheffield Railway. By July 1, 1888, the Nashville, Florence & Sheffield Railway was completely equipped to the L&N main line at Columbia, Tennessee, and coke bound for Sheffield District furnaces was flowing over this line from as far away as Virginia. Even though the Old Reliable extended low freight rates to these enterprises, the furnaces were so far removed from the coal fields that transportation costs eventually became prohibitive, and some of the iron companies were forced out of business.[42]

As land prices continued to rocket upward in Gadsden and various parts of north Alabama, many thoughtful people wondered if the speculative fever might lead to a disastrous bust. The March 17, 1887, issue of the *Gadsden Weekly Times and News* posed this question to an "expert" in an article entitled "Will the Boom Collapse?" "We had a conversation recently with the president of a large publishing company of Baltimore," the author confided, "and in course of the conversation remarked to him that we had some fears as to the permanency of the boom, and rather thought that real estate had reached fictitious valuations. He said: 'By no means. You have no idea of the tendency of the north in the direction of North Alabama, and the immense amount of money that will in a short time be invested there, and the number and character of the vast industries which will be erected.' This was the substance of his remarks, and he is a man who travels extensively, has an office in New York and speaks advisedly."[43]

For the time being, this big-city prognosticator was right. Northern capitalists continued to pour money into Alabama mineral invest-

Furnace workers, lunch pails in hand, arrive for duty at Cherokee County's Rock Run Furnace as the locomotive builds steam for the day's work. (Photograph ca. 1890, courtesy of Robert A. Scarboro, Scarboro Photo Shop, Gadsden, Alabama)

Prospective investors boarded Fort Payne & Eastern Railroad trains in 1890 to tour the mineral properties and furnaces at Fort Payne. (Courtesy of Robert A. Scarboro, Scarboro Photo Shop, Gadsden, Alabama)

ments and the boom reached a towering crescendo. As the speculation increased, money found its way into properties that were of marginal value at best, and within a few years the concerns of prudent men were realized. When the seemingly limitless boom finally exploded in a tragic bust, a less pretentious pundit would refer to Gadsden as "a quaint old town."[44]

As the boom matured, more and more money was wasted on hopeless speculations. One of the more notable examples of wild speculation occurred in Wills Valley where a considerable brown hematite ore field of questionable quality was found. In 1886–87 promoters bought several thousand acres of this land and formed a marketing organization known as the Fort Payne Land and Improvement Company, which sold an incredible five million dollars worth of stock to unsuspecting investors throughout the country. The promoters also formed an iron company in 1889 and hyped its stock throughout New England. Trainloads of potential investors traveled to Fort Payne to see the golden goose and eagerly snapped up the stock. It was said that every New England governor became a stockholder in a Fort Payne iron company. Furnaces were soon erected and the eleven-and-one-quarter mile Fort Payne & Eastern Railroad was constructed to haul the ore down the mountain. This railroad owned at least three switching locomotives

Fort Payne & Eastern Railroad 2-6-0 locomotive, ca. 1890. (Courtesy of Robert A. Scarboro, Scarboro Photo Shop, Gadsden, Alabama)

and some passenger cars to pull excursion trains laden with prospective investors.

Suffering the same destiny as all latecomers to the iron boom, the Fort Payne investors lost millions. When the first furnace went into blast on September 3, 1890, the unfortunate shareholders discovered that the coal did not coke satisfactorily and that the ore was of poor quality. This furnace lost money for about a year before it was closed down. Work also stopped on another furnace that had been scheduled to use the same substandard coal and iron ore. In 1895 the furnaces were purchased by Henry DeBardeleben, who intended to refire them or move them to Bessemer. Nothing came of either scheme, however, and all of the Fort Payne industries, including the short-line railroad, were eventually dismantled.

Some time later it is said that a Confederate and Union veteran were reminiscing about the war when the Yankee boasted: "We sure gave you Rebels hell at Gettysburg."

"Yes," came the quick reply, "but we sure got even at Fort Payne!"[45]

11

MATURITY

THE IRON BOOM reached its climax in 1892 when the Tennessee Coal, Iron & Railroad Company acquired both the DeBardeleben Coal and Iron Company and the Cahaba Coal Company. When Aldrich and DeBardeleben joined the Tennessee Company, an overexpanded mammoth resulted that would be extremely vulnerable when the day of reckoning arrived. That day came suddenly in 1893. The price of pig iron plummeted and credit dried up as another severe financial panic engulfed the country.[1]

In the Birmingham District, practically the sole source of loans was industrialist Braxton Bragg Comer, who was cultivating a constituency that would later place him in the governor's mansion. Comer advanced the TCI&RR Company credits in flour and grain valued at $19,000 from his mills. Each day Comer could be found at the office of Truman Aldrich, who was now general manager of the Tennessee Company, inquiring after the solvency of the company.

"Going to bust today?" quipped Comer.

"Not to-day, Mr. Comer, but I can't tell about tomorrow," was the tongue-in-cheek reply.[2]

Throughout the panic Milton H. Smith also remained a staunch supporter of the Birmingham District. During its darkest days, he gathered the coal and iron managers together and exhorted, "Keep in blast. It don't make a deuced bit of difference what the freight rate is, keep in blast! I'll carry the product to market if I've got to haul it on my back!"[3] Ironically, Comer and Smith would eventually be pitted against each other in a bitter feud. But for now, men like these helped Alabama industry weather the panic of '93.

At the height of the panic, as large amounts of Tennessee Coal Iron & Railroad Company stock were being liquidated, DeBardeleben was tempted to leave the company and go to Wall Street, where he intended to scoop up the depressed shares at bargain prices. Although he appeared to have a good scheme for gaining control of the company, DeBardeleben was relatively inexperienced in Wall Street manipulations and went broke trying to execute his plan.[4] Indeed, all the rulers of Alabama's Gilded Age quickly discovered that pent-up forces of change were unleashed in 1893 that would shake the foundations of their autocratic empires.

For many years these industrialists and railroad managers had pressed their enterprises forward with scant regard for the safety of their employees. Operating the trains was especially hazardous work, and no crew member faced more daily dangers than the freight-train brakeman. Usually, no more than three of these brave souls were assigned to the typical freight train in Alabama, which was about fifteen or twenty cars long. As these trains rocked and swayed over winding grades, the brakeman patiently awaited the engineer's signal to apply the car brakes. When the whistle blast came, he hurriedly tightroped along the narrow roofwalk until he reached the brakewheel at the end of the car. After securing a precarious foothold, the brakeman turned the wheel until the biting brakes slowed the car. Then, with reckless abandon, he jumped to the next car to repeat this perilous chore. Just one mishap—one broken link of the brake chain or an untimely lurch of the car—and the hapless workman could be thrown from the rolling stock and mangled beneath the train. Tunnels, bridges, and other overhead structures also claimed their share of victims. In icy or rainy weather, the danger increased exponentially, and even though the brakeman armed himself with buckets of sand or salt that he sprinkled ahead to improve traction on the slippery car tops, his rooftop dance all too often ended in tragedy.[5]

As risky as the brakeman's aerial duties were, his perils were compounded when he climbed to the ground to couple and uncouple the cars. Although a simple chain link had joined one car to another since antebellum days, this antiquated method of coupling was still considered safe, at least theoretically, in the late nineteenth century. In operation, the chain link was secured by a pin in a slot at the end of the first car; the engine pushed the first and second cars together so that the uncoupled side of the link slipped into a corresponding slot in the second car. If a pin had been tilted at just the right angle in the slot of the second car, the impact of mating would cause it to fall into place and secure the link, while the workman stood back and safely watched. In practice, however, things seldom worked out so neatly. Often the two slots didn't mate, or the pin wouldn't fall into place, and the brakeman or switchman had to get between the cars to complete the coupling. Some uncoupling techniques also required the operative to run between the moving cars or to lie across the coupler beam while the train was in motion in order to remove the pin at the right moment.[6] This primitive link-and-pin coupling method inevitably led to countless reports of severed fingers and crushed bodies along Alabama tracks, which the government bureaucrats in Montgomery consistently attributed to employee negligence. Although hundreds of innovative coupling devices were invented throughout the nineteenth century, railroads across the country continued to use the link-and-pin coupler not only because it was deemed safe by vested interests but also because the railroad companies were not generally held liable for the carnage it caused. As one writer explained: "So long as brakes cost more than brakemen we may expect the present sacrificial method of car coupling to be continued."[7]

All this began to change in March 1893 when President Benjamin Harrison signed into law the federal Safety Appliance Act. The Act essentially outlawed the link-and-pin coupler as well as manual braking systems and required that all railroads replace them with automatic couplers and the Westinghouse air brake.

The safer couplers were pioneered by a New York store clerk named Eli Janney who had whittled the prototype from a block of wood. The basic Janney design worked like two hooked fingers. A pin behind the knuckles locked the couplers, and as long as the moving train maintained pull-tension upon the hooks, the pin could not be removed. When the train halted, the tension was relieved and the pin could be withdrawn easily using a lever that protruded safely away from the coupler.[8]

George Westinghouse had patented his brake in 1868 but many years elapsed before it was perfected. At first, compressed air from a tank in the locomotive was transmitted through a hose to activate each car's brake shoes. But the air pressure dropped to ineffective levels at the rear of long trains, and although the forward cars were effectively slowed, they were rear-ended by the unbraked following cars. This problem was addressed by installing compressed-air tanks in each car and activating the entire system with electricity. The inherent safety of the Westinghouse invention was further improved when the system was modified so that the brakes were activated by removing, rather than applying, air pressure. This meant that accidentally uncoupled rolling stock would be stopped automatically when air escaped from the broken hose.[9]

Development work continued, and by 1887 the Westinghouse air brake was finally suitable for freight-train operation. But some of the earliest versions of this system worked well on shorter trains, and the air brake had been featured on almost every main-line passenger train in Alabama since the early 1880s. Railroads were less eager to equip freight trains with expensive air brakes, however, and dragged their feet when the federal government mandated their use. Years after the Safety Appliance Act became law, Alabama freight trains still lacked air brakes. Milton H. Smith argued that the L&N was unable to bear such an expense in the wake of the recent depression and another costly yellow fever epidemic. The federal government agreed with Smith and extended the L&N's deadline for installing both air brakes and couplers. It was 1904 before all L&N rolling stock was fitted with automatic couplers, and air brakes were not installed on all the cars until 1914.[10]

Passage of the federal Safety Appliance Act was a long-overdue triumph for the hard-working railroad man, but other events also marked 1893 as a pivotal year in labor-management relations on railroads in the Heart of Dixie. Railway trade unions had been growing nationally since 1870, when the Brotherhood of Locomotive Engineers opened its first lodge. This brotherhood's first Alabama lodge was chartered in Birmingham in 1881. In 1887 a second lodge was established at Selma, followed four years later by a Montgomery local. Later, other railway unions organized in Alabama, including the Order of Railway Conductors and the Brotherhood of Locomotive Firemen. The long-abused brakemen and switchmen also organized, and finally protested their plight by striking in 1887, assisted by the Knights of Labor.

Nevertheless, labor unrest on the railroads had been relatively subdued in Alabama until 1893, when the brotherhoods decided to flex their collective muscle in a wage dispute with the L&N Railroad. Even though he had been assured by local officials that everything was under control, Governor Thomas Jones dispatched troops to New Decatur when he heard that violence was imminent. "Our fight is a legal one," a union spokesman protested, "and not accompanied by violence to persons or property whatsoever." Finally, the governor received a wire from the mayors of Decatur and New Decatur: "No disorder. Strikers claim to have had no unlawful intention. Sensational press dispatches without foundation." With this assurance, the governor withdrew the soldiers. Still, there is little doubt where the governor's sympathies lay. After all, Jones was ex-attorney for the L&N Railroad.

The face-off with the governor in 1893 was merely a prelude to a more crucial confrontation the following year. When Birmingham District coal miners went on strike, they appealed to the railway unions for support. The striking miners desperately needed to interrupt the flow of coal from mines that continued to be worked by convict laborers and notorious strikebreakers called "blacklegs," but the brotherhoods refused to get involved and kept running the trains. When the cooperation of the railroad brotherhoods could not be obtained, some of the coal miners resorted to sabotage. But no amount of trestle burning would assist the miner's cause as much as repercussions from another distant labor disturbance.

In 1893 a nationwide group of railroad labor activists headed by Eugene V. Debs became dissatisfied with the fragmented brotherhoods and formed the American Railway Union, which was opened to all railroad workers. During the summer of 1894, representatives of the ARU came to Alabama to recruit members. The organizers met little success in Montgomery and Mobile but attracted a substantial following in the turbulent Birmingham District. Meanwhile, workers had struck the Pullman Palace Car Company in Chicago, and Debs called for an ARU boycott of Pullman Company products. Since Pullman cars were carried on passenger trains that stopped in Birmingham, yardmen on the Kansas City, Memphis & Birmingham, and L&N railroads walked off their jobs in sympathy with the Pullman strikers. Firemen on the Queen and Crescent Route soon joined the strike, and railroad operations throughout the Birmingham District were effectively shut down—just what the miners wanted.[11]

The walkout immediately led to a showdown with the governor. Striking miners and ARU members converged upon Union Station on July 8 and attempted to convince nonstriking trainmen to leave their jobs. Bickering among strikers and working crewmen soon attracted a large crowd of spectators, and a hectic melee ensued. An observer reported that a "vast throng looked on, jeered and yelled, and hourly became more disorderly and reckless."

Governor Jones had already made plans to deploy state troops, contingent upon developments at Birmingham. When the governor came to the Magic City at midnight, the mayor and sherrif urged him to act, and Jones immediately ordered the state militia to clear the railroad station and secure the surrounding area. The next morning six hundred guardsmen dispersed the crowd at Union Station and took up positions in the trainyards and shops. As patrolling soldiers scattered demonstrators, the strike was broken.

These actions were hailed in conservative newspapers. "The public highways must be kept open, the mails must move, life must be preserved, and the government must be protected," proclaimed the Union Springs *Herald*. Talladega's *Our Mountain Home* concluded that the walkout had "degenerated into anarchy" leaving "no excuse under Heaven for the course pursued by the striking railroad men."[12] The ARU strikers could find few sympathizers, even among their fellow workers. The Birmingham chapter of the Brotherhood of Locomotive Firemen would have no part in the strike and threatened to oust participants from its organization. As the brotherhoods fell into line, the railroads savored their victory by taking retaliatory steps to consolidate their hold over labor. Reasoning that they would be less likely to rebel, L&N management assigned the majority of fireman, brakeman, and switchman jobs in the Birmingham District to nonunion blacks.[13]

The railroads had survived the most serious challenge yet by labor, but some actions taken in 1893 came back to haunt them. In 1900 the Order of Railroad Telegraphers struck three Alabama railroads that had reacted to the economic downturn by imposing a 10 percent wage reduction. The strikers wanted the pay restored, as well as a minimum wage, overtime pay, and establishment of a grievance committee. This time, the union garnered much local support, but the railroads continued obstinately to reject their demands.[14]

Meanwhile, Alabama coal miners continued their struggle, only to meet uncompromising opposition from a solid alliance of mine operators and state government. A liberal dose of heavy-handed police tactics broke a particularly nasty strike in 1908 and essentially crushed union activity in the state until World War I.[15] Major railroad strikes were also quelled in Alabama until the federal government enacted sweeping legislation in 1920 that facilitated settlement of railway labor disputes.

The economic troubles of the early 1890s were the catalyst that brought attention to labor problems that had been ignored far too long, but the financial distress inflicted at the furnaces also revealed a fundamental technological problem that menaced both management and labor. Indeed, this vicissitude imperiled the very livelihood of everyone in the mineral districts of Alabama.

The panic of 1893 was not as severe as its 1873 granddaddy, and recovery was relatively rapid in most parts of the country. But the price of pig iron remained low because steel was steadily gaining favor as the construction material of choice, and the rebound in the iron business was anemic at best. Once more the Birmingham District was at a crossroad. Just as the efficacy of Alabama ores for iron production had to be proven twenty years earlier, those same ores were now being judged for their suitability in steel manufacture. Once again the very survival of the Alabama mineral industry was at stake; and, once again, the railroads would be lifesavers.

Before steel could be made, Alabama ores would have to produce iron with low silicon content. This was called basic iron. Countless skeptics, with pronouncements evocative of the ridicule heaped upon Alabama minerals twenty years earlier, condemned Birmingham ores as unfit for making basic iron. In 1891 a breakthrough was accomplished at Bessemer's Little Belle furnace when a small amount of basic iron was cast, but this endeavor only proved the potential of the state's ores, and the viability of a commercial-scale steel operation was yet to be demonstrated in Alabama. Undaunted, the Tennessee Company doggedly continued to experiment. Finally, on July 22, 1895, in a triumph reminiscent of the success that had launched Birmingham's iron industry, the Alice furnace produced a large commercial-scale cast of basic iron. A four thousand-ton sample of the Alice basic iron was sent to the Andrew Carnegie mills in Pittsburgh for evaluation and proved to be so good that a 21,000-ton follow-up order was soon received. The feasibility of commercial steel manufacture in Alabama was proven.

As shipments of basic iron to the mills at Pittsburgh increased, thoughts of Alabama entrepreneurs turned to the possibility of erecting steel mills in Birmingham. Steel could be made more easily if the basic iron were in its initial molten state, and tremendous transportation savings would accrue to any company making steel in Birmingham instead of a thousand miles away in Pittsburgh. The impetus for steel manufacture in Alabama culminated with the construction of the Birmingham Rolling Mills, which produced its first steel cast in July 1897. The Tennessee Company immediately invested $100,000 to increase this mill's capacity to five hundred tons and the Old Reliable again lived up to its sobriquet by matching this outlay.

A year elapsed, however, and little progress was made in upgrading the Birmingham Rolling Mill facilities. Smith of the L&N and Tennessee Company president Nat Baxter became so frustrated that they invited Southern Railway president Samuel Spencer to join them in building a new steel plant. Spencer accepted the invitation and soon both railroads invested $250,000 to organize a consortium known as the Alabama Steel and Shipbuilding Company. In 1899 the Alabama Steel and Shipbuilding Company erected ten huge open-hearth furnaces at Ensley, and as a result of the cooperative efforts of the L&N and Southern Railway System, Alabama's steel industry became a successful reality.

The Birmingham Southern Railroad was also incorporated in 1899 in order to acquire the old Pratt mining line that ran from Birmingham to Pratt City. Needing more transportation facilities for their expanding operations, the TCI&RR Company bought the Birmingham Southern Railroad, extended it to the new furnaces at Ensley, and consolidated all other TCI&RR Company rail operations within Alabama under the Birmingham Southern's corporate title. The L&N and the Southern Railway immediately broadened their cooperative alliance in Alabama by purchasing the twenty-eight-mile-long Birmingham-Southern, which they operated jointly until 1907, when all of the trackage, except for the section between Woodstock and Blocton, was repurchased by the Tennessee Company to become the nucleus of a terminal railroad that connected its expanding industrial complex.[16]

The spirit of cooperation between the L&N and Southern was not confined to the Birmingham steel ventures. Nor were their business deals always above reproach. The L&N had emerged from the depression stronger than ever, and the Southern, backed by Wall Street's powerful House of Morgan, became a formidable system in Alabama when it was formed in 1894 through the consolidation of several southeastern railroads, including the Georgia Pacific and the East Tennessee, Virginia & Georgia Railways. With established monopolies throughout the South, managers of both the L&N and Southern now looked about suspiciously for possible competition. The chief threat stemmed from the many poorly financed lines within these giant's territories that were vulnerable to takeover. Milton H. Smith and Samuel Spencer feared that competing systems might invade their territories by acquiring these impoverished roads. Cutthroat rate wars would inevitably result that would slash profits for both the L&N and Southern.

To guard against such an eventuality, the L&N and Southern adopted a policy of defensive acquisition through which they would purchase these small derelict lines in order to keep them out of competitor's hands. With this in mind, Smith and Spencer took steps to secure their regional monopolies through mutual cooperation. By precisely defining their respective realms and agreeing to reciprocally respect them, the competitive threats might be thwarted and rate stability could be maintained. To come to an agreement with respect to territorial division, an extraordinary summit meeting took place on October 28, 1894, when Smith and Spencer faced each other in a railroad car at Kennesaw, Georgia. The two men planned to formulate a policy of cooperation by agreeing on territories that each company "owned," reviewing the status of independent roads within those territories, outlining possible expansion plans, and drafting joint strategies to deal with competition and rates. Most importantly, they would decide which independent roads were to be swallowed up and which were to remain free.

Smith acquiesced to Spencer's desire to have the Southern obtain control of certain major unattached lines, including the Memphis & Charleston, the Mobile & Birmingham and the Alabama Great Southern. With these acquisitions, the Southern would join the L&N as one of the two preeminent rail systems in Alabama. The discussion then drifted to the smaller roads. Smith expressed a great deal of concern about the ninety-six-mile Birmingham, Sheffield & Tennessee River Railway between Sheffield and Parrish, Alabama. Although this road was in receivership, Smith had learned from DeBardeleben that capital was being raised to extend the route to Birmingham. The L&N already had plenty of western competition from the Kansas City, Memphis & Birmingham Railroad, and Smith hoped to defend against the rumored move by persuading Spencer to assimilate this line into the Memphis & Charleston. But Spencer declined to promise immediate action. "I do not want to imply any disposition upon our part to put money in any of these properties," he asserted. "We prefer not to do so unless we are forced to it. We must, if necessary, do the needful to protect existing interests. All that can be accomplished now is to reach, if possible, some general understanding, as to our mutual interests, and such divisions of territory as appears feasible, but without obligations on the part of either to buy any thing." Smith concurred in a most colorful

way. "I think both of us would be very glad if we could feel assured that these miserable abortions would remain status quo," he grumbled.

As the meeting wore on, a line connecting Gadsden with Chattanooga received special attention. "I overlooked another abortion down there," Smith said, "the Chattanooga Southern. I do not know who in the world wants it."[17] This "abortion" had been incorporated in 1890 by Chattanooga capitalists Russell Sage and C. E. James to service the coal, iron ore, and timber industries along its ninety-two miles of main line track, which paralleled the Alabama Great Southern on the opposite side of Lookout Mountain. Although the Chattanooga Southern aspired to enter Birmingham as an AGS competitor, one look at its existing roadbed showed how unrealistic such ambitions were. Freight trains usually required ten to twelve hours to haul as little as 750 gross tons over the flimsy fifty-six-pound rail between Gadsden and Chattanooga. After falling into receivership in 1892 the Chattanooga Southern became a takeover candidate. Smith and Spencer considered the possibility that the Chattanooga Southern together with the East & West Railroad of Alabama might be consolidated into a larger system such as the Kansas City, Memphis & Birmingham, but after some discussion, the men dismissed the likelihood of such a development.[18] Smith surmised that Eugene Kelly, chief executive of the East & West Railroad of Alabama, was "getting too old and too conservative to throw away any more money there." Likewise, the Savannah, Americus & Montgomery Railway was thought to be beyond hope of salvation.[19]

Smith and Spencer were correct in their assessment of the Chattanooga Southern. Nobody wanted this road, and it struggled through a series of reorganizations until reincarnated as the Tennessee, Alabama

Steam power of the Tennessee, Alabama & Georgia Railway consisted mainly of 2-8-2 Mikados and 2-8-0 Consolidations. Consolidation No. 100 was acquired new from Baldwin Locomotive Works in 1920. Six other Consolidations were on the TAG Route's locomotive roster, as well as fifteen Mikados. (Courtesy of the Railroad Museum of Pennsylvania [PHMC], Strasburg)

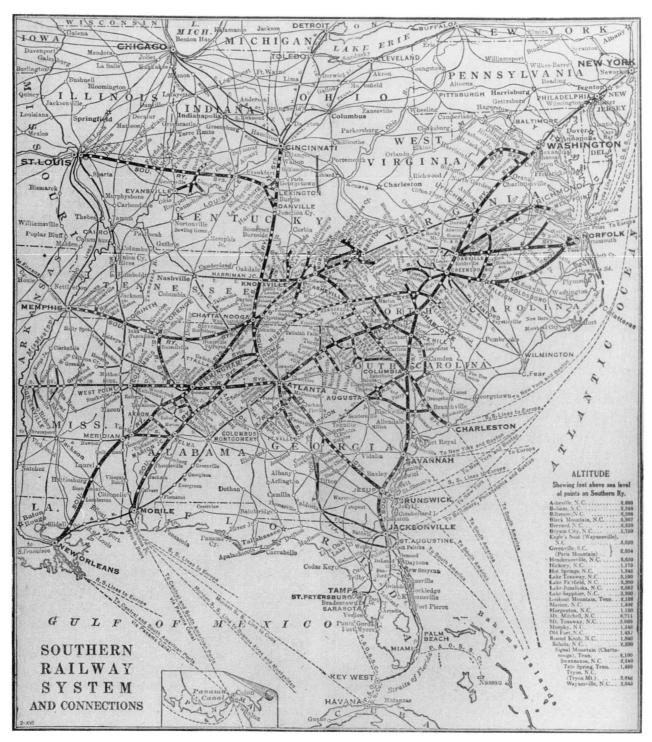

Southern Railway System Map for 1917. (Courtesy of William Stanley Hoole Special Collections Library, The University of Alabama, Tuscaloosa)

& Georgia Railway in 1911. Affectionately christened the TAG Route, the Tennessee, Alabama & Georgia Railway remained independent, and continued to courageously compete with the powerful AGS throughout the first half of the twentieth century. The only knight-in-shining-armor who stepped forward to help the little road was one of its original builders, C. E. James, who rescued it from abandonment in 1922.[20]

LOOK AHEAD-LOOK SOUTH

This advertisement appeared in the Southern Railway's public timetable of February 14, 1904. By this time the Southern Railway was so dominant in the southeast that it was not only the popular route to many sunbelt vacation spots but also in many cases the only route. Several of these resorts were located in Alabama. A few, such as the Monte Sano Hotel near Huntsville, operated their own short-line railroads to transport guests directly from the depot to the hotel door. (Courtesy of William Stanley Hoole Special Collections Library, The University of Alabama, Tuscaloosa)

But the conferees missed the mark with respect to the Savannah, Americus & Montgomery Railway, as well as the East & West Railroad of Alabama. A few years later the Seaboard Air Line Railway would acquire both lines to gain entrance into the important Montgomery and Birmingham markets. In fact, the Chattanooga Southern was one of the few railroads in Alabama that escaped the grasp of major railway systems. Although Smith adamantly denied any conspiracy to carve up territory, the ultimate disposition of Alabama's independent railroads essentially mirrored the Kennesaw agreements. The Birmingham, Sheffield & Tennessee River Railway was reorganized as the Northern Alabama Railway in 1895 and came under control of the Southern Railway in 1899. The Southern also acquired both the Memphis & Charleston Railroad and Mobile & Birmingham Railway in 1899. In 1917 the AGS formally joined the Southern family.[21]

Meanwhile, the L&N had its hands full fending off its archrival in south Alabama. With valuable timberland and cotton fields beckon-

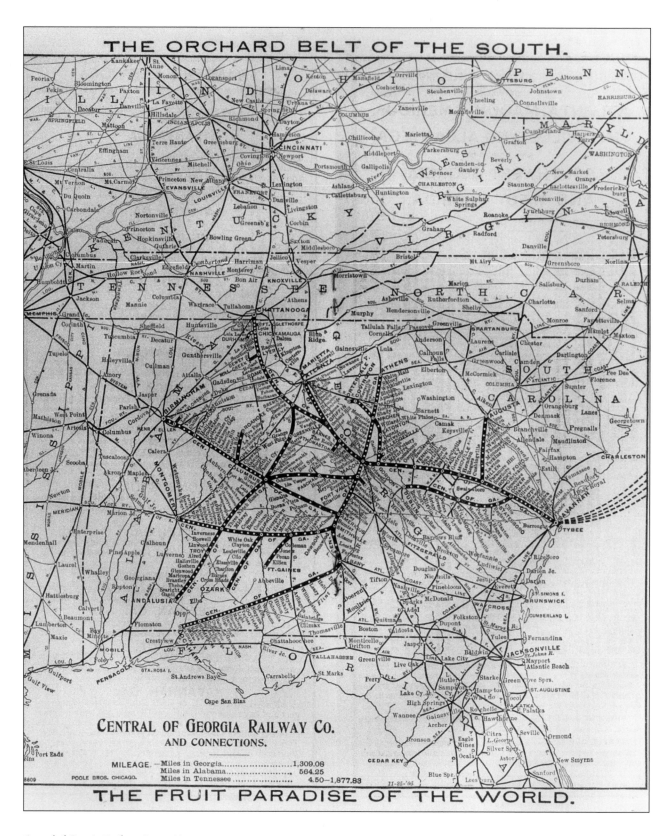

Central of Georgia Railway System Map for 1906. (Courtesy of William Stanley Hoole Special Collections Library, The University of Alabama, Tuscaloosa)

L. & N. Depot.   FLORALA, Ala.

ing, the Central Railroad & Banking Company started a campaign to exploit the region. In 1895, reorganized as the Central of Georgia Railway, this company absorbed the 121.6-mile Mobile & Girard Railroad, which had been recently completed between Columbus, Georgia, and Seawright, Alabama, as well as the 80.3-mile-long Montgomery & Eufaula Railroad. In 1899 the Central of Georgia continued to press forward in Alabama by extending the old Mobile & Girard route nearly seventeen miles to Andalusia. The Central's march through Alabama continued in 1904 when the company took over the Chattahoochee & Gulf Railroad to gain a 91.5-mile line that ran from Columbia through Dothan, to access a huge lumber operation at Lockhart, Alabama.[22]

To counter these moves, the L&N initiated an extension from its main line at Georgiana that would lead to Graceville, Florida. Work was slow, but the branch was finished on July 16, 1902. At this time traffic into the Sunshine State was steadily building as two famous railroad moguls, Henry Flagler of the Florida East Coast Railway and Henry Plant of the Plant System, were opening Florida for settlement and tourism. The L&N intended to capture a greater share of this traffic by augmenting its Pensacola connection. A suitable bridge line to northwest Florida was established when the L&N bought the Yel-

This little wood-burning 4-4-0 engine at the L&N's Florala Depot in 1913 is likely a holdover from the Yellow River Railroad that was acquired by the Old Reliable. The Yellow River Railroad owned two 4-4-0 locomotives, nos. 83 and 84. Its other loco, No. 85, was a 4-6-0. (Postcard from the author's collection)

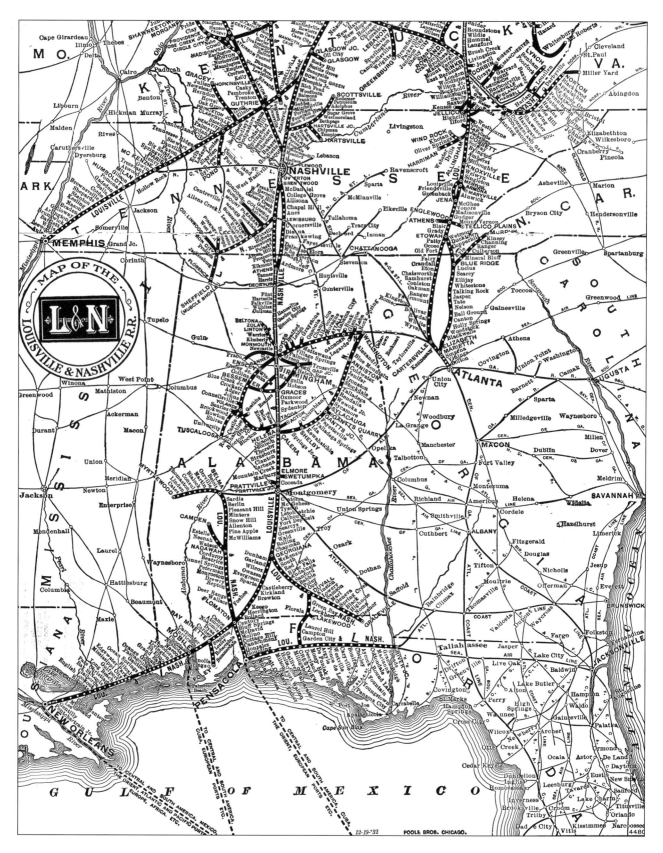

*The Louisville & Nashville Railroad's
Lines in Alabama, 1932. (From a January 4, 1933, L&N timetable)*

low River Railroad. Originally a standard-gauge logging pike, the Yellow River extended from the L&N main line at Crestview, Florida, to the state line at Florala. The Florida connection was completed in 1902 when the L&N built a branch from Duvall, on its new Graceville extension, to Florala.[23]

Assimilation of the Yellow River Railroad exemplified Smith's defensive acquisition strategy. By purchasing the Yellow River Railroad, he protected the L&N monopoly at Pensacola by effectively blocking the Central of Georgia's bid to reach a Gulf port via Florala. Meanwhile, in 1900, Smith had also tackled a long-neglected project that further secured his Pensacola operations when he closed the forty-six-mile gap between Repton and Pine Apple, giving the L&N a direct connection between Selma and the Gulf. The Old Reliable exercised its defensive acquisition strategy once again in 1900 when the defunct Birmingham, Selma & New Orleans Railway, successor of the Reconstruction era New Orleans & Selma Railroad, was added to its corporate structure. Two hundred forty miles of track between Selma and New Orleans had originally been projected for the failed pike, but only twenty miles of this promise was fulfilled when the L&N came on the scene. The road was immediately extended from Martin to Myrtlewood, Alabama, where a connection into Meridian, Mississippi, was effected over a short line titled the Meridian & Bigbee River Railway.[24] At Choctaw City, on the Meridian & Bigbee, another short line called the Sumter & Choctaw Railway headed north to connect with the Southern Railway's main line into Meridian at Lilita, Alabama.[25]

Smith could not fend off all competitors, however, especially giants like the Plant System. This railroad system was founded by Henry B. Plant of Connecticut, who had served as southern superintendent of the Adams Express Company from 1854 until the beginning of the Civil War. In 1861 Adams Express offices in the South broke away from the parent company. With the support of southern stockholders, Plant organized the rebellious fragments into a new shipping enterprise called the Southern Express Company. Plant operated the Southern Express Company on behalf of the Confederacy until 1863, when he sailed for Europe because of illness. After the war, Adams Express agreed to let the Southern Express Company remain independent, and Henry Plant returned as company president. Southern Express continued to serve railroads throughout the South for many years, including many in Alabama. Then, in 1879 Plant began a series of railroad acquisitions that burgeoned into a vast railroad empire, and eventually became one of the largest and strongest combinations in the South.[26]

One of Plant's lines, the Savannah, Florida & Western, extended across southern Georgia to connect Savannah with Bainbridge. From Bainbridge, Plant wanted to extend the tentacles of his combine into Alabama, and his opportunity came in 1887 when he was approached by Montgomery cotton factor Joseph Washington Woolfolk. Woolfolk was president of the Alabama Terminal and Improvement Company, which was organized to construct the Alabama Midland Railway between Montgomery and Troy, Alabama. Woolfolk had been frustrated in his attempts to gain financing for the Alabama Midland Railway and suspected that the Central Railroad & Banking Company of Georgia was actively obstructing his efforts. Central tracks already connected Troy with Columbus, Georgia, and the Alabama Midland threatened their monopoly. Woolfolk charged that the Central Railroad had gone so far as to hire detectives to follow him in his search for capital in New York.

Woolfolk walked into Plant's New York office at a most propitious time. After being assured that the Alabama Midland would be extended from Troy to connect with the Savannah, Florida & Western at Bainbridge, Plant was glad to lend a helping hand. In exchange for a loan, Woolfolk agreed to let the Plant System operate the Alabama Midland when it was finished.

Surveying of the Alabama Midland began in 1888, and by March 1889 the route had been graded from Bainbridge to the Chattahoochee River. When Woolfolk was ready to lay track over this section, he placed the initial orders for Alabama Midland engines and equipment. Unfortunately, the cars and locomotives were to be delivered to Bainbridge, and had to be carded over Central tracks. The Central was determined to impede its rival's progress and appropriated much of Woolfolk's shipment for its own use. Some of the rolling stock was found in Michigan and Ohio, loaded with Central freight. Other cars ended up on Central work trains. The Central was also accused of negligently damaging two locomotives while en route to the construction site.

After the equipment was finally retrieved, Alabama Midland trackmen hammered ahead until they reached Ozark, Alabama, where the feud with the Central Railroad & Banking Company was about to intensify. The approach to Ozark ran along a ridge north of town, and although Woolfolk had obtained a deed to this ridge in 1887, he was astonished to find Central track gangs occupying this property just as Alabama Midland crews were about to enter the village. Woolfolk discovered that the Central Railroad was extending a branch from Clayton to Ozark, and had decided to ignore his deed and lay track over the ridge in a manner that would deny use of the right-of-way to anyone else. Woolfolk complained that the Central Railroad was deliberately laying its track "in a zig zag manner, more resembling the course of a worm fence, which completely covered the ridge from side to side at some points, excluding absolutely the occupancy of said ridge by any other road subsequent to themselves." This action forced the Alabama Midland to radically alter its route so that a hill had to be excavated before it was possible to lay track into Ozark.

The escalating dispute with the Central Railroad & Banking Company reached its climax in the summer of 1889 when Woolfolk ordered four hundred tons of steel rails to be delivered to Ozark. Again, the Alabama Midland had no choice but to let the Central Railroad handle the shipment. After a two week delay, the rails were finally brought to the Central depot at Ozark, but the only way they could reach the Alabama Midland right-of-way was by building a spur track across the Central's roadbed. Continuing its obstructionist policy, the Central obtained a temporary injunction preventing the crossing, an act that drew fire from the editor of the Troy *Enquirer:* "If the Central is to be the 'petted darling' before whom judges, courts and everybody shall bow in humble obeisance, and at its mercy, the state government had best issue an edict giving it kingly prerogatives," the indignant writer declared. But Woolfolk and the Alabama Midland did not intend to bow before the Central Railroad & Banking Company of Georgia. The temporary injunction expired on Saturday, July 20, 1889. At sunrise the following Monday, one hundred Alabama Midland laborers, guarded by two hundred sentries carrying Winchester rifles, scrambled into action and began laying track across the Central's roadbed. All had been carefully prearranged. The guards had filtered into Ozark over the weekend in secrecy. Alabama Midland sympathizers had also seized the telegraph to make sure communications were paralyzed when the Central tried to wire for help. Rendered powerless, Central Railroad men watched in frustration as the trackwork moved to completion in the early afternoon. Woolfolk's Winchester diplomacy had achieved its purpose, and henceforth the Alabama Midland would experience little more trouble with its nemesis.[27]

The Alabama Midland found it easier to enter Montgomery by acquisition than by construction, and the next step on the way to the first Capital of the Confederacy was to purchase the Montgomery & Florida Railway. The Montgomery & Florida was originally incorporated as the narrow-gauge Montgomery Southern Railway, which was built from Montgomery to Ada, Alabama in 1882. This road failed and was taken over by lenders who reorganized it as the Montgomery & Florida Railway in 1884. It was extended fifty-one miles south to Luverne before it failed again and was bought by the Alabama Midland. Following this transaction, the short line was renamed the Northwest & Florida Railroad. The Northwest & Florida track was upgraded to standard gauge in 1889 and the twenty-mile segment between Montgomery and Ada became the western end of the Alabama Midland's main line. By 1890 the rest of the Alabama Midland main line was in operation between Ada and Bainbridge.[28] A reporter who rode over the new road from Bainbridge to Troy sent an enthusiastic dispatch to the Troy *Messenger* proclaiming that "a new era and new hopes are opened to the people of Southwest Georgia and Southeast Alabama with the completion of this splendid railroad."[29] A new era was also opened to Henry Plant: On July 9, 1890, the road was sold to Plant's Savannah, Florida & Western Railway Company.

The first passenger train on the Abbeville Southern Railway, November 27, 1893. Locomotive No. 1, a Rhode Island 4-4-0 manufactured in 1887 and previously owned by the Savannah, Florida & Western Railway, was the only locomotive assigned to this subsidiary of the Alabama Midland Railway. (Courtesy of the Alabama Department of Archives and History, Montgomery, Alabama)

Three subsidiary Alabama Midland lines were eventually constructed. The twenty-seven-mile Abbeville Southern Railway connected Abbeville with Abbeville Junction in 1893, and the thirty-seven-mile Southwestern Alabama Railway was built from Waterford to Elba, Alabama, in 1898. To perform switching duties for the Alabama Midland at Montgomery, the Plant System organized the Belt Line Railway Company, which constructed approximately two miles of track through the streets of the capital city. The company operated two dummy locomotives and became known as the Montgomery Belt Line.[30]

The ever-ambitious Plant intended to extend the Alabama Midland westward from Montgomery to effect a connection with the Illinois

Central Railroad at Grenada, Mississippi. In 1890 a large force of mule-driving laborers were busily grading the portion of this extension between Montgomery and Tuscaloosa, and Plant expected to have the entire extension in operation by the summer of the following year. Although this extension was advertised as the most direct route from the Mississippi Valley to the Atlantic seaboard and was to constitute a vital connection for the Plant System, the Alabama Midland was not destined to complete it. The panic of '93 interrupted the work, and no further progress was made until the Mobile & Ohio Railroad became interested in the project.[31]

The M&O wanted to build a branch from Columbus, Mississippi, leading toward Florida in order to generate more traffic for the northern end of its system, and in 1896 decided to use essentially the same route that had been partially completed by the Alabama Midland. Construction was started in 1897 and in April 1898 the sixty-one-mile section from Columbus to Tuscaloosa was placed in full operation. The entire line between Columbus and Montgomery, complete with an eleven-mile branch to Blocton and a nine-mile branch to the Warrior coal fields was finished in July 1899.[32] In that same year the M&O laid thirty-nine more miles of track in Alabama when the Mobile & Bay Shore Railway was opened between Mobile and the southwest Alabama villages of Alabama Port and Bayou La Batre.[33]

By the turn of the century the Plant System dominated important rail routes in the southeast, but this supremacy was soon to be challenged by a head-to-head competitor, the Seaboard Air Line Railway, aided largely by a key Seaboard acquisition in Alabama. In 1891, one year after Plant's gigantic combination reached Montgomery, the Savannah, Americus & Montgomery Railway was extended into Montgomery from Lyons, Georgia, a distance of 265 miles. The SAM failed financially and was purchased at auction by the Georgia & Alabama Railway, headed by John Skelton Williams, a Virginia capitalist. Williams finished the old SAM route into Savannah and initiated a series of acquisitions that gave the Georgia & Alabama Railway, also known as the Savannah Short Line, a total of 460 miles of southeastern trackage. On July 1, 1900, Williams consolidated this property with other routes along the eastern seaboard to form the Seaboard Air Line Railway. The Seaboard, in hot pursuit of the Plant System, could now proudly advertise that its tracks ran "Through the Heart of the South."[34]

The Seaboard paralleled many of Plant's routes and competition

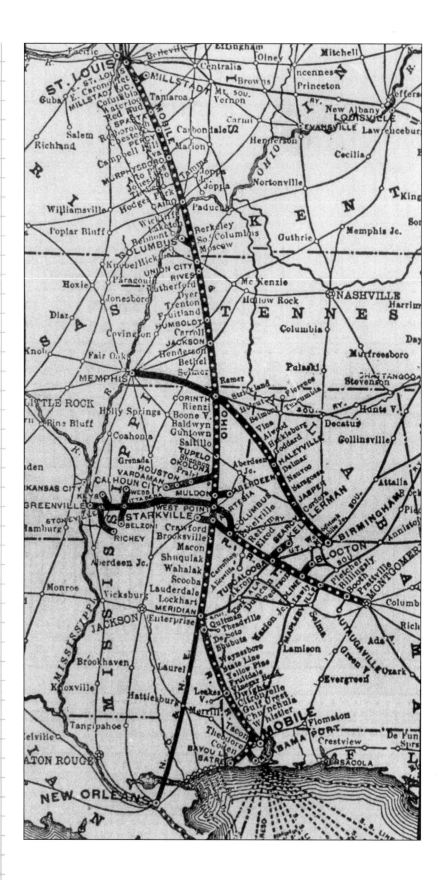

This Mobile & Ohio Railroad system map for 1921 indicates that the M&O had trackage rights over other railroads from Corinth, Mississippi, into Birmingham. These trackage rights, negotiated in 1908, were for freight trains only. (Courtesy of William Stanley Hoole Special Collections Library, The University of Alabama, Tuscaloosa)

between the two roads became fierce, but the Seaboard lacked the Plant System's strong financing and depended on the prudent and resourceful leadership of its president, John Skelton Williams, to outmaneuver its rival. Williams promptly demonstrated his skills in this regard when he negotiated a bargain entrance into Birmingham. Williams saw an exceptional opportunity in the East & West Railroad that twisted through the hills of west Georgia and east Alabama to a junction with the Southern Railway at Pell City. This line was the successor of the bankrupt East & West Railroad of Alabama that had been purchased by the Kelly brothers of New York in 1893. By 1896 the Kellys had built a three-and-one-half-mile feeder for the East & West Railroad called the Tredegar Mineral Railway that ran from Tredegar to Jacksonville, Alabama. After absorbing this line, the East & West Railroad had 121 miles of trackage in operation, and plans were being formulated to extend the pike into Birmingham; however, John Skelton Williams harbored similar plans. By taking over the E&WRR, the Seaboard could enter Birmingham by building only forty-three miles of additional trackage from Howells to Rockmart, Georgia, plus thirty-seven miles from Coal City to the Magic City. This was indeed an economical way to reach such a major new market as Birmingham. Williams purchased the East & West Railroad and established a new subsidiary called the Atlanta & Birmingham Air Line Railway to carry out the work of straightening and leveling the old roadbed. Nearly three thousand feet of tunnels, including two long ones in Alabama, were required between Atlanta and Birmingham in order to hold ruling grades to one percent or less. By 1904 all the trackwork was finished and the Atlanta & Birmingham Air Line Railway was transferred to the Seaboard Air Line Railway.[35]

By the turn of the century, mergers and acquisitions were the order of the day, and many smaller railroads were gobbled up by larger systems. Soon, even the giants could not escape the feeding frenzy. By 1902 the Plant System was consolidated with other southeastern lines to form the Atlantic Coast Line Railroad. Then, in a series of intricate Wall Street manipulations, J. P. Morgan obtained a majority interest in the L&N. Much to the chagrin of Milton H. Smith and other executives of the Old Reliable, the Atlantic Coast Line bought all of Morgan's stock and became the parent of the proud L&N system. Smith, who had little respect for Wall Street operators, reacted scornfully. "Mr. Morgan's idiosyncrasy is the creation of enormous combinations," Smith

In 1914 the Sipsey branch of the Frisco Railway served the Maryland Coal & Coke Company mines, some thirty miles northwest of Birmingham in Walker County. (Courtesy of the Birmingham Public Library Department of Archives and Manuscripts)

scoffed. "He is in the position of a strong man in the circus, on his back, feet up, keeping an enormous cask revolving in the air, which sooner or later must come down."[36] The change of ownership had little affect on L&N policies and operating practices, however. The L&N continued to operate as an independent line and Smith remained in control, freely running the Old Reliable as he saw fit. Overall, the ACL and L&N found much unity of purpose and cooperated more closely. Nonetheless, in the next few years the L&N lost its Pensacola monopoly and two major rivals reached Birmingham.

The St. Louis–San Francisco Railway, better known as the Frisco, had already entered Birmingham by acquiring the Kansas City, Memphis & Birmingham Railroad, and was now on the lookout for a Gulf connection. While Milton Smith fretted over J. P. Morgan's machinations, the Frisco was eyeing a small northwest Florida lumber line, the Pensacola & Perdido Railroad. On October 15, 1892, the Pensacola & Perdido had established a subsidiary called the Pensacola, Alabama & Tennessee Railroad which was projected to run from Pensacola to Memphis. Driven by blind ambition, Pensacola & Perdido managers forgot about day-to-day business and concentrated almost entirely on laying shiny new rail. Neglected shippers found no reason to continue patronizing the preoccupied company and revenues dried up before fifteen miles of track could be finished. In 1913 the Pensacola, Mobile & New Orleans Railway was organized to purchase all the failed properties.

Wishing to avoid previous mistakes, management scaled back and modified the new company's objectives. The Pensacola, Mobile & New Orleans would simply try to reach Mobile, while a subsidiary called the Gulf, Florida & Alabama Railway was loosely targeted for some point on the Alabama, Black Warrior or Tombigbee River in the state of Alabama. With luck, this subsidiary might actually reach Memphis someday. The Pensacola, Mobile & New Orleans Railway made slow and tentative progress until its tracks reached Pemona, Alabama, two thirds of the way to Mobile. At that point, a long and costly bridge consumed the railroad's remaining capital, and the dream of reaching Mobile was brought to an abrupt and desolate end. It is regrettable that funds vanished before the ultimate goal was attained, since this route would have placed Pensacola forty miles nearer to Mobile than the L&N's circuitous right-of-way.

The Gulf, Florida & Alabama made better progress as it crossed the remote pine forests of south Alabama. One hundred twenty miles of backwoods railroad connected the quaint little towns of Atmore, Mortimer, McCullough, Hadley, Hixon, and Coy before the last dollar for the project was expended. The area through which the line ran was simply too sparsely populated to support the venture. In 1924, all property of the Pensacola, Mobile & New Orleans and the Gulf, Florida & Alabama was purchased by a subsidiary of the St. Louis–San Francisco Railway. The Frisco used these acquisitions as stepping-stones to the Gulf. Following the path laid out fifty years earlier by Nathan Bedford Forrest, Frisco tracks pushed from Amory, Mississippi, to Kimbrough, Alabama, in 1928. The Gulf, Florida & Alabama roadbed led the rest of the way to Pensacola. The Frisco brought the outside world to dozens of tiny, secluded communities as it sliced across southwest Alabama en route to the Gulf. Unfortunately, the incomplete Mobile line was abandoned.[37]

In a separate development, the Frisco had entered into a rather odd agreement with the Illinois Central Railroad in 1899. The Illinois Central was seeking a coal source for its operations in the South, and the

Frisco allowed the IC to build an eight-mile spur from the old Kansas City, Memphis & Birmingham main stem at Winfield leading to some coal mines at Brilliant, Alabama. The Illinois Central was permitted to haul the coal over Frisco track to connect with the IC main line at Aberdeen Junction, Mississippi. The peculiar Winfield-Brilliant spur, far from the IC main line, was so isolated and lonely that it was dubbed "The Orphan."

Concurrently, Illinois Central strategists foresaw significant increases in foreign trade via the new Panama Canal and resolved to get a bigger share of this growing southeastern traffic. After establishing a traffic office in Birmingham, the IC made plans to extend a 216.6-mile branch from Jackson, Tennessee, to Birmingham. Only a portion of this route required new construction, since trackage rights could be negotiated for the balance. The Illinois Central built the eighty-mile section from Corinth, Mississippi, to Haleyville, Alabama, and used forty-one miles of Southern Railway trackage from Haleyville to Jasper as well as forty miles of the Frisco's route from Jasper to Birmingham.

Trackwork underway on the Illinois Central Railroad near the northwestern Alabama community of Vina in 1908. (Postcard from the author's collection)

After the sparkling new steel rail of the Illinois Central reached Haleyville on April 19, 1908, coal tonnage from Alabama mines steadily grew over the IC system. The Illinois Central doubled its coal car fleet during the first ten years of the new century in order to handle a 78 percent increase in yearly coal traffic. On June 16, 1909, the Illinois Central pulled off another power play in Alabama by gaining control of the Central of Georgia Railway. Birmingham then became a strategic gateway for Illinois Central traffic between the Midwest and important southeastern cities. Through this alliance, the Illinois Central could participate fully in the expanding Florida, Cuba, and Panama Canal trade by sending its trains directly to the port of Savannah over Central of Georgia tracks.[38]

Another road destined for Birmingham was born in 1905 when the Atlanta, Birmingham & Atlantic Railroad was incorporated by the original organizers of the Georgia Power Company, H. M. Atkinson and Preston S. Arkwright. The AB&A came into existence when Arkwright and Atkinson decided to take over the three-hundred-mile

long Atlantic & Birmingham Railway, which had only been completed from Brunswick to Montezuma, Georgia. They acquired the Atlantic & Birmingham Railway in 1906 and immediately extended it to Manchester, Georgia, where the track was split into two branches, one leading to Atlanta and the other heading for Birmingham. Now called the Atlanta, Birmingham & Atlantic Railroad, its Birmingham branch followed the roadbed of the defunct Macon & Birmingham Railway through Roanoke and Pyriton, Alabama. At Pyriton the roadbed of the old Eastern Railway of Alabama was reworked to become part of the main line to a point a few miles east of Talladega.

The twenty-mile-long Eastern Railway of Alabama had been built in 1903 to connect the L&N with the Alabama Pyrite Company mines at Pyriton. General offices of this short line were maintained at Talladega but daily operations were contracted to the L&N. A seven-mile branch of the Eastern Railway of Alabama, finished in 1905, veered off to Ashland and had been operated by the L&N for about a year before the AB&A came along. In 1907 this extension, known as the Alabama Northern Railway, was acquired by the AB&A as a branch line. In 1915 the Ashland branch again reverted to independent ownership as the Alabama Northern, and later became known as the Ashland Railway.

After reaching Pelham, the AB&A obtained trackage rights over the L&N into Birmingham and trains were running into the Magic City by September 1908. In 1910 the AB&A ceased to rely on the L&N when its own track was laid into Birmingham. Beginning in 1913 the Woodward Iron Company used a fourteen-mile branch of the AB&A, with steep 1.75 percent grades, to reach the Mulga Mines.[39] With its winding route and heavy grades, trips over the AB&A were seldom speedy. One rider who had to make a connection to Birmingham via the Central of Georgia's Roanoke branch said with understatement, "It took much time to get to Birmingham from Opelika."[40]

The Atlanta, Birmingham & Atlantic Railroad was in financial difficulty as early as 1909, when it first went into receivership and H. M. Atkinson lost his personal fortune. The railroad could not recover and

Extremely rare view of the Atlanta, Birmingham & Atlantic depot at Erin near Clairmont Springs in northwestern Clay County. Erin was typical of the many sawmill towns that were established along rural main lines in Alabama. Approximately fifty people populated the town when this photograph was taken around 1910. (Postcard from the author's collection)

Atlanta, Birmingham & Coast brakemen performing their routine but terribly hazardous chores. (Photograph ca. 1930s, from the author's collection)

faced foreclosure again in 1915. It was reorganized as the Atlanta, Birmingham & Atlantic Railway, but was still unable to pay its creditors and went into receivership once more in 1921 with Colonel B. L. Bugg acting as receiver. In 1926 it emerged from another reorganization as the Atlanta, Birmingham & Coast Railroad and, with the backing of the powerful Atlantic Coast Line, became a going concern. In 1946 the Atlanta, Birmingham & Coast became the Western Division of the ACL Railroad.[41]

Although the L&N had lost considerable ground to encroaching competition, the Old Reliable still dominated the eastern approaches to Mobile. In contrast, Mobile bristled with western connections. In addition to the L&N and M&O routes, another important road called the Mobile & Northwestern led from the Port City into the pine forests of southeastern Mississippi. The Mobile & Northwestern had been organized in 1870 to haul timber from these dense woods into Mobile, where it was exported to growing markets in the North and East. Optimistic promoters had originally projected the right-of-way through Hattiesburg and Jackson, Mississippi, to a location on the Mississippi River opposite Helena, Arkansas. Complete surveys were done and some

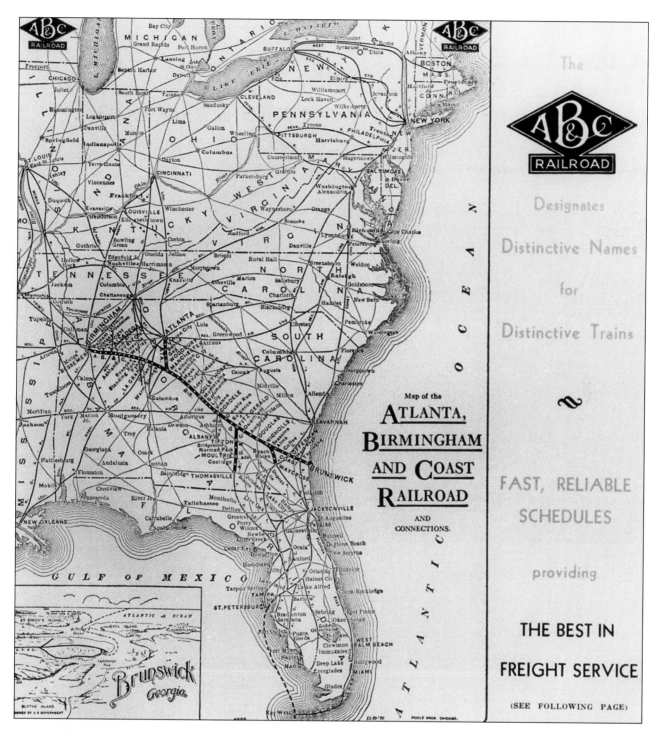

Map of the

ATLANTA,

BIRMINGHAM

AND COAST

RAILROAD

AND
CONNECTIONS.

grading was accomplished at each end of the line, including twenty-four miles between Mobile and Wilmer, Alabama, but the project languished until February 20, 1890, when surging demand for southern pine lumber led to its reorganization as the Mobile, Jackson & Kansas City Railroad Company. A few more leisurely surveys were conducted, but little of substance was achieved until Mobile's Frank B. Merrill assumed control in December 1896. Merrill expedited fifty miles of

Atlanta, Birmingham & Coast Railroad public timetables of the 1930s contained advertising for the road's hot-shot freight trains as well as passenger-train schedules and a system map. (Courtesy of William Stanley Hoole Special Collections Library, The University of Alabama, Tuscaloosa)

Baldwin delivered this beautiful 4-4-0 to the Mobile, Jackson & Kansas City Railroad in 1903. (Courtesy of the Railroad Museum of Pennsylvania [PHMC], Strasburg)

Depot at the south Alabama town of Jackson, on the Southern Railway's Mobile Division. (Postcard ca. 1909, from the author's collection)

trackwork leading to an uninhabited spot on the Pascagoula River in Mississippi that received his name. Merrill also moved the location of the company's Mobile Bay docks to Choctaw Point, two miles from the old harbor. A twenty-three-foot channel was dredged to Choctaw Point, piers were installed, and by 1904 vast quantities of lumber were being loaded aboard ships for export. All this occurred while tracklaying continued on the main stem.

Inevitably, the forward march of the MJ&KC was soon interrupted by the maladies that typically afflicted developing railroad enterprises in Alabama. A yellow fever epidemic broke out in 1905, and quarantines in Alabama and Mississippi from July 29 to October 23 hurt profits considerably. The heavily indebted company was unable to withstand a rapidly ensuing business slump and sank into receivership on the day after Christmas, 1906. Business was so bad during the first six months of 1907 that only seventeen of approximately 197 sawmills along the line were operational, and they were on "short time."[42] Two years later the company continued to drink from a cup of woe as floods crippled the road for several days in May and June. "Five miles of track were under

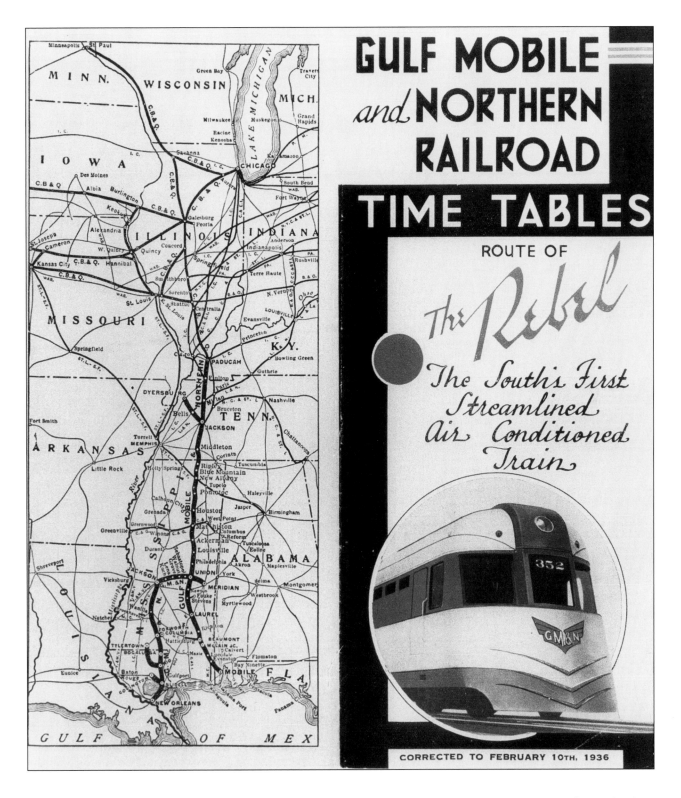

water for the period named," the company reported, "though this track had been raised two feet above the highest recorded watermark; and since the recent flood these banks have been raised another three feet."[43]

In 1909 the piney woods pike was reorganized again with what was described by a company official as "another high-sounding name," the

New Orleans, Mobile & Chicago Railroad. By 1912 the road had been extended to Middleton, Tennessee, 368 miles from Mobile. Nevertheless, the enterprise failed once more and was reorganized yet again in 1916 as the Gulf, Mobile and Northern Railroad.

The Gulf, Mobile & Northern was overtaken by World War I and, like most railroads throughout the country, became a ward of the U.S. government under the control of the director general of railroads, W. G. McAdoo. As McAdoo frugally allocated resources, he decided that the Mobile & Ohio would suffice as the main through route to the North out of Mobile, and kept this road in a goodly state of repair while practically abandoning the GM&N right-of-way. Soon after the war, Isaac Burton Tigrett became president of the Gulf, Mobile & Northern—just in time to receive the road from the federal managers in what he termed "deplorable condition." Many years later, Tigrett jocosely recalled his rather inauspicious rise to power. "The owners soon decided to build into Jackson, Tennessee, a distance of forty miles," Tigrett remembered, "and it was then, in 1917, that I was first elected a Director of the Gulf, Mobile and Northern Railroad. . . . In October 1919, when the return of the railroad from Federal control was imminent, the names of two experienced railroad men were presented for the Presidency, at a GM&N Directors' Meeting. The Board was divided between them. Finally, some Director suggested that 'we elect Tigrett temporarily until we can agree on a competent man.' We never could agree and, therefore, I am still serving."

Actually, Tigrett proved to be a very able manager and restored the company to profitability rather quickly, even though he faced an almost impossible rebuilding task when he took the helm. "The GM&N had not been too well constructed in the first place," he admitted, "and by this time it was quite dilapidated. Freight trains were frequently derailed and sometimes it took two or three days to travel from Jackson to Mobile."

A passenger train crosses the Tennessee River at Florence in 1909. A highway bridge spanning the river at this site was blown away by a tornado on March 10, 1854. Later, the Memphis & Charleston Railroad, when building its Florence branch, laid track on top of the rebuilt highway bridge. The bridge was rebuilt again in 1869–70, and in 1888 the Nashville, Florence & Sheffield Railway acquired trackage rights across the bridge. Trolleys subsequently shared the upper level with trains. In 1939 automobile traffic was discontinued on the lower level when a new highway bridge was placed in operation. (Postcard from the author's collection)

To illustrate the poor condition the railroad was in after the war, Tigrett related the following anecdote: "The private car which went along with my job as President, though not much by present standards, was a source of great pride. One of my first guests on a trip to Mobile was the pastor of my church at Jackson, Tennessee. We left Jackson one evening and sometime during the next day when we were still en route he said to me: 'Brother Tigrett, the Lord is with this Railroad. Only the Lord could have brought us safely through that ride last night.'"

Under Tigrett's leadership the GM&N was put in good order and prospered during the 1920s. The GM&N also weathered the Great Depression, although the economic stringency sometimes called for extraordinary measures. "I recall that when we were at our lowest ebb we asked our employees to take a ten percent wage reduction," Tigrett recounted. "We called it a voluntary contribution. I later learned that one of our supervisory officials told his men that he wanted the ten percent to be purely voluntary and if they knew what was best for them they would not fail to come across."

During the 1930s Tigrett began merger negotiations with the

Like a structure from a fairy tale, this gingerbread depot served the little hamlet of Epes in west Alabama. The community was originally called Epes Station in honor of John W. Epes, who donated the right-of-way through this area to the Alabama & Chattanooga Railroad. (Postcard ca. 1918, from the author's collection)

Mobile & Ohio Railroad, but the negotiations did not reach fruition until 1940, when the two companies became one. "This was the first merger of two parallel, competitive railroads," he explained. "It was a natural, though, since the M&O had already long been in bankruptcy and needed the GM&N as much as the GM&N needed to reach the St. Louis gateway. The merged properties became known as the Gulf, Mobile & Ohio, thus retaining a part of the names of both constituents."[44]

The compulsive drive toward cooperation among railroads that began in the late nineteenth century was alive and well. But Alabama's railway map was essentially complete long before the M&O–GM&N combination. By the turn of the century this map bore the colors of only a few large systems—the L&N, Southern, Central of Georgia, ACL, Seaboard, IC, and Frisco. Competitive pressures had forced consolidations and cooperative practices that left railroad service in Alabama concentrated within a handful of powerful companies. These developments would not go unnoticed—especially at the state capitol, where politicians were eager to claim them as issues.

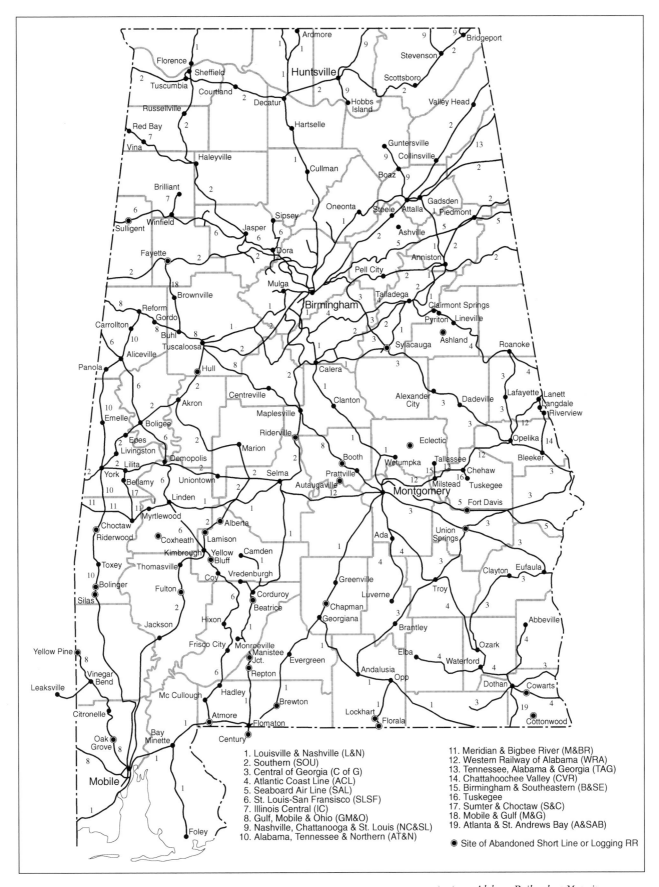

1. Louisville & Nashville (L&N)	11. Meridian & Bigbee River (M&BR)
2. Southern (SOU)	12. Western Railway of Alabama (WRA)
3. Central of Georgia (C of G)	13. Tennessee, Alabama & Georgia (TAG)
4. Atlantic Coast Line (ACL)	14. Chattahoochee Valley (CVR)
5. Seaboard Air Line (SAL)	15. Birmingham & Southeastern (B&SE)
6. St. Louis-San Fransisco (SLSF)	16. Tuskegee
7. Illinois Central (IC)	17. Sumter & Choctaw (S&C)
8. Gulf, Mobile & Ohio (GM&O)	18. Mobile & Gulf (M&G)
9. Nashville, Chattanooga & St. Louis (NC&SL)	19. Atlanta & St. Andrews Bay (A&SAB)
10. Alabama, Tennessee & Northern (AT&N)	

⊙ Site of Abandoned Short Line or Logging RR

Alabama Railroads at Maturity, ca. 1950s

Alabama Great Southern depot at the village of Steele in St. Clair County, ca. 1920s. (Courtesy of the Birmingham Public Library Department of Archives and Manuscripts)

Although the railroad that owned these shops at Montgomery is unidentified, the buildings bear an architectural design that is characteristic of L&N engine houses. Note the nineteenth-century fire protection system on each structure's roof. (Photograph ca. 1880s–90s, courtesy of the Alabama Department of Archives and History, Montgomery, Alabama)

Alabama Great Southern freight train running extra at Attalla with a consignment of Alabama-hewn crossties. Locomotive No. 6570, a 2-8-0 Consolidation type, was manufactured by Richmond Locomotive Works in 1905. (Photograph taken sometime before 1924, courtesy of Robert A. Scarboro, Scarboro Photo Shop, Gadsden, Alabama)

Birmingham's Tutwiler Hotel was scheduled to open on June 16, 1914, and a carload of furniture for its lobby had been lost in transit. The car containing the furniture was not found until June 13, when it was located in Atlanta. To make sure the furniture arrived in time for the hotel's opening, the Seaboard Air Line Railway coupled the car to one of its fastest locomotives, hitched a caboose behind, and cleared the main line for one of the fastest runs ever made between Atlanta and Birmingham. The proud crew of this unique train is shown in front of the roundhouse at the Seaboard's Birmingham yards after the furniture was successfully delivered on June 15. (Courtesy of the Birmingham Public Library Department of Archives and Manuscripts)

Southern Railway shops at the Birmingham suburb of Avondale around 1908. (Postcard from the author's collection)

Southern Railway Train No. 7, displaying the name Samuel Watkins on the Locomotive cab, met disaster on December 19, 1921. Samuel Watkins was widely known as the engineer-parson of the Southern Railway. The thirty-seven-year veteran railroader was also an ordained minister who converted thousands as he preached the gospel wherever he could along his run between Atlanta and Birmingham. A feature article honoring Watkins appeared in the New York Times and was reprinted in the December 18, 1921, edition of the Anniston Star. "When the Rev. Samuel T. Watkins is not at the throttle of his mountain climbing engine . . . he generally can be found at work trying to reclaim unfortunates in the prisons of Alabama and Georgia," the article reported. Affectionately called "Dad," the ever-smiling sixty-four-year-old engineer was loved by everyone, especially children. "In the cab of No. 6442 he carries a stock of candy and little pocket Testaments," the article continued. "When he sees a girl or boy within throwing distance of his engine he pitches them a packet of candy or gum and . . . he includes one of the Testaments." The very next day after this feature ran, Watkins was guiding the westbound Kansas City–Florida Special through Tarsus, five miles west of Anniston, when spreading rails threw the speeding engine from the track. After turning over several times, the locomotive slammed into a little trackside depot and finally lay demolished in a ditch. The tragic mishap claimed the lives of the fireman and mail clerk, as well as the famed and beloved engineer. (Courtesy of the Alabama Room, Public Library of Anniston-Calhoun County)

12

REGULATION

WITH THE APPROACH of the twentieth century, Alabama's main line railroad system was almost complete. Railroads had brought the industrial revolution to Alabama, together with all the change and upheaval associated with it, and it was only natural that conflicts would arise between the railroad corporations and their customers. Disagreements between overworked agents and impatient shippers became more and more commonplace as the railroad gained greater importance in the commercial life of communities.

A notable example of the strained relations that were developing between the populace and the railroads occurred in 1881 when Ashville residents complained of abusive actions taken by the Alabama Great Southern agent at Whitney Station. Although three and one-half miles away, Whitney Station was the nearest depot, and vital to Ashville's interests. Various accusations were leveled against the agent, including the allegation that he refused to allow patrons use of the depot's waiting room on bitterly cold nights. When belligerent area merchants sued to have the agent removed, the AGS reacted by downgrading Whitney Station to a flag stop. This further inconvenienced Ashville customers, since prepayment was required for all shipments to flag stations. Furthermore, parcels were not cared for after they were unloaded. Without notification, flag station freight was simply thrown onto the depot platform, where it remained unprotected until the owner came to claim it. Since the AGS monopolized rail transportation through St. Clair County, the disconcerted complainants had little recourse. They were at the mercy of the railroad.[1]

As large systems began to dominate the state, rivalry between competing lines gave way to cooperative efforts to defend the vested interests of the industry. The agreements between Smith and Spencer proved that the concerns of railroad managers had shifted to issues of common interest. Emphasis was now placed on protection of established territory, maintenance of stable and profitable rates, and resistance to regulation.

As southern railroad systems evolved, many evils crept into their operating practices. In Alabama, for example, free transportation passes had been granted to furnace owners as part of the industrial development policies instituted by the railroads. This practice was soon extended to many other businessmen, legislators, newspapermen, and others with whom the railroads wished to curry favor. After a few years, the free transportation privilege came to be considered a prerogative by special interests. More frequently, it constituted a bribe. The apogee of free pass abuse occurred in 1899 when the L&N provided every member of Alabama's legislature with a free ride to Mobile's Mardi Gras festival.[2]

The evil bringing the loudest protest, however, was inequitable freight rates. Selective discrimination saddled some shippers with high rates while more favored clients enjoyed discounts for the same service. Rebates and overcharges gradually became commonplace. All of these problems had been addressed by 1870s legislation, but many of the laws were becoming outmoded and unenforceable. Neither were these problems unique to Alabama. Increasingly, railroad reformers were at work throughout the nation, and Alabamians took notice.

The most prickly of the freight tariff problems was the differential between local and through rates. Competitive factors had forced the railroads to institute the discriminatory basing-point system, which required higher rates for local traffic than for long hauls. The basing-point system evolved largely as a result of competition between pioneer railroads and steamboat companies. The railroads attempted to attract traffic away from the river steamers at important river landings such as Montgomery, Selma, and Mobile by instituting low freight rates at these points. These cities, called competitive points, became flourishing major trade centers as the low rates attracted long-haul traffic from the North. From these distribution centers, higher local rates prevailed to outlying towns. The rate to small interior Alabama towns would be the sum of the through rate to the competitive point plus the higher local rate. Thus, the interior towns paid considerably more in transportation charges when compared to the basing-point cities. For example, it cost $3.75 to ship a bale of cotton from Montgomery or Selma to New York in 1882. In contrast, the same bale cost $4.65 to ship from Opelika and $5.90 from Goodwater. Predictably, small-town leaders complained that the high local rates were unfairly discriminatory and inhibited development of their communities. The railroads retorted by claiming that traffic density was so low in rural areas, particularly in poorer sections of Alabama, that the high local rates were justified.[3]

Since through traffic was the lifeblood of railroads, long-haul rates were fiercely competitive, and every system did everything possible to reduce their long-haul operating costs. Ruling grades were reduced; trackwork was improved by using heavier steel rails and straightening curves; bridges were rebuilt; stronger locomotives were placed in service; and better terminal facilities were constructed to lower the cost of operations. The most dramatic example of the effort to facilitate interstate train movements was the universal switch to standard-gauge track. But in spite of the intensive modernization efforts in Alabama, demand did not keep pace with competition, and the railroads suffered from overcapacity. To preserve profitability, the railroads would go out of their way to maintain rate stability. In 1900, for example, a shipment from the North to Montgomery could be made more cheaply by routing it to Mobile and back to Montgomery, an additional distance of 350 miles compared to a direct line-haul. The railroads would rather do this than reduce Montgomery's rate. If Montgomery's rate were reduced, the public would clamor for similar reductions at Eufaula and Columbus, where the same rate was in force. Anyone wishing to lower local freight rates in Alabama would be met with stubborn opposition from the railway companies.[4]

Southerners wanted more railroads, but there was also a lingering public suspicion and animosity toward them in the wake of the scandals and economic hardships of Reconstruction, particularly in rural and farm regions. In 1879 this mistrust boiled to the surface in Georgia when a stringent law was enacted that established a railroad commission with rate-making authority. The Georgia law stemmed from an 1877 U.S. Supreme Court ruling that sanctioned state regulation of private property when it was devoted to public use. In later cases, this decision was reversed, as the Supreme Court declared rate fixing by states to be an unconstitutional breach of the Fourteenth Amendment. But this ruling did not come until 1890, and by then the low rates mandated in Georgia had become institutionalized and were so in-grained that they were almost impossible to change.

Managers of railroads operating in Alabama were deeply concerned that the state legislature would decide to establish a powerful commission modeled after the Georgia body, and made special efforts to appease proponents of regulation. The inevitable push for regulation in Alabama came from the city of Montgomery in 1881. As impoverished railroads were absorbed by the larger systems, the L&N and Central Railroad & Banking Company of Georgia soon controlled all of the lines serving the capital city. Montgomery businessmen feared that these railroads might discriminate against their city in favor of a rival trade center and persuaded their senator, Daniel S. Troy, to draft legislation establishing a sympathetic railroad commission. After some initial opposition, the railroad interests decided that more intensive resistance might precipitate the formation of an antagonistic Georgia-like regulatory body and soon acceded to the establishment of a railroad commission with subdued, advisory power. A bill largely contoured after Troy's recommendations was passed on February 26, 1881.

The new law, declared by the *Selma Times* to be "as mild as a May morning and as harmless as a dove," called for a three-member commission that, while authorized to make recommendations regarding tariffs, was powerless to actually regulate freight or passenger rates. The commission's primary responsibilities were to conduct hearings, straighten out complaints, investigate accidents, compile statistics, and make sure no one was unfairly discriminated against. The commissioners were to conduct yearly inspection tours of the state's railroads, carefully insuring that tariffs were posted at depots. A special tax on railroad earnings would pay operating expenses.[5]

Using the Georgia commission as a model, Alabama's first railroad commission included a seasoned lawyer and a railroad expert. The legal scholar was Walter L. Bragg, who was appointed commission president. Bragg was a respected Montgomery attorney who had been instrumental in the 1874 ouster of the Radicals. The railroad authority was Charles Pollard Ball, former superintendent of the AGS and Western of Alabama railroads. James Crook, a planter and attorney from Calhoun County, rounded out the commission.

Crook and Ball wasted no time in taking up their mandate. They boarded special trains in May and June 1881 to be chaperoned on a tour of the state's railroads by one or more officials of the roads they inspected. After the tour, they immediately compiled their observations and issued the first comprehensive assessment of Alabama's railroads. Bragg proved to be an able and conscientious leader. He had a good deal of success in rectifying the common overcharge abuse and also offered many constructive recommendations regarding rates. The railroads didn't want to arouse antirailroad sentiment and be faced with concomitant hostile juries, so they went along with Bragg's early recommendations. Bragg was also careful to use restraint in rate reduction due to the poor financial condition of many Alabama railroads. Therefore, although considerable progress was made in establishing more equitable long-haul tariffs, little was done about the troublesome local rates.

By 1884, despite the fact that several of the state's railroads were in serious financial difficulties, Bragg could no longer ignore the inequities of the basing-point system and decided to take action on a complaint filed by citizens of Opelika. Through its Columbus & Western and Western of Alabama subsidiaries, the Central Railroad & Banking Company of Georgia dominated transportation at Opelika. When the Central made Columbus a competitive point, Opelika merchants were placed at a distinct disadvantage as they continued to pay the higher local rate on shipments. A compromise settlement offered by the Central fell short in Bragg's eyes, and he ordered the Columbus & Western to make Opelika a competitive point. The Central was afraid that this would start a chain reaction of other way stations demanding similar treatment and obstinately resisted the order. Bragg was uncompromising and introduced several bills in the state legislature aimed at procuring enforcement authority for his commission in the Opelika case.

The Central Railroad & Banking Company held its ground, however, and Bragg soon found himself confronting a determined railroad lobby. In an attempt to arouse public support for the railroad, the lobbyists secured petitions expressing opposition to the proposed legislation and published them in newspapers across the state. "This railroad lobby swarmed around the hotels of Montgomery at night," Bragg said with vexation, "and around the Capitol by day. It prepared petitions in Montgomery against this legislation and sent them up and down the railroad lines of the State procuring the signatures of the merchants generally, at country towns along their lines, and also sent petitions signed by a large number of merchants of Montgomery, Selma, Mobile, Birmingham, and Eufaula. The object of these petitions thus obtained was to produce upon the legislature the impression that the people were generally opposed to such legislation. The counsel of these railroad companies meanwhile argued against this proposed legislation before the committees of the legislature, and prepared and printed arguments which were furnished to the legislature generally, and plied them generally and individually with arguments and appeals against it."

Bragg tried a petition campaign of his own, but was only able to solicit significant support from the Opelika area. Bragg's proposals were given a fair and thoughtful hearing in the legislature, but after much debate they were defeated. The large number of signatures on the railroad's petitions, as well as the legislative decision itself, showed that there was almost no sentiment in Alabama to expand the power of the railroad commission. Despite the intrinsic unfairness of the basing-point system, railroads were held in high public esteem, and Alabamians refused to scare away the capital needed to build them. This railroad triumph sealed the fate of the railroad commission for the next twenty years.[6]

Neither Bragg, Ball, nor Crook was reappointed to third terms, primarily because of their opposition to incumbent Governor E. A. O'Neal in the election of 1884. Bragg, however, was appointed to the first U.S. Interstate Commerce Commission by President Grover Cleveland in 1887. Bragg's position with regard to the basing-point system was initially upheld by a provision of ICC legislation declaring that higher rates could not be charged for a shorter versus longer hauls. The basing-point debate continued to rage before the ICC, however, and was not fully resolved until 1910 when the Mann-Elkins Act expressly prohibited a higher tariff for short-hauls.[7]

Meanwhile, Alabama's railroad commission degenerated into a moribund body of self-serving professional officeholders. With paramount concern for remaining in office, the commissioners rubber-stamped railroad activities. In 1890, when the railroads also had the good fortune to place a close friend of Milton H. Smith in the governor's chair in the person of ex-L&N lawyer Thomas G. Jones, railroad domination of the state was assured. An observer in the early 1890s noted: "More than commonly kind relations exist between the railroads and the people of Alabama. A railroad commission of limited powers, established in 1881, has tended further to harmonize these relations."[8]

The movement for regulation simmered until 1896, when Governor Joseph F. Johnston called for strengthening the railroad commission. Although the proposal failed, one of its supporters, Braxton Bragg Comer, was determined to fight another day. Comer was an ambitious Barbour County cotton planter when the Georgia Pacific Railway came to Alabama in 1884. He concluded that the Georgia Pacific would bring outstanding trade opportunities to east Alabama, and moved to Anniston to engage in the wholesale grocery business. In Anniston, Comer got his first exposure to the inequities of the basing-point system and discriminatory freight tariffs. He found penetration of business territory east of Anniston to be exceedingly difficult due to the lower freight rates in effect at competing west Georgia towns. In 1890 Comer protested to the railroad commission but discovered that body to be impotent. Finding no relief as he vigorously fought the system, an exasperated Comer moved to Birmingham.

The entrance of the Georgia Pacific Railway and Kansas City, Memphis & Birmingham Railroad into Birmingham had brought reduced rates to both the east and west and had raised the Magic City's stature as a trade center. Comer rode the rising tide of Birmingham trade to build several prosperous business enterprises. He was associated with Avondale Mills and joined a partnership that operated the Western Grain Company, famous for its "Jim Dandy" products. Within a few years, Comer became one of the richest men in the state.

Comer had not forgotten the galling freight rate experience at Anniston, and subsequent experiences convinced him that railroad rate structures also unfairly discriminated against Birmingham merchants in favor of jobbers in Memphis, Nashville, St. Louis, and other cities. The railroads did little to soothe Comer's growing outrage when they instituted other rate policies that hurt his milling operation. Comer could no longer tolerate these perceived injustices and initiated a determined campaign for rate reform. He enlisted the aid of prominent Birmingham businessmen, including Rufus Rhodes, editor of the *Birmingham News,* and formed an organization called the Commercial Club, which strove to improve the rate situation. Slackening mercantile business brought on by the panic of '93 only served to exacerbate the rate controversy. Comer attacked Governor Jones and accused him of acting on behalf of the railroad interests rather than for the commonweal of the state. The personal feud between Comer and Jones was just beginning. After Jones's gubernatorial term expired, he was appointed to the federal bench, where he would preside over Comer's rate reform crusade in the courts for years to come.

Even though Comer's appeals to the railroad commission, governor, and legislature were in vain, his philosophy regarding Alabama railroads had crystallized. He came to believe that the state's economic problems could be traced principally to low farm income and reasoned that lower freight rates would give poor farmers more disposable income, which they could use to purchase locally produced goods. This would eventually lead to the development of diversified regional industries, with a consequent increase in local railroad traffic. Comer backed up his contention by showing that Georgia, with the low tariffs imposed by her railroad commission, was more prosperous than Alabama; and that Georgia railroads were also more profitable than those in Alabama. He was convinced that the railroads were charging more in Alabama out of greed rather than necessity. According to Comer's figures, Alabama's rates were 20 to 120 percent higher than those of other states. Moreover, Comer wanted to free Alabamians from the control of outsiders. As things stood, Alabama was locked in the shackles of a colonial economy where money and control of industrial development reposed outside the state. Freight rate savings could be plowed back into the state's economy to lift it by the bootstraps through local initiatives.

Comer's first real opportunity to institute reform came on May 21, 1901, when a constitutional convention was called to address the suffrage issue and to correct deficiencies in the state constitution of 1875. At this convention Comer and his colleagues planned to introduce provisions expanding railroad commission power and changing it to an elective body. Comer was unable to incorporate his specific proposals into the new constitution, but got something just as good. The new document was patterned after the 1877 Georgia constitution and gave the state legislature comprehensive power to control freight and passenger rates.[9] It was now up to Comer to ensure election of legislators who advocated the reforms he wanted. Comer promptly established a committee to certify candidates favoring a strong elective commission and appointed a prominent Birmingham lawyer, Frank S. White, as committee chairman. The committee soon drafted railroad regulating resolutions and obtained antirailroad pledges from certified candidates.

Comer had declared war on the railroads, and the L&N responded by calling up the old Confederate veteran Jefferson M. Faulkner, who gallantly made the following proclamation in an interview with the *Birmingham News:* "I do not magnify this movement, but I say to you and the paper which you represent, which is saying it from the house-top, that the Louisville and Nashville railroad is going to fight this movement with all the weapons that are recognized as fair in political warfare. We come out boldly into the open field."

Chairman White met with Birmingham merchants on July 21 and urged them to "make the sacrifice and go out two by two, . . . and spread the doctrine." Following his orders, two merchants went south on the AGS, two took the Central of Georgia to east Alabama, and two went north on the L&N. Comer himself bravely sallied forth to the western front on the Frisco, and soon returned to the home front with this stirring war story:

> I had never made a speech in my life, except one, and that was on the free silver issue, up at Decatur—I was heartily in favor of it; that was the only time I ever made a speech. Now the first talk we had was at Sulligent. I got off at the station, from the Frisco Railroad, and the hotel-keeper met me at the car door, and I told him my name was Comer, I had come up to make a talk on the elective Commission. He had never heard of it before, and didn't know whether to call me Mr., Colonel, Captain, or what not. He went around with me, to see the different men, and says here is a man who has come to talk to you this evening on something he will explain to you. I got them to come out to the door-steps of the store a little bit elevated, they stood on the steps while I stood on the ground and talked. I made them a talk of perhaps an hour and a half. Going back to the hotel, he called me "Colonel." . . . It was the first time I was ever called Colonel.

Faulkner, meanwhile, noted that L&N crews had longer "layovers" in Birmingham than anywhere else, and warned that his company might "find justification for removing these crews to some other point." For good measure, Faulkner also threatened to raise the rates on coal and iron and have L&N employees boycott Birmingham businesses. The propaganda machine worked incessantly for both sides as the battle raged furiously across the pages of Alabama newspapers.

After the smoke cleared, the antirailroad interests had won a handy victory. Comer had painted a picture of extortionistic rates holding back progress in Alabama while Georgia prospered under commission imposed tariffs—and the voting public viewed this picture as a masterpiece. When the antirailroad legislators took office, they immediately presented a bill calling for a powerful elective railroad commission with the authority to set rates. The railroad lobby tenaciously fought this legislation and it passed only after some adroit legislative maneuvering. Some portions of the bill succumbed to the intensive lobbying efforts, however, and the final measure was not as strong as the antirailroad legislators originally intended. The law provided for the election of three commissioners to four-year terms beginning in November 1904.[10]

Incumbent commissioner Wiley C. Tunstall was soon reappointed, and William T. Sanders joined him as associate commissioner. These men were by no means reform crusaders. When the legislature reconvened, the law was materially amended so that the commission president was to be elected in 1904 while the two associate commissioners would not stand for election until 1906. This meant that the new commission president would be stuck with Sanders and Tunstall for two years, like it or not.

Who would the new commission president be? Who else but Comer, who declared himself a candidate in 1904. His chief rival, among many announced competitors, was incumbent John V. Smith, who was vigorously supported by the railroad interests, led by Milton H. Smith of the L&N Railroad. Comer opened his campaign in Selma on January 28 with a speech outlining a platform that called for reduced freight rates, better car service, and prompt claims settlement. Smith countered by challenging Comer's contentions regarding freight rates. Both men ignored the other candidates and engaged in a series of exhausting statewide speeches and debates. On February 25, the *Montgomery Advertiser* noted the effect nonstop campaigning was having on the candidates. "All day canvassing, continued speaking far into the night, daylight rising to catch early morning trains had subdued the spirit and enthusiasm of the debaters," the paper observed.

From well-staffed headquarters in Birmingham's First National Bank building, Comer saturated the state with campaign literature. On the back of each envelope mailed from this office could be found the declaration "A vote for B. B. Comer for Railroad Commissioner is a vote for cheaper local freights." The candidate invested heavily in these mailings and proudly characterized them as a public service. "I put up eight thousand dollars myself," Comer boasted, "to carry education to the people of Alabama . . . and it was money well spent. . . . I am perhaps the only man in the State that can tell you what it will cost to send the voters of the State a circular. I don't reckon there is a man in the State besides me that can tell you what it would cost to send electors of the State a letter. I know. I did it. Along this whole line every dollar of this money that was spent was spent for the purpose of education; was spent to take you out of the hands of these great corporations, and to put you where you belong; a free and independent State . . . ; wherever I went I could get off at the stations, I have noticed this myself, 'this is Comer,' he says, 'B. B.' 'Yes, I got your letter.'"

Another Comer weapon was newspaper advertising. Railroad representatives retaliated in kind and plastered newspapers with a barrage of anti-Comer ads. A favorite railroad tactic was to instigate editorial attacks upon Comer in leading papers and then pay other journalists to publish quotations from these editorials. The editor of the *Daphne Standard* stated that he received a one-hundred-dollar bid for three days of anti-Comer editorial comment immediately preceding election day. The agent making the offer stated that no other state publication had refused similar payments.

The mudslinging culminated with ads in the *Birmingham Ledger* and *Birmingham Age-Herald* accusing Comer of using meal sacks to ship flour from Tennessee to his Birmingham milling facilities so that he fraudulently received a lower freight rate. W. E. Knox, superintendent of the Alabama Mineral Railroad, signed the advertisement after promulgating the rumor for weeks. Next day, the accusation was affirmed by an affidavit appearing in the *Age-Herald* signed by the L&N's general freight agent, E. A. DeFuniak. Less than a month later, on the day preceding the primary election, the railroad interests ran an affidavit charging that Comer had conspired to defraud the L&N of money due for track repairs.

As the vilifying attacks turned viciously personal, emotions ran high on election day. Lucklessly, Comer and DeFuniak chanced to meet on a Birmingham sidewalk outside a polling place, and fists flew. A newspaper account of the altercation stated that "no harm was done besides a bloody nose." Without revealing which of the combatants received the bloody nose, the paper reported that both men were fined five dollars in the inferior criminal court the following day. A separate article in the *Montgomery Advertiser* chronicled the congratulations that were rolling in for the Comer victory. A casual glance at this headline may not have readily revealed whether the compliments were for the election win or his triumph in the street fight.

Comer won handily throughout the state, outdistancing his opponents' combined vote total by eighteen thousand ballots. He was strong everywhere except in the major cities, all of which were competitive points and therefore beneficiaries of the existing system. Comer's election marked a sea change in Alabama politics. The railroad had reached every corner of the state, and Alabamians no longer felt the need to tolerate unrestrained laissez-faire capitalism. Comer had stirred the seething suspicion and resentment of the railroads, and rugged individualism ceased to receive a blanket endorsement in Alabama. The significance of the election was duly noted by the *Montgomery Journal:* "Aside from any affect his election may have on the railroads and their interests, the result of Mr. Comer's election means a re-arranging of political lines in this state. It means a new force and a new power in state politics. It means that all the old leaders are to be relegated to the rear and new leaders, new policies and a new order of things are to prevail. This is as certain as anything can be in the future. Mr. Comer is the new leader in Alabama politics and this fact cannot be disguised."[11]

Comer eagerly took over as chairman of the railroad commission on March 6, 1905, and immediately put his shoulder to the wheel of reform. On April 3, after diligent preparation, he confidently convened a hearing on fertilizer rates. As an army of railroad lawyers marched to the witness stand to defend against Comer's assertion that fertilizer rates were too high, the chairman was suddenly ambushed. Without warning, the associate commissioners demanded that the hearing be expanded to embrace the entire intrastate rate structure. Thunderstruck, Comer realized that he had been tricked into a hopeless confrontation with the railroad crowd. He was completely unprepared to face single-handedly the largest assembly of railroad officials ever to appear before the commission and argue for reform of the whole spectrum of rates. Comer pleaded to the governor for help, but got none. The chairman fought courageously, but associate commissioners Sanders and Tunstall sided with the railroads, and Comer's cause was lost. Comer then realized that the changes he sought could not be made at the commission level. They would have to be accomplished from a higher office. "From my associates' decision against the people, there is no appeal except to the ballot," Comer cried, and he decided to run for governor.[12]

Unquestionably, public discontent over rates was growing, and Comer was confident that the voters would support him. As Chambers County teacher J. J. Newman remembered, some communities could not wait for political action. "Some LaFayette folks thought the Central of Georgia Railroad was not being fair in their freight rate," Newman said. "About 1905 they set up the LaFayette Railroad with Edgar McGhee as president. . . . The line was built from LaFayette by

Oakbowery to Opelika. It joined the Central of Georgia line about a mile south of LaFayette. . . . Area for tracks was surveyed from LaFayette to Davidston by way of Rock Springs and Marcoot. This was never built. The company operated for a number of years. Many lost money in this venture. Papa lost $550."[13]

Comer threw his hat in the ring on October 20, 1905, and rode the developing wave of antirailroad sentiment with determination, as he assembled a unified slate of sympathetic legislative candidates who hoped to be swept into office on Comer's coattails. His opponent was the popular lieutenant governor, Dr. Russell M. Cunningham. Cunningham's platform was very similar to Comer's and called for more railroad regulation. Therefore, the railroads saw no reason to support either man and the race essentially boiled down to a personality contest. Comer focused so intensely on the railroad issue that the *Montgomery Advertiser* said he was playing a "lyre with one string." Despite this taunt, Alabama voters danced to the one-note tune, and Comer chalked up another convincing victory.

With Comer at the governor's desk, the railroad commission was invigorated as at no other time since the Bragg Commission. In 1907, armed with widespread public endorsement, he rammed an avalanche of regulatory legislation into law. A new railroad commission was established with rate-making authority and plenary power. Issuance of free passenger passes as well as campaign contributions to politicians was strictly prohibited. One of the new laws sought "to define corrupt solicitation of legislators and provide adequate punishment therefor." Maximum freight and passenger rates were established and statutes were put on the books specifying rules for posting, filing, and changing rates. The state also enacted a complicated system of laws designed to block judicial relief from the regulatory legislation. The most controversial of these laws was called the "outlaw" provision, which stipulated that any railroad company doing business in the state would lose its license to conduct intrastate activities if it appealed an order of the state to a federal court or otherwise transferred a case from the state court to federal court. The antirailroad legislative menu was so extensive that split sessions were required to pass all the legislation.

Just as the legislature finished dishing out its first heaping helping of railroad reform, another financial depression struck. Railroad interests quickly pointed fingers at the reformers and alleged that the antirailroad legislation had caused the economic decline. When the

Western of Alabama and Atlantic Coast Line closed their shops at Montgomery, the new laws were speciously blamed.

Ignoring the new laws blocking access to the federal judiciary, railroad lawyers planned to fight in federal court on the grounds that the Alabama statutes were an unlawful confiscation of property and violated the Fourteenth Amendment. This defense had worked before, and it worked again. Former Alabama governor Thomas G. Jones, reputed to be the railroads' friend, had been appointed to the United States Circuit Court. In unison, the railroads asked Jones for an injunction preventing enforcement of the Alabama legislation. Alabama attorneys were no match for the slick railroad lawyers, and Jones granted temporary injunctions barring implementation of the laws. Railroad officials were delighted. They knew that temporary injunctions were just as good as permanent ones, since the railroads had the resources to indefinitely drag the cases through the federal courts.

On July 9, the legislature reconvened for its second session and churned out more regulatory legislation. This time a law was enacted giving the railroad commission plenary power to adjust rates up or down at its discretion. Unlike the first session, however, some proposals encountered heavy resistance. One bill mandating the use of electric lights on locomotives was rejected with the argument that "the electric headlight is a novelty and its use is extending over the country in the form of a fad."

Soon after the gavel fell at the end of the second legislative session, the Southern Railway defiantly transferred a rate case to federal court. The resulting confrontation would test the governor's resolve and the power of the state. The federal court had thrown out the legislature's "outlaw" provision when the temporary injunctions were granted, but Secretary of State Frank N. Julian dug through the Alabama Code until he uncovered an expedient club to wield against the renegade railroad. Citing a corporate licensing act that was unrelated to the rate cases and therefore not subject to the injunctions, Julian revoked the Southern's license to do business in the state of Alabama. Without a license, Southern employees risked criminal prosecution if trains continued to run through the state. J. P. Morgan hastily reacted to the crisis by calling the various railroad interests together for a New York strategy session. Milton H. Smith, who was uncompromising in his belief that Alabama's actions were unlawful, was in attendance and became so exasperated with Morgan's lack of resolve that he walked out of the meeting. After a week of controversy and useless bargaining, the Southern finally gave in and agreed to obey the new laws until a test case could establish their constitutionality. A Southern Railway spokesman stated that his company had yielded in order to maintain a harmonious relationship with the authorities. Admitting that "the sacrifice of its revenue is a matter of no small moment, and a surrender of its legal rights a matter of serious concern," he maintained that the Southern "is willing to make such sacrifice and surrender rather than enter into or prolong what might become an angry contest with the authorities of the State of Alabama."

One by one, other railroads operating in Alabama capitulated and accepted the state-imposed rate reductions. But those lines with the greatest interest in the state, principally the L&N and Central of Georgia, continued to disobey the regulatory laws. Governor Comer was determined that these companies would "take the Southern's medicine." Furthermore, he lifted the crisis to a higher plane when he wrote that "It is not now so much freight rates, as it is State rights." Judge Jones agreed that the impasse transcended a mere dispute over business practices, and announced that it tested "whether we shall have anarchy or a government of laws." With confidence that the U.S. government would enforce his decisions, Jones issued restraining orders prohibiting further action against the defiant railroads.

Comer applied persistent pressure to bring the railroads into compliance with the mandated rate structure. The threat of a special legislative session induced the Southern Railway to drop its lawsuits regarding the statutory rates in exchange for a slight increase in passenger fares. But the L&N, under the leadership of Milton H. Smith, steadfastly refused to yield. Smith's followers were captivated by his leadership and the coalition of disobedient roads held together.[14] Comer conferred with lawyers and legislators as he searched for legal snares that would selectively entrap the recalcitrant roads while causing little harm to those that had come to terms. A face-to-face meeting between Comer and Smith produced no progress. The two men were equally uncompromising. Smith complained that "it was not a question of the amount of reduction which the state would make in their published rates, but that there should be any reduction at all." Meanwhile, the recession continued unabated, and public backing for Comer flagged as Alabamians worried more about winning their daily bread than supporting political initiatives.

Left: *Milton Hannibal Smith, ca. 1910. (Courtesy of the L&N Collection, University of Louisville Archives and Records Center)* Right: *Braxton Bragg Comer, ca. 1910. (Courtesy of the Alabama Department of Archives and History, Montgomery, Alabama)*

On November 7, 1907, an extraordinary session of the legislature convened in Montgomery. Asserting his intention to fix "whether or not the people of Alabama have the right to dominate their intrastate affairs and make laws to regulate them," the governor presented a long list of viciously punitive proposals contrived to bring the resisting roads into line. The proposals were passed with little amendment and, once again, Alabama's statute books bulged with laws aimed at denying the railroads access to federal courts. Smith, who had taken up residence at Montgomery, directed a counteroffensive from his private car. In short order the L&N, South & North Alabama, Central of Georgia, NC&StL, and Western of Alabama obtained temporary restraining orders enjoining enforcement of the legislation.

Litigation painfully crawled through the courts, and the state failed to muster enough legal force to wiggle out of the injunctions. As economic hardships lingered, weary Alabamians despaired of the railroad issue and it came to be disparagingly assailed as "Comerism." Comer's opposition to Smith and Judge Jones eventually degenerated into a bitter feud with ugly consequences. As each side hurled virulent invective at the other, the animosity between Comer and Smith grew into unremitting hatred.[15]

Courts handed down conflicting decisions as the cases dragged on. The state of Alabama won a rare victory in 1909 when the New Orleans Circuit Court of Appeals reversed Judge Jones's rulings and ordered dissolution of his temporary injunctions. Undeterred, an L&N lawyer proclaimed that "Austerlitz has been lost, but Waterloo is yet to be fought," and the railroads took their cases before specially appointed masters in chancery. Once again the state was woefully short of qualified attorneys and the masters accepted the railroad arguments hook, line, and sinker. On April 2, 1912, based upon the resulting reports, Judge Jones issued permanent injunctions against the state.[16]

In 1911 Comer was succeeded as governor by Emmett O'Neal, who was also in favor of railroad regulation. Public passion for regulation continued to wane, however, and Governor O'Neal took a more moderate course. Minnesota and Missouri cases before the U.S. Supreme Court involved many of the same issues that were in question in Alabama, and O'Neal decided to save litigation costs by postponing appeals until these cases were decided.

As the adversaries waited for these momentous decrees, Comer made plans for his next gubernatorial campaign. Anticipating the ex-governor's moves, Milton H. Smith renewed his newspaper campaign against Comer. Smith used over $34,000 of L&N money to publish antiregulation advertisements in approximately 130 Alabama papers. When company money was not available, he dipped into his personal account to blast Comer in these journals.[17] In some of the articles, he used his father's name, Irulus, as his pen name. An example of Smith's derisive characterization of Comer is found in an excerpt from an article entitled "Comeritus—A Jim-Dandy One-Man Comer-dy."

> My fond ambition's goal is the limelight glare
> And exercise of constant public function,
> In which to exploit myself and court applause
> And, posing as the people's dearest friend,
> Hold power to carry out my fell design
> To wreck upon the railroads rank revenge.[18]

But Comer had long since ceased to be a realistic threat to the railroads, and the propaganda directed against him was largely a waste of ink. Most voters were tired of the long court battles and scurrilous exchanges and turned their attention to more appealing issues such as Prohibition. Soon, an accelerating cascade of fateful events would resolve the railroad crisis in Alabama.

On June 16, 1913, the Supreme Court handed down its anxiously awaited Minnesota and Missouri decisions. Elaborate interpretations of the relevant principles of law sent a joyous message to Comer and the railroad reformers. By setting aside flawed arguments that had handcuffed railroad commissions for over fifteen years, the Supreme Court decision effectively affirmed the right of states to regulate intrastate rates. Now confident that the rate cases could be won, Governor O'Neal filed appeals with the U.S. Supreme Court in December 1913. But the governor knew the judicial process might take years to complete, and he was also growing sensitive to Comer's campaign rhetoric criticizing the state's management of the cases. It was time for compromise.

In a practical move designed to strip Comer of his political agenda, the railroads struck a deal with the state. On February 21, 1914, all parties accepted a compromise settlement in which the state promised to withdraw its appeals in exchange for concessions on passenger fares. Since freight rates were not specifically included in the compromise, Comer angrily accused the O'Neal administration of selling out to the railroad interests after the state had already won its battle. But Comer failed to mention one of the most important aspects of the compromise. Even though the compromise agreement called for the injunctions against the Comer regulatory statutes to remain in effect, the railroads also conceded that the Alabama railroad commission should be free to discharge its lawful duties with regard to freight and passenger rate revision.

As Comer was well aware, the compromise was politically motivated. Voters had had enough of controversy and conflict. The railroads had had enough of Comer. And politicians had had enough of the railroad issue. All these interests knew that resolution of the railroad dilemma would destroy Comer's platform. And it did. O'Neal resented Comer and threw his support behind the ex-governor's opponent, Charles Henderson. Henderson, a former railroad commissioner, became governor of Alabama in 1915.

The railroads had acknowledged the right of the Alabama railroad commission to regulate rates, and the commissioners wasted no time in exercising their authority. On March 3, 1914, the commission called for hearings on freight rates. By July, the Central of Georgia and Western of Alabama had adopted the same rates that were in effect on the Southern Railway System following its capitulation to Comer. Diehard L&N lawyers continued to argue futilely, but by September the

Old Reliable had also fallen into line. Comer's freight rates were universally in force on Alabama's railroads.

The compromise signaled a new beginning in the relationship between the state and the railroads. The contentiousness of the railroads had served only to further alienate the public and cause even more mistrust of corporations. This led to more regulation than ever. By the same token, Comer's actions had been extreme and may have scared capital investment away and hurt the reputation of the state. But with the compromise, politicians and railroad executives could now attempt to deal realistically with the investment and operational needs of Alabama's rail system.[19]

In 1914 Charles Henderson correctly summarized the political mood in Alabama: "We have had enough of rainbow chasing. We have had enough of men riding into office on hobbies and diverting the public mind from material things right here at home. We have had enough of strife. We have had enough of dictatorship. We need a government that will administer affairs in an orderly economical way, as a business man would administer the affairs of his personal business. We want peace, tranquillity and prosperity in Alabama, and unless the signs of the times fail we are going to have it soon."[20]

Heavy coal and freight drags in Alabama's hill country required mighty motive power, such as this Central of Georgia 2-10-2 Santa Fe type engine. This Baldwin locomotive, with a full load of coal in its tender, is shown at the road's Birmingham engine house on July 25, 1931. The Illinois Central and Seaboard also used Santa Fe types in Alabama. The Southern resorted to even larger locomotives and regularly employed mammoth 2-8-8-2 articulated Mallets (with a total of sixteen drive wheels) on ponderous mainline hauls. (From the author's collection)

Barrels of watercress await shipment at Huntsville Depot in the 1930s. Huntsville was considered the watercress capital of the world in the 1930s and 1940s. (Courtesy of the Heritage Room, Huntsville-Madison County Public Library, Huntsville, Alabama)

To handle the extraordinary increase in freight tonnage between Montgomery and Atlanta during World War I, the Western Railway of Alabama purchased two 2-8-2 Mikados from the Lima Locomotive Works in 1918. The performance of these locomotives was so impressive that the company ordered four more, slightly larger ones from Lima between 1923 and 1925, including No. 376, shown here at Montgomery in the 1930s. These were the most powerful engines on the W of A until their 54,700 lbs. of tractive effort was eclipsed by the 63,000 lbs. generated by a new Baldwin 2-8-2 that joined the loco roster in 1944. (From the author's collection)

*Cupolas adorned the roofs of many South-
ern Railway depots along the old Georgia
Pacific right-of-way in Alabama. The
Choccolocco Depot, located on well-mani-
cured grounds a few miles east of Anniston,
exemplified this distinctive architectural
style. (Photograph ca. 1929, courtesy of
the Alabama Room, Public Library of
Anniston-Calhoun County)*

13

SHORT LINES AND LOGGING RAILROADS

INDUSTRIAL DEVELOPMENT followed Alabama's main lines into the Cotton Belt and lumber regions as well as the mineral districts. As cheap labor rates attracted more and more textile companies to the Heart of Dixie, spur tracks radiated to several new cotton mills at Eufaula, Huntsville, Selma, Tuscaloosa, and many other towns. In the decade from 1890 to 1900 the number of cotton manufacturing spindles operating in the state soared from 79,324 to 411,328.[1] In east Alabama, cotton manufacturing had flourished on the banks of the Chattahoochee River since the close of the Civil War, when mills were constructed at River View and Langdale. Cotton duck fabric manufactured in the region known as "the Valley" was used worldwide for ship sails and was also utilized as covering for pioneer wagons in America's great westward expansion.

The Langdale mill was acquired by the Lanier family in the 1880s and reorganized as the West Point Manufacturing Company. In the 1890s the West Point Manufacturing Company purchased the mill at River View, built a new mill at Lanett, and established the Lanett Bleachery and Dye Works.[2] This rapidly growing cotton manufacturer soon needed a railroad of its own, and in 1897 a ten-mile-long standard-gauge line called the Chattahoochee Valley Railway was placed in operation between West Point, Georgia, and River View, Alabama. This short line kept pace with the growth of the West Point Manufacturing Company and was later extended to connect with the Central of Georgia main line at Bleecker, Alabama.[3] The passenger schedules of the CVR were slow, inefficient, and inconvenient, however, and the few travelers who used this line had to flag down the slow-moving trains to make connections with equally dilatory Central of Georgia locals.[4] Inevitably, the Chattahoochee Valley Railway discontinued passenger service in the 1940s, but CVR trains continued to contribute to the growth of the Valley region by providing almost a century of excellent freight service.[5]

In Macon County, the historic town of Tuskegee and its famous Tuskegee Institute enjoyed the benefits of a short-line railroad that branched from the Western Railway of Alabama at Chehaw. The Tuskegee Railroad was incorporated in 1860 and the entire six miles of track were in operation between Chehaw and Tuskegee when the Civil War began. All the trackage was destroyed during the war, but in 1871 several Tuskegee investors, led by E. T. Varner, purchased a 2-4-2 Tank locomotive, a passenger coach, baggage car, two boxcars, and two platform cars, and restored the road to full operation as a three-foot-gauge line. Varner eventually widened the road to standard gauge, obtained better equipment, and diligently labored to provide a reliable rail connection for the citizens of Tuskegee until his death in 1918. The railroad subsequently changed hands several times, but until it stopped operating in 1963, thousands of passengers bound for Tuskegee Institute changed cars at Chehaw to ride the steam powered trains of the Tuskegee Railroad.[6]

A few miles to the west along the Western Railway of Alabama's track, another short-line railroad was carving out a niche in central Alabama's cotton trade. One of the oldest cotton mills in the state, owned by the Tallassee Falls Manufacturing Company, was perched upon the banks of the Tallapoosa River at Tallassee. With power supplied by a dam across the river, the mill grew steadily until mule teams were unable to keep up with the plant's output, and the owners decided to build an eight-mile short line to connect the mill with the Western Railway of Alabama at Milstead, Alabama. The Tallassee & Montgomery Railway was soon chartered and the first sections of standard-gauge track were spiked into place in September 1895. On February 6, 1896, a train pulled by a locomotive called the *Anna Roman* steamed into Tallassee. The engine was named for a mill owner's daughter and was a wonderment to myriad river residents who had never before encountered an iron horse. To reach mill structures on the west side of the river, the company erected a new bridge that accommodated both trains and wagons.

On April 15, 1912, the Tallassee & Montgomery Railway was purchased by the Union Springs & Northern Railway Company, headed by noted Alabama contractor William Blount. Blount had built this seven-and-one-half-mile short line in 1901, giving Union Springs an interchange with the Seaboard Air Line Railway at Fort Davis. In 1904 the Union Springs road obtained trackage rights over the Seaboard into Montgomery, but Blount was not satisfied with this arrangement. In 1911, reflecting his ambitions, the US&N changed its corporate title to become the Birmingham & Southeastern Railway, and Blount unveiled plans to link Fort Davis with the soon-to-be-acquired Tallassee & Montgomery Railway as the first step on the way to Birmingham. Twenty miles of new Birmingham & Southeastern trackage was operational between Fort Davis and Milstead by June 1912, and one year later the road reached Eclectic, Alabama, fourteen miles northwest of Tallassee. Blount was well on his way to Birmingham.

Blount's blueprint called for a continuation of the line through the pine forests of central Alabama to Pell City, where coal could be picked up for southbound trips to the newly opened port at Panama City, Florida. But Blount's aspirations stalled at the town of Eclectic when World War I brought an abrupt end to short-line financing. Nevertheless, Blount had overcome considerable adversity in forging his forty-eight-mile short line. On one occasion the Central of Georgia Railway characteristically resisted Birmingham & Southeastern plans to cross Central track at Union Springs. The crossing was sanctioned by the city, however, and Blount kept laying track until he reached the Central's right-of-way. Just as the crossing was about to be installed, the C of G defiantly blocked the way with a column of boxcars. This provocation caused Blount to burn with indignation, and he impulsively ordered his locomotive to ram the barricade. A ravaging blow left the cars in splinters and paved the way for installation of the crossing diamond. Although the crossing was made, the bitterness and suspicion wrought by this action forced Blount to maintain a guard at the crossing for years to come.[7]

The hardships of World War I were followed quickly by the disastrous floods of 1919, which swept away large sections of the roadbed from Tallassee to Milstead. A surging torrent of muddy water also fractured the upriver dam, and it had to be replaced at great expense. All this adversity led to receivership in 1920. Passenger traffic dwindled, and patronage of any note was found only between Tallassee and Milstead. Seeking to reduce expenses wherever possible, the receivers replaced steam passenger trains with cost-efficient gasoline coaches in 1923. In that fateful year the company's fortunes began to improve, however. The railroad received a vital shot in the arm when the mills were expanded by 50 percent and the Alabama Power Company started a massive dam construction program on the Tallapoosa River.

Two years later the railway was reorganized as the Birmingham & Southeastern Railroad, and joint projects were initiated in collaboration with the Alabama Power Company to support work at the river sites. Alabama Power crews added a branch to the Eclectic line near the Elmore County community of Kent that snaked to the site of Martin Dam, ten miles from Tallassee. Over the next ten years, as many as 125 cars per day followed this circuitous route over high trestles, as the B&SE moved gigantic volumes of material and equipment for the dam projects. Traffic was so heavy that the B&SE had to rent locomotives from the Western Railway of Alabama in order to haul the 22,000 carloads of material eventually required to build Martin Dam. Track was laid across Martin Dam after it was finished so that supplies could be moved to the east side of the Tallapoosa River to be used in the construction of Yates Dam, three miles upriver. The business boom on the B&SE continued with the construction of Thurlow Dam at Tallassee.

The power plant projects were extremely profitable and represented the zenith of glory for the Birmingham & Southeastern. Unfortunately, this work tapered off just as the Great Depression descended upon America. Boom-time business fell relentlessly into an abyss of desolation, and by the mid-1930s the B&SE had abandoned the Eclectic branch. Soon only a single mixed train survived on the Tallassee–Union Springs run. It left Tallassee each day at 5 P.M. and sometime between two and nine o'clock next morning it ascended the three-quarter-mile grade into Union Springs. More often than not, the combination coach and baggage car that trailed behind the freight cars was devoid of passengers. Finally, in May 1937, the engine pulling this train took on water and rode the turntable at Union Springs for the final time.

The Birmingham & Southeastern Railway owned two steam locos: a Rogers 4-6-0 and this secondhand 2-8-0 manufactured by the American Locomotive Works (Alco) in 1912. Number 200 is pictured at Tallassee, Alabama, on July 21, 1938. (From the author's collection)

The B&SE struggled to provide a full range of services on its remaining Tallassee-Milstead line, but trucks were taking more and more of the mill business. The quaint little gasoline coaches, called doodlebugs, hauled riders until 1955, when patronage slipped to less than a hundred paying customers per month and all passenger service had to be discontinued. While freight and passenger business decreased in proportion to the increase in the numbers of automobiles and trucks rolling along Route 229, the little railroad still retained a profitable U.S. Postal Service mail contract. Beginning in 1955 the B&SE operated three mail trains a day between Tallassee and Milstead. At Milstead, speeding Western of Alabama express trains caught mail sacks on the fly and threw incoming mail to the platform to be retrieved by waiting B&SE crews. In 1964 operating expenses were trimmed further when a section-gang motor car was modified to handle the mail runs. But it was too late. The B&SE lost the mail contract three months later. Despite determined cost-cutting and modernization measures, including the complete dieselization of the road on May 18, 1953, business continued to vanish. Finally, on March 5, 1965, the B&SE was abandoned entirely.[8]

In a throwback to antebellum days, the trams of this lumber mill at Mount Vernon used primitive wooden rails. (Postcard ca. 1908, from the author's collection)

The Birmingham & Southeastern went the way of dozens of short-line railroads in Alabama. Unlike the B&SE, however, the preponderance of Alabama short lines did not depend upon a manufacturing base such as the textile trade. In the Heart of Dixie, short-line railroads were mainly needed for one purpose—to gain access to natural resources and bring them to the main-line railheads.

Alabama has been blessed with an abundance of natural resources. In addition to the rich mineral wealth of the central and northern counties, virgin forests covered the state, with great stands of yellow pine timber particularly plentiful in south Alabama. For decades these ample forests were scarcely exploited, and trees were more often felled for subsistence needs than for commerce. Then, about 1880, things began to change. As the white pine forests of the Great Lakes and New England were inexorably depleted, lumbermen turned to Alabama tim-

The Lathrop-Hatten Lumber Company had an extensive rail operation at Riverside, near Pell City. This turn-of-the-century photograph shows a quaint Lathrop-Hatten 0-6-0 locomotive working the St. Clair County woods. (Courtesy of Robert A. Scarboro, Scarboro Photo Shop, Gadsden, Alabama)

ber to replenish their rapidly dwindling supplies.[9]

In 1879 Alabama mills produced 17 million board feet of hardwood and 235 million board feet of softwood lumber. Twenty years later, these figures stood at 109 million board feet and 992 million board feet, respectively. This phenomenal growth brought attendant transportation problems. No longer could logs be hewn exclusively from easily accessible waterfront tracts and floated down creeks and rivers to the mills. Lumbermen were pushing deeper into the woods, and they needed reliable methods to extricate the timber from the forest depths. After experimenting with primitive log-moving methods such as gravity trams and pole-roads, Alabama lumbermen realized that the steam locomotive was the answer to their transportation needs.[10]

Special geared locomotives, such as the Shay and Heisler designs, were well adapted for forest operation and eventually became commonplace throughout Alabama's piney woods.[11] The Lima Locomotive Works manufactured nearly three thousand Shays between 1880 and 1945, and a large number of them ended up in Alabama. In the basic Shay design, the boiler was shifted slightly to the left to make room for vertical cylinders on the right side of the locomotive. The cylinders

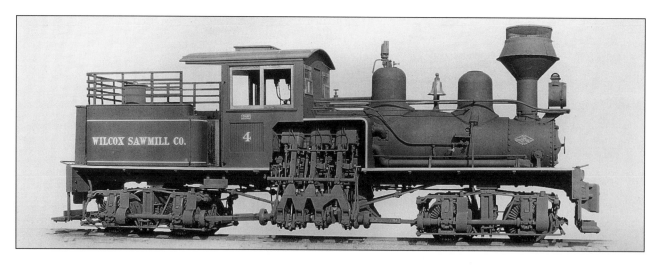

The Shay was a popular locomotive on the logging railroads of Alabama. These engines were identified by the number of wheel assemblies (each carrying four wheels) called trucks, *which were used to power them. Both two-truck and three-truck Shays were employed in the state. This two-truck version, built in 1920, was used by the Wilcox Sawmill Company on its three-foot-gauge line at Flatwood, Alabama. (Courtesy of DeGolyer Library, Southern Methodist University, Ag82.232)*

turned a shaft that was connected by beveled gears to the trucks. The Heisler operated in a similar manner but looked much different. A cylinder was mounted at a forty-five degree angle underneath each side of the Heisler's boiler. These two cylinders acted on a shaft that ran the length of the Heisler and turned axles at the extreme ends of the engine. The other wheels of each truck received power through outside connecting rods.

The Shay was commonly employed on Alabama logging railroads because it could efficiently work the steep grades encountered in the forest. This engine typically could manage a speed of four to six miles per hour while pulling a heavy load on a 7 or 8 percent grade.[12] Before the Shay became so popular, however, some of the earliest logging locomotives to be used in Alabama were traditional road switchers that the logging companies obtained secondhand from the major interstate railway companies. Although all these types of locomotives represented a huge initial capital investment, they provided great cost advantages. One engine could replace as many as thirty teams of oxen, with resulting cost savings of up to 75 percent.[13]

The iron horse largely defined the nature of the lumber business in Alabama. Expensive logging railroads were cost-effective only when employed amid vast concentrations of dense forest. It was estimated that one million board feet of timber had to be cut along each mile of track for rail operations to be profitable. Only large, well-financed businesses could afford the hefty investments in extensive expanses of timberland as well as the railroads necessary to work them. To increase their revenues per track-mile, the big operators purchased small, widely dispersed tracts and consolidated them into compact, well-wooded empires that could be effectively serviced using a minimum of track-

age. The dominant enterprises therefore had a voracious appetite for timberland that they satisfied by buying out small operators, who were unable to compete with the efficiently tracked giants and sold out to them. On the other hand, the large operators realized the importance of concentrating holdings into cohesive units and generally respected each other's territorial claims.[14]

Among the largest pioneer logging enterprises in the state was the W. T. Smith Lumber Company, with extensive operations near Chapman, Alabama. In 1891 Smith purchased the Rocky Creek Lumber Company, which had placed a one-locomotive logging line in operation three years earlier. Smith built an extremely successful business and by 1895 was ready to lay twelve more miles of track. Alabama loggers prudently trimmed expenses by purchasing or leasing used equipment whenever possible, and Smith was no exception. Smith planned to lease used steel rails from the L&N in an effort to reduce construction costs for this new section of track. With the money saved, he could purchase more land. A letter regarding this lease from the Old Reliable's traveling freight agent to the general freight agent at Montgomery yields some interesting insight into the competitive structure of Alabama's logging industry and the influence the iron horse had upon it. "Mr. Smith wishes this matter settled as quickly as possible," the agent wrote, "in a manner which will leave his capital largely in his own hand, so that he can at once proceed to buy up and otherwise secure the timber throughout as much of this section as possible, thus

Coxheath Lumber Company No. 5 is typical of the two-truck Heislers used in Alabama. Note the rods connecting the wheels of each truck. (Photograph ca. 1920, courtesy of DeGolyer Library, Southern Methodist University, Ag82.232)

The SS Trunk B. Jordan *proved that the Shay locomotive could go almost anywhere, when this diminutive engine crossed the muddy Tallapoosa River in Elmore County with its train of two log cars. (Photograph ca. 1900, courtesy of the Alabama Department of Archives and History, Montgomery, Alabama)*

cutting off the supply from the various little mills already existent there, *thus stopping them,* and securing the product via Chapman at the same time. . . . By helping Mr. Smith to get his road in, we not only place ourselves in position to handle this business, lumber and all, but we assist in developing a section of the country agriculturally, whose outlet will naturally be our own line." The L&N's development policy in this case was clearly discriminatory. Nonetheless, the main-line railroad executive and logging entrepreneur alike considered their monopolistic actions to be merely sound business practice that would bring lasting benefits to the entire region.[15]

Although all main-line roads traversing lumber company territory obligingly accommodated the loggers whenever possible, conflicts were not unknown. In one celebrated case, Tuscaloosa's J. L. Kaul wanted to build a branch of his lumber railroad across the Mobile & Ohio's main line. If Kaul did this, all through traffic on the M&O would be forced to stop at the crossing in compliance with ICC regulations. The M&O

refused to allow the crossing, but was rebuffed in court and Kaul laid his track as planned.

Even though lumber company executives tried to minimize their track mileage, many of the woodland roads grew to comprise a considerable right-of-way. Many lines were narrow gauge and some were standard gauge, but all emphasized cost-cutting and efficiency. Engineers and firemen frequently doubled as shop personnel when repairs were needed.[16]

Kaul's track layout was typical. Forty-five miles of branch track radiated from a main stem that extended for thirty miles into the woods. Unfortunately, every ounce of timber along a branch was hewn down to justify the expense of building the line. Even small trees were chopped to the ground to be used for fence posts. Virtually all the loggers practiced clean cutting, and when the timber along a branch was totally exhausted, the light rail was torn up and moved to an unexploited section.[17]

Dozens of these little railroads dotted the state in the first quarter of the twentieth century. Almost all of them have disappeared into the mists of time, but for a while they were a fascinating part of Alabama's landscape. The following brief sketches describe some of the more notable of these quaint old railroad companies.

Alabama Central Railroad. At least four different companies proudly assumed this name. The South & North Alabama Railroad was originally called the Alabama Central, and shortly after the Civil War the Selma & Meridian Railroad also used this name. Then, an Autauga County sawmill road organized in 1903 decided to adopt the same corporate title. This nine-mile road connected Autaugaville with Booth and served the intervening sawmill at Forrest, Alabama. The company abandoned the track between Forrest and Autaugaville in 1936, and by 1940 the same fate befell the entire line.[18] The fourth incarnation of the Alabama Central was incorporated in 1906 and operated as a sub-

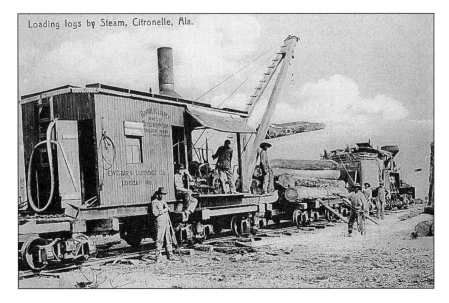

Loading logs by Steam, Citronelle, Ala.

Steam log loader and log car pulled by a Shay type locomotive at Citronelle, Alabama, near the turn of the century. (Postcard from the author's collection)

stantial nine-mile coal-hauler extending from Marigold to an interchange with the Frisco, Southern, and Illinois Central at Jasper. Although a coal-hauler, this line used at least one logging locomotive—a 2-truck Shay—as well as two 2-6-2s, a 2-6-0, three 4-6-0s, and three 2-8-0s.[19]

Alabama, Florida and Gulf Railroad. On August 16, 1910, W. S. Wilson and E. L. Marbury organized a sawmill road called the Alabama, Florida & Southern that ran northward from Malone, Florida, to join the Atlantic Coast Line Railroad at the Houston County village of Ardilla. Wilson bought Marbury's interest in the road and then acquired another Houston County sawmill pike that operated between Cowarts and Cottonwood, Alabama. In 1917 Wilson laid additional track to Greenwood, Florida, and incorporated the consolidated standard-gauge system as the Alabama, Florida & Gulf.

Wilson was quite proud of his two-locomotive line, and each year he sent annual passes to the presidents of all the country's big-time railroads, expecting them to reciprocate. One year, Wilson didn't receive a free pass from the Pennsylvania Railroad, and when business took him to Philadelphia, he decided to find out why. He boldly dropped into the office of the president of the "Standard Railroad of the World" and demanded to know why he had not been issued a complimentary pass. "I appreciate your pass, Mr. Wilson," the PRR president offered, "but it is impossible for us to send annual passes to every small railroad president in the country. After all, our railroad is thousands of miles long, and yours is only 32 miles long." "Well," Wilson huffed, "your road may be longer than mine, but mine's just as wide as yours." With that, Wilson got his pass. His railroad never achieved the status he thought it deserved, however, and the Alabama, Florida & Gulf went out of business around 1934.[20]

Alabama & Mississippi Railroad. Fifteen years after being organized in 1902 by the Vinegar Bend Lumber Company, this standard-gauge pike wound through seventeen miles of pine forests between Vinegar Bend, Alabama, and Leaksville, Mississippi. The road used at least one Shay of 1910 vintage.[21]

Alabama & Tombigbee Railroad. Incorporated in 1898, this line was operated by the Scotch Lumber Company and extended from Eugene to Fulton, Alabama. Connection was made at Fulton with the Southern Railway's Mobile branch. This railroad had a marvelously diversified stable of engines, including a 2-4-0, three two-truck Shays, four

three-truck Shays, a 2-4-4 Tank locomotive, two 4-6-0s, one 2-6-0, and a 2-8-0.[22]

Brewton Railroad and Transportation Company. This road's lone locomotive was a hand-me-down from the Wabash Railroad. Could this have been the legendary *Wabash Cannonball?* Actually an Alabama Great Southern express that ran through Birmingham in the 1880s was referred to in local newspapers as the "Cannon Ball."[23]

W. P. Brown and Sons Lumber Company. A far-flung enterprise for a logger, the corporate offices of this company were located in Louisville, Kentucky, and its plants were situated in Florida and Mississippi as well as Alabama. The Brown company got its start in Alabama when it purchased the Baskett Lumber & Manufacturing Company in July 1919. Sometime around 1912 Baskett had organized a logging road to serve its mill at Fayette, and had twenty-five miles of track in operation along the swampy Sipsey River bottomlands when Brown acquired the road. The little town at the end of the track became known as Brownville, and by 1926 the railroad's main stem was extended south from this point to join the M&O at Buhl, a few miles west of Tuscaloosa. All the property was then transferred to a newly incorporated subsidiary that Brown optimistically called the Mobile & Gulf Railroad. As a common carrier, the Mobile & Gulf operated a daily mixed train between Fayette and Buhl, but riders were hard to find. For the entire year of 1934 the conductor punched tickets for only sixteen passengers. Passenger business ended for good in 1948 when the mill at Fayette burned and all the trackage between Fayette and Brownville was abandoned.[24] A single 2-6-0, which the engineer kept parked in his back yard when not in use, continued to run on the remaining trackage until 1970, when it was traded for a diesel.[25] This was said to

In 1915 the Lima Locomotive Works manufactured this 2-8-0 for the Scotch Lumber Company, owner of Alabama & Tombigbee Railroad. The Alabama & Tombigbee Railroad lasted longer than most logging pikes in Alabama, but when the road faltered in 1928, this loco was relieved of its piney-woods chores and banished to duty at a Selma gravel pit. (From the author's collection)

be the last steam engine to see regular service on a common carrier in the United States.

In the early days, Brown Lumber Company had an impressive, eclectic array of locomotive power. Rosters listed at least eleven engines, including two 2-6-0s, 0-4-0 and 0-4-2 Tank Locos, three two-truck Shays, two 4-6-0s, and a 2-8-0. This railroad presumably also owned a Heisler or two.[26]

Choctaw Lumber Company. The little Choctaw County hamlet of Bolinger was named for Sanford Henry Bolinger, the Kansan who came to Alabama in 1915 to acquire land and build the Choctaw Lumber Company. He soon had standard-gauge trains working the Choctaw and Washington County woods all the way to Silas and Yellow Pine. It must have been a locomotive enthusiast's dream to behold the variety of engines Bolinger used. In addition to four common Shays, a two-truck Heisler, two Climax locos, a 4-6-0, and an old 4-4-0 imported from the Galveston, Harrisburg & San Antonio Railway also roamed the woods in the finest logging railroad tradition.[27]

Escambia Railroad Company. Organized around 1890 by a group of Mobile and Pensacola investors, the Escambia Railroad was a subsidiary of the Alger-Sullivan Lumber Company, which operated a big sawmill at Century, Florida. With 197 miles of track stretching through Escambia, Monroe, and Conecuh counties, as well as the Florida panhandle, the Escambia Railroad was one of the longest sawmill roads in the state, and probably operated the largest fleet of logging locomotives in the Southeast. In Alabama, the Escambia Railroad effected a connection with the L&N at the village of Mous, near Manistee Junction, in Monroe County. With such a large amount of main line, the Escambia Railroad used more traditional types of road locomotives, mostly 2-6-0s and ten-wheelers.[28]

Frost-Sibley Lumber Company. Lamison, Alabama, was a real railroad town. Established in 1888 on the Mobile & Birmingham Railway, it was named for the community's first depot agent. In 1900 the Frost-Sibley Lumber Company built a good-sized logging railroad into the piney woods from Lamison. The sights and sounds of the log trains abounded until the mill burned in 1928 and all the railroad equipment was relocated to Alberta, Alabama, where it functioned faithfully until 1932. Meanwhile, in the spring of 1923, Frost-Sibley established another line that ran for about eight miles out of Yellow Bluff, Alabama.

Frost-Sibley owned an interesting mixture of both narrow- and standard-gauge motive power. At least four two-truck Heislers, an 0-4-0 Tank, three two-truck Shays and a two-truck Climax graced the road's roster.[29]

E. E. Jackson Lumber Company. The E. E. Jackson Lumber Company was one of the most extensive lumbering concerns in the state and was responsible for the creation of at least two Alabama towns. With a Mr. Rider as company president, this firm was logging the prolific woods of Choctaw County as early as 1840, and the community of Riderwood bears this pioneer president's name. In 1910 the company entered Covington County and founded the town of Lockhart, while erecting the largest lumber mill in the state. The company also maintained substantial lumbering facilities at Riderville, in Chilton County, although this town's name is not credited to the lumber establishment's president. Although Lockhart track was standard gauge, a curious forty-one-inch gauge was used at Riderville and Riderwood.

Eventually, the Jackson Lumber Company railroads acquired new names. The rousing title of Dixie Route was bestowed upon the Jackson Lumber Company successor at Riderwood, while the property at Riderville became known as the Riderville, Centerville & Blocton Railroad.[30]

Kaul Lumber Company. Another of the major builders of logging railroads in Alabama, J. L. Kaul had interests in standard-gauge railroads at Birmingham, Sylacauga, and Tuscaloosa. At peak activity, Kaul had more than seventy-five miles of right-of-way. With such extensive trackage, Kaul motive power was generally heavier than that of other logging lines. Four three-truck Shays were the mainstays at Tuscaloosa. An ex–New York Central 2-4-4 of 1891 vintage is said to have been acquired in 1919. Several Kaul locomotives eventually were transferred to the Sylacauga & Wetumpka Railroad, the company's Talladega County subsidiary.[31]

Kentucky Lumber Company. Two Frisco Railroad officials were honored in Lamar County when their names, Sullivan and Sargent, were combined to name the town of Sulligent. Sulligent's railroad heritage was embellished when Harris, Cole & Company bought a Porter 0-4-0 Tank locomotive from Birmingham Rail and Locomotive Company in 1911, painted *No. 1* on the cab, and started hauling logs out of the woods. Pleased with the results, the railroad expanded by purchasing a new Lima Shay in 1911. This successful operation did not go unnoticed, and in 1915 the Kentucky Lumber Company came to town and bought the railroad. Not only green trees but cash of the same color abundantly flowed from this operation, and as more new locomotives were added to the roster, the line provided a steady source of income for a goodly number of Lamar County citizens over the years.[32]

Manistee & Repton Railroad Company. In 1900 the Bear Creek Mill Company built this railroad through the thick Monroe County forests to connect its big but isolated piney woods sawmill with the L&N Railroad some twenty miles to the east at Repton. The county seat at Monroeville shared the sawmill's isolation and its inhabitants also yearned for a connection with the L&N. In 1912 Monroeville's dreams came true when the Manistee & Repton Railroad was extended five miles to reach this ambitious little town in the center of the county. A few years later the M&R also made a connection with the Gulf, Florida & Alabama Railway. Although the Manistee & Repton Railroad was a great benefit for Monroeville, it was never profitable, and eventually all the original trackage was abandoned in favor of a new four-and-one-half-mile connection into Monroeville from the L&N's Selma-Pensacola main line.[33]

T. R. Miller Mill Company. In 1848 a water-driven timber mill was opened in a rustic section of Escambia County by the Cedar Creek Mill Company. The mill grew over the years under various owners, including T. R. Miller, and was eventually relocated to Brewton as a steam-powered plant. The company laid some railroad track in 1904 and joined the half-dozen or more logging firms whose railroads laced the Escambia County forests. Under T. R. Miller's enlightened management, the company was one of the first to practice selective cutting, initiate other conservation programs, and build more than sixty miles of woodland railroad.[34] These astute business decisions enabled T. R. Miller Mill Company to grow and thrive over the years, and a great number of steam engines consequently appeared on its locomotive roster, including six 2-8-0s, two 2-6-0s, a 4-6-0, a 2-6-2, a couple of tank locos and a two-truck Heisler.[35]

Nadawah Lumber Company. In keeping with the widespread trend in Alabama, many Monroe County communities owe their existence to the railroad. The little village of Beatrice was named in honor of the daughter of the general superintendent of construction for the Selma-Pensacola branch of the L&N as it cut through the center of the county. Meanwhile, the Pine Forest Lumber Company quietly brought logs to this railhead. In 1910 the Nadawah Lumber Company bought this little logging line and established a town bearing the company name. Standard-gauge track eventually connected Nadawah with Beatrice, and for several years echoes of Shays and Heislers drifted across the tranquil landscape of this isolated region. After the logging trackage was abandoned in 1928, the L&N continued to keep Nadawah in touch with the outside world by sending a daily passenger coach to the lonely little community for another six or seven years.[36]

Oak Grove & Georgetown Railroad. The M. L. Davis Lumber Company originally established this narrow-gauge line, sending three Shays and two 4-4-0 type locomotives scurrying through the Mobile County forests to fetch carloads of timber for interchange with the M&O at Oak Grove. The Oak Grove & Georgetown took over and expanded operations by adding more equipment. In 1916 the OG&G owned six locomotives, forty-four log cars, three flats, a boxcar, and a caboose. The flourishing right-of-way must have been well maintained, since a rail loader, tie car, and a couple of camp cars were also on the property list. Twenty-five years later, nothing remained of the Oak Grove & Georgetown Railroad.[37]

W. T. Smith Lumber Company. Smith's railroad was one of the most expansive in the state, eventually growing to more than one hundred miles of track. The company was owned by Birmingham businessman W. T. Smith, who bought and developed an established Butler County lumbering enterprise in 1891. His efforts were highly successful, and by 1895 the L&N was hauling more than two million pounds of Smith's forest products each year. Shortly after the turn of the century Smith had five locomotives of his own in service. It is said that three of them were named *Helga, Georgia,* and *Mary* in honor of Smith's daughters.

Smith's policy regarding personal use of railroad equipment was typical of the industry. The sawyers were generally permitted use of the motive power for trips from the isolated campsites to town and to church. Large groups of workmen and their families made such journeys sitting on benches nailed to the flatcars. A big barrel of drinking water was a welcome amenity as a sweltering sun filtered through the pines onto the converted flatcars.

Will McGowan, who inspected the camps for Smith, tells of one Sunday when a locomotive was mysteriously missing from the Black Rock Camp. It was learned that one of the loggers had "borrowed" the loco to go to Chapman. On the return trip, the engine collided with another locomotive, causing extensive damage. The loghand-turned-

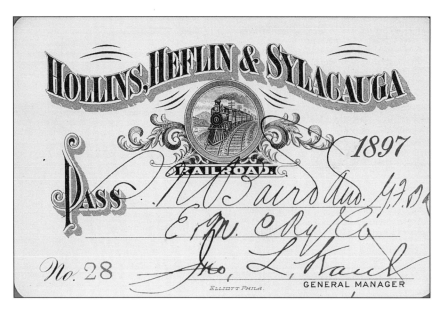

engineer escaped, and needless to say, was never heard from again. Later, Smith tried to provide adequate passenger service by using a gasoline powered coach, but the experiment failed because of the want of passing-tracks.[38]

Sylacauga & Wetumpka Railroad. The Sylacauga & Wetumpka Railroad bears a distinction not shared with many other Alabama logging railroads: It shows up on old railroad maps. Originally organized under the name Hollins, Heflin & Sylacauga Railroad, the road comprised approximately sixty miles of main line that eventually stretched between Sylacauga and Wetumpka. The Sylacauga & Wetumpka Railroad was a Kaul subsidiary and six Kaul standard-gauge Shays found their way onto this road before it was abandoned in 1927.[39]

Vredenburgh Sawmill Company. The countryside along the Alabama River in Wilcox and Monroe counties supplied enough forest products to keep several logging companies in operation. In fact, business was so brisk in 1900 that the Louisville & Nashville Railroad built a sixteen-mile branch from its Selma-Flomaton main line to serve the growing community of Camden. A few miles south of Camden Junction, at the settlement of Corduroy, the standard-gauge track of the Vredenburgh Sawmill Company also joined the high iron of the L&N.

Using at least eight Shays, a Baldwin 4-6-0, and three Baldwin 2-8-0s, Vredenburgh Sawmill Company delivered log tonnage to the L&N at Corduroy and to the Gulf, Florida & Alabama Railway at Vredenburgh Junction.[40]

As the twentieth century dawned, the logging industry continued to grow steadily in Alabama, motivating the L&N to join the lengthening list of roads dedicated to its development. In 1905 a new L&N subsidiary called the Bay Minette & Fort Morgan Railroad penetrated the thirty-seven miles of dense Baldwin County pine forests between Bay Minette and Foley, Alabama. After a few years of intensive logging, however, the forests in this part of the state were depleted, and the area was in danger of becoming a wasteland of pine stumps. But the L&N continued the colonization policy that had brought thou-

Few artifacts remain from Alabama's logging railraods. Among them is this 1897 annual pass for the Hollins, Heflin & Sylacauga Railroad, predecessor of the Sylacauga & Wetumpka Railroad. The pass is signed by John L. Kaul, a major builder of logging railroads in the state. (From the author's collection)

sands of settlers to Alabama, and the Old Reliable's agricultural development incentives eventually attracted many new immigrants to Baldwin County. Working closely with the L&N Railroad, these new settlers cleared the stumps from the clean-cut acreage and developed it into excellent farmland. Over the years, these farms yielded bumper crops that were hauled over what came to be known as the Foley branch of the Louisville & Nashville Railroad.[41]

The vast majority of other logging railroads in Alabama were not as fortunate as this branch of the L&N, however. Trucks relentlessly replaced the log-hauling locomotives, and by the 1940s most Alabama lumber lines lay abandoned, their roadbeds choked with thick underbrush. Nevertheless, a few of the woodland roads successfully diversified and became thriving regional short lines.

In 1905, wood-burning locomotives of the Enterprise Lumber Company, owned by wealthy forester A. B. Steele, scurried over extensive land holdings south of Dothan. As Steele's light rail penetrated Florida's Panhandle, he set ambitious goals for his modest pike. With the L&N's northwest Florida main line within reach, Steele planned to extend his road and connect it with the Old Reliable at Cottondale, Florida. Steele would then have an important bridge line to ferry Central of Georgia traffic from Dothan to the Sunshine State.

Steele was keenly aware that his railroad occupied a strategic location between Atlanta and the Gulf of Mexico. Atlanta was rapidly becoming the commercial hub of the South, and the Panama Canal was about to open. Just south of Steele's railroad lay undeveloped St. Andrews Bay, touted as the most promising spot to locate a Panama Canal shipping port. The alluring prospect of owning exclusive facilities for funneling vast volumes of trans-Canal traffic between Atlanta and the superb deep water of St. Andrews Bay was irresistible.

Ink was barely dry on the contract for the Cottondale extension when Steele resolved to press his railroad to the Gulf. As he cast about for a suitable terminus on St. Andrews Bay, G. M. West of the Gulf Coast Development Company suggested a site near the little fishing village of Harrison. Steele and an entourage of planners trekked across the state line to examine potential terminal properties and were highly impressed with the Harrison location. Harrison was not the largest town on the bay, but it was most favorably situated with respect to the deep-water shipping lane. Steele selected Harrison as the terminus, and chose a route that would also serve the German-American Lumber

A. & St. A. R.R. Wharf, Panama City, Fla.

The Atlanta & St. Andrews Railway acquired six 4-6-0 Tenwheelers between 1907 and 1913. Numbers 105–107, 120, and 121 were Baldwin locomotives. Number 110 was a Brooks product of 1892 that was purchased as a used loco in 1907. (Postcard ca. 1909 from the author's collection)

Company at Millville, which employed approximately fifteen hundred workers, as well as the oystering center of St. Andrew, with a population of 600. Numerous turpentine stills along the right-of-way also promised additional traffic. The principal outlet for area products had been Pensacola, but now thousands of northwest Floridians looked hopefully to Steele to provide a gateway to northern markets.

Steele incorporated the Atlanta & St. Andrews Bay Railway and moved construction rapidly forward until June 29, 1908, when 250 passengers swarmed aboard A&SAB coaches at Dothan and rode to St. Andrews to celebrate the road's grand opening. The A&SAB built terminal facilities at Harrison that stimulated the settlement's growth. In 1909, the town of Harrison further promoted its Panama Canal prospects by formally changing its name to Panama City.[42]

Lean times almost immediately befell the A&SAB, however, and they lingered after Steele's death. Minor C. Keith, an executive of the United Fruit Company, purchased the struggling short line as part of a plan to establish a banana terminal at Panama City that would rival the largest one on the Gulf at Tampa. But these plans fell through when the railroads serving Tampa collectively reduced their freight rates, making it impossible for the proposed Panama City banana port

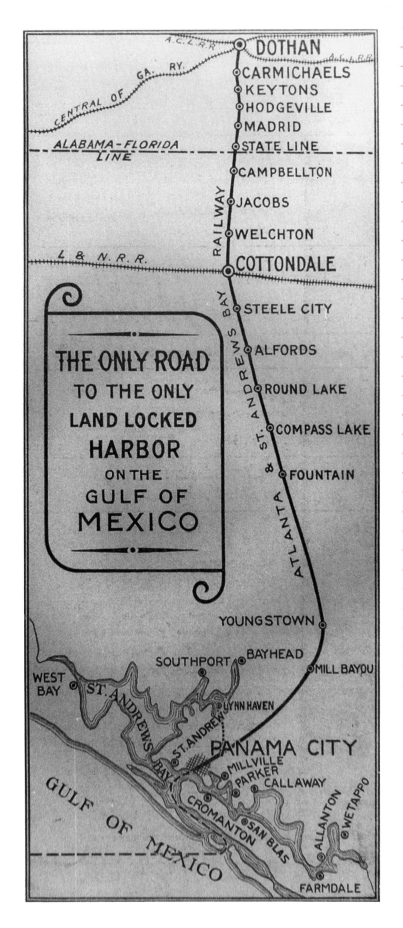

Atlanta & St. Andrews Bay Railway Route Map. (From the August 28, 1913, public timetable, courtesy of William Stanley Hoole Special Collections Library, The University of Alabama, Tuscaloosa)

to be competitive. Thus, on the eve of the Great Depression, the A&SAB barely survived by hauling meager ladings of forest products, naval stores, and a few other commodities, and by operating underutilized passenger trains. The outlook for the railroad could hardly have been more bleak, but in 1929 the Southern Kraft Division of International

Paper Company announced that it would build the first paper mill in Florida at Panama City. An International Paper Company affiliate, the Saint Andrews Bay Holding Company, purchased the A&SAB and appointed John A. Streyer, former vice president of the American Short Line Railroad Association, as general manager. Streyer initiated a modernization program that called for heavier rail and new diesel-electric loco-

Bay Line No. 143 was one of six Alco 4-6-2 Pacific type locomotives acquired from the Florida East Coast Railway in 1934 and 1935. Numbers 142, 143, 145, and 146 were built in 1920, while No. 131 was built in 1917, and No. 154 was new in 1922. (From the author's collection)

motives, and in 1937 he became president of a much healthier road. Under Streyer's expert guidance, the A&SAB became one of the premier short lines in the country. Annual revenues soon topped the one-million-dollar mark, enabling the line to be ranked as a Class I railroad, and in June, 1947, the Atlanta & St. Andrews Bay Railway became the first Class I railroad in the United States to become fully dieselized.

During World War II the defense buildup at Panama City greatly boosted traffic. A&SAB trains worked Wainwright Yards, a shipbuilding center that produced 106 big cargo ships, as well as Tyndall Field Army Air Base and other military installations. At the Panama City suburb of Lynn Haven, the U.S. Navy operated a petroleum terminal that generated 60,000 tankcar loads of oil that the A&SAB transported to inland points using 110-car unit trains. Passenger traffic was discontinued on July 15, 1956, because of slack demand, but freight traffic kept growing in the decades after the war, and the A&SAB continued to prosper. Although Panama City never fully achieved its ambitions as a Gulf shipping center, the city still developed into an important industrial location and tourist destination. Dothan and Panama City owe a large measure of their dynamic achievements to the railroad that came to be called affectionately the Bay Line.[43]

In the center of west Alabama's logging country, another story of short-line success may be told. In the late nineteenth century, Pickens County residents were unhappy when they were bypassed by the M&O's Montgomery extension, and clamored for rail service when rumors that the M&O would build a branch from Reform to Carrollton proved to be unfounded. In 1900, John Cochrane of the Tuscaloosa Belt Line satisfied this demand when he started laying track from Reform to Carrollton. The ten-mile-long connection, called the Carrollton Short Line, was immensely popular when placed in service in 1902. A Pickens County old-timer recalled the excitement created by the Carrollton Short Line. "Often there would hardly be standing room on the trains," he recollected. "Most of the travel was from one station to the next, and often the entire train would change crowds at a station. Whole families would go to Tuscaloosa or Columbus by train just to be riding a train."

People flocked to the railroad to escape the vexations of riverboats and muddy turnpikes. The insignificant settlement of Reform was transformed into a bustling railhead, and Gordo became a big sawmill town. It seemed that everyone wanted to live near the iron pike, and the resulting migration eventually turned many river communities into ghost towns.

Even before the Carrollton Short Line reached its namesake terminus, a movement was afoot to extend the line further southward. Cochrane would have pushed ahead immediately but was delayed when a quarrel erupted over the possibility that a Vicksburg-Birmingham rail project might preempt the extension. Undeterred, Cochrane bought thirty-six acres of disputed land in 1902 and prosecuted the extension with bold determination. In the middle of his newly acquired property, Cochrane laid out a new town to be named after his wife, Alice. Soon trains were running through Alice City and all the way to Bridgeville.

Initially, the Carrollton Short Line was far from a first-class road. Minor accidents were commonplace, and train service was often suspended for several days at a time while repairs were made. Still, Cochrane

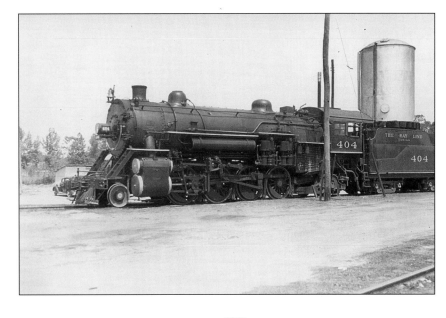

The Bay Line acquired its first Mikado type locomotive in 1936 when a thirteen-year-old Brooks 2-8-2 was added to its motive-power roster. During the next two years the road obtained four additional Schenectady-built Mikes from the New York Central Railroad. A&SAB nos. 401, 402, and 403 were built in 1907. Number 404, shown here in 1940, was built in 1905. (From the author's collection)

Alabama, Tennessee & Northern passenger train, pulled by a Baldwin Tenwheeler No. 302 at Mobile in the 1920s. The AT&N employed at least seven 4-6-0s at various times. Number 302 was ordered new from Baldwin in 1910. (Courtesy of Robert A. Scarboro, Scarboro Photo Shop, Gadsden, Alabama)

persevered, and in 1907 his newly founded village of Alice City was incorporated as the town of Aliceville. Three years later, as the Carrollton Short Line continued to creep southward, Aliceville's population had surged to all of sixty-four inhabitants. Despite this slow growth, Cochrane was convinced that Aliceville would become one of many railroad boom towns if his tracks could reach the Gulf.

With this in mind, Cochrane moved to Mobile in 1905 and acquired the narrow-gauge Tombigbee & Northern Railroad. Changing both the gauge and the name, Cochrane pushed his Tombigbee Valley Railroad northward with the same energy he had shown in Pickens County. When the Tombigbee Valley and Carrollton Short Line finally converged at the lumbering center of Riderwood, Cochrane revealed his ultimate aim by assigning the name Alabama, Tennessee & Northern Railroad to the conjoined system.

Like Steele's Bay Line, the AT&N never totally fulfilled Cochrane's ambitions. Likewise, even though Cochrane's tracks could advance no further north than Reform, his road developed into a vital lifeline for

isolated west Alabama communities. In 1928 the AT&N reached the docks at Mobile and made another important connection when the Frisco crossed its tracks at Aliceville.

In 1932 the AT&N became the only railroad in Mobile to own marine facilities when car ferries were purchased to transport freight cars from the west bank of the Mobile River to industrial locations on the east bank, as well as Blakely Island. This equipment was of great advantage during World War II, as 26,000 cars were ferried to and from the shipbuilding sites on Blakely Island. After the war, the AT&N became one of the first fully dieselized line-haul railroads in the United States. The AT&N further modernized its equipment over the ensuing decades, and eventually consummated an operating alliance with the Frisco.[44]

Like many of her main-line predecessors, the Alabama, Tennessee & Northern Railroad had opened extensive areas of west Alabama for settlement and development. In addition to Aliceville, the little hamlets of Panola, Emelle, Lisman, and Toxey were brought to life by the AT&N.

Alabama, Tennessee & Northern Railroad No. 204 is shown as it rolled off the Lima Locomotive Works assembly line on a snow-covered day in January 1922. After it was shipped to its home in South Alabama, this 2-8-0 would seldom again encounter snowy weather. Altogether, Lima constructed five of these Consolidations, nos. 202–205 and No. 250, for the AT&N between 1920 and 1925. The AT&N also owned another Consolidation, No. 201, that had been purchased new from Baldwin in 1912. (From the author's collection)

Alabama, Tennessee & Northern Railroad tracks paralleled the Alabama-Mississippi border for about 200 miles northward out of Mobile. This map, from an AT&N public timetable of November 14, 1937, gives the impression that the route was much longer. (Courtesy of William Stanley Hoole Special Collections Library, The University of Alabama, Tuscaloosa)

To this list may be added the names Allison, Bellamy, Buhl, Fulton, Hull, Kellerman, Manchester, Searles, Sanford, Wadsworth, and other communities that were founded by various short-line and logging railroads. This list grows larger and larger when the towns established by the major roads are considered. From Atmore to Birmingham, from Frisco City to Tunnel Springs, from urban centers to rural waystations, Alabama was built with railroad track, and much of it was laid by short lines and sawmill pikes.[45]

The AT&N joined the Bay Line as an example of survival and growth through competent management. Both roads found their niche as reliable freight haulers and were content to continue to serve the little towns along their line faithfully. The more glamorous aspects of railroading were left to their powerful regional brethren that graced Alabama main lines with fast expresses and streamlined flyers.

14

ALABAMA VARNISH

Heavy coats of varnish were applied to early passenger cars to protect and improve the appearance of their wooden bodies. This practice earned passenger trains, especially the more elegantly appointed ones, the nickname of "Varnish." In the earliest days of railroad travel, however, elegance was something totally lacking. Sultry Alabama summers brought stifling heat to the cramped cars and when relief was sought by opening windows, billowing smoke and flying cinders added to the discomfort. Winter travel was even worse. With no ventilation, cars were stuffy and became choked with a smoky haze when the wood-burning stove was fired up. Passengers closest to the stove suffered suffocating hot blasts, while those further away shivered in an unwarmed draft as the heat dissipated before reaching them.[1]

In horse and buggy days, the average Alabamian seldom traveled; and he watched in awe as the varnished trains raced past the family farm en route to mysterious, faraway destinations. Nevertheless, infrequent travelers in remote stretches of the state welcomed the convenience of passenger trains. Timid first-time railroad patrons often greeted the newfangled contraptions with expressions of wonderment. Mrs. Ella S. Witherill was a telegrapher on the Alabama & Chattanooga Railroad shortly after the road opened and related the following anecdote: "After the road was completed, on one trip there was but one passenger for some distance. At one station he stepped off in time to see an old man and his wife in the act of boarding the train. It was so evidently their first experience in traveling that the passenger watched them through the car window. As they entered the door the man reverently removed his hat. Both of them gazed about with wonder at the red plush-covered seats and the small stove at the end of the car—for in those days steam heat had not yet arrived. Slowly they advanced down the aisle. At length the wife started to sit down, when the old man frantically clutched her arm, exclaiming: 'Ol' woman don't set down on that thar little bed! They'll bring us some chairs purty soon.'"

Trains were slow and schedules were light in the early days. As a consequence, conductors frequently took unusual liberties. Mrs. Witherill explains: "The writer was on that road [A&C] more than once, when it would suddenly stop right in the woods, near a blackberry patch, and the call would ring out: 'Twenty minutes for blackberries,' when train crew and passengers would join in picking and eating as many as they could, even filling any stray receptacle that might be found on the train."[2]

For a while, meandering local passenger trains adequately served the modest needs of most Alabamians. But steadily advancing operating and safety improvements inexorably quickened the tempo of travel. In 1869 George Westinghouse invented the air brake and liberated brakemen from the treacherous hand-braking chore that had claimed too many lives. Then automatic couplers came on the scene to prevent countless other tragedies. Reluctant railroads were forced to adopt these exigencies when the Safety Appliance Act was passed in 1893.[3] Heavier steel rails were installed that could withstand the pounding of speedier and more powerful locomotives and, with the standardization of track gauge, the way was paved for the fast through trains that were destined to glamorize rail travel. Soon, long-distance travelers could comfortably settle into one of George Pullman's sleeping cars for rapid interstate journeys. The era of the Limited had dawned.

As early as 1874 the New Orleans, Mobile & Texas Railroad showcased a fast 4-4-0 locomotive that sped two coaches of theatre aficionados on a quick round trip between New Orleans and Mobile. Riders on the well-publicized *Barrett-Lightning Matinee Train* arrived at the theatre in Mobile two hours and forty-seven minutes after leaving New

Central of Georgia and Western of Alabama tracks crossed at Opelika. The depot was on one side of the crossing diamond and Hick's Cafe was on the other. The dining room was a welcome sight for hungry train crews and passengers. (Postcard ca. 1908, from the author's collection)

Orleans. They were back home in New Orleans three hours and eleven minutes after the final curtain.[4]

By the early 1880s the L&N advertised Pullman Palace sleeping cars on two northbound and two southbound runs out of Birmingham (train nos. 1, 2, 3, and 4). These cars ran straight through to Louisville and New Orleans without change, although meal stops were made at Mobile, Montgomery, Birmingham, and New Decatur. Schedules for these trains were quickly accelerated. Train no. 2 maintained the benchmark time between Louisville and the Crescent City of thirty-five hours. Train no. 3 soon shaved three hours from this time. Finally, nos. 1 and 4 cut their running time to a mere twenty-six and one-half hours. By the 1890s traffic grew so heavy over this route that two more trains were required. Train nos. 5 and 6, with a New York–New Orleans–Galveston sleeping car in the consist, were placed in service south of Montgomery. When the Old Reliable added three dining cars to its passenger fleet in 1901, two of them were assigned to train nos. 1 and 4 between Birmingham and New Orleans.[5]

By the 1890s, old open-platform coaches were supplanted by closed-vestibule cars. Glamorous names had not yet been assigned to varnish, and trains with these cars were simply but liberally advertised as "Vestibules." The East Tennessee, Virginia & Georgia Railway built solid vestibuled trains especially for the 1893 Chicago World's Fair. The *World's Fair Limited* was touted in Alabama newspapers as the fastest through service to the fair from the South.[6] Also in 1893, the Queen & Crescent Route advertised the regularly scheduled *New Orleans Vestibule,* "a solid vestibuled, gas-lighted, Pullman-built, quick-scheduled train, solid from baggage car to sleepers," that ran between Cincinnati and New Orleans via Birmingham.[7]

About the same time, the Southern Railway operated its *Vestibule* between Washington and New Orleans using a route that would prove to be increasingly popular. The Southern pulled the train to Atlanta, where the West Point Route took over for the trip to Montgomery. The West Point Route was the holding company for the roads that connected the capital cities of Alabama and Georgia—the Atlanta & West Point Railroad and the Western Railway of Alabama. At Montgomery, an L&N locomotive was coupled to the *Vestibule* for the run to New Orleans. This train was a grand success. Its route was extended to New York and it became known as the *Washington and Southwestern Vestibuled Limited.* The New York–New Orleans run was soon being made in the unheard-of time of forty hours. Included in the train was the first dining car to be placed in service between the Big Apple and the Big Easy. After vestibules became a familiar sight on most railroads, this train became simply known as the *Washington and Southwestern Limited*. In 1906 a club car and observation car were added and the name was again changed. This time it was called the *New York and New Orleans Limited* and was advertised as a "year round exclusive Pullman car train."[8]

Near the turn of the century, this West Point–L&N route through Alabama formed part of a famous transcontinental run known as the *Washington Sunset Route*. "Sunset Tours" Pullman Tourist Sleeping Cars were carried over this route between Washington and the West Coast. The train ran three days per week and made the trip from Washington to San Francisco in five and one-half days. The West Point Route operated the train from Atlanta to Montgomery, where L&N train nos. 2 and 3 took over.[9]

The 4-6-0 Tenwheeler was the Western Railway of Alabama's standard passenger and freight locomotive from the 1880s until the second decade of the twentieth century. When the company purchased new Pacific and Mountain types for high-speed passenger runs, and Mikados for mainline freight hauls, the proud, once-dashing Tenwheeler was relegated to thankless duty on W of A locals. In this scene, No. 131, an Alco-Richmond product of 1913, waits patiently for baggage handlers to perform their duties at Montgomery's Union Station on September 5, 1934. Two sister 4-6-0s built by Alco-Richmond in 1911 and 1912 remained on the W of A loco roster when this photograph was made, as well as eight Tenwheelers manufactured by Rogers between 1899 and 1907. (From the author's collection)

The increased traffic along this Washington–Atlanta–Montgomery–New Orleans route justified a new depot at Montgomery. For years, Alabama Railroad Commission reports had complained of insufficient and dangerous depot facilities at Montgomery, and in 1896 the L&N Railroad took steps to rectify these deficiencies. The Old Reliable planned to build a splendid Romanesque structure covering two and one half acres near the Exchange Hotel that would serve all the railroads entering the capital city. When Union Station opened with much fanfare on May 6, 1898, passengers were no longer subjected to the dangers of crossing congested terminal trackage to reach their trains. Engineering techniques used to construct the Eiffel Tower in Paris were adopted to equip Union Station with an impressive six-hundred-foot-long train shed that spanned three sets of platform-separated tracks.[10]

From December 1902 until January 1907 one of the most famous passenger trains in history thundered over this famous route through Montgomery. *Fast Mail Train No. 97* originated in Washington, D.C., with a solid consist of mail cars bound for Atlanta over the Southern Railway. At Atlanta, passenger accommodations were coupled to the

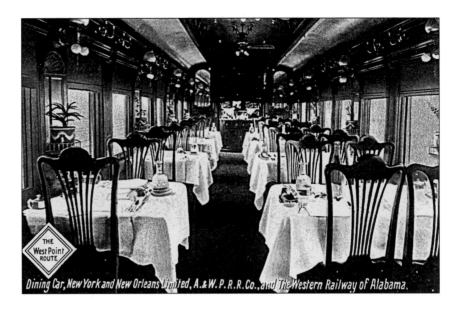

Dining Car, New York and New Orleans Limited, A.&W. P. R.R. Co., and The Western Railway of Alabama.

With its ornate decor, fine dinnerware, and excellent service, the dining car of the West Point Route's New York–New Orleans Limited *was the epitome of luxurious train travel. (West Point Route advertising postcard, ca. 1907, from the author's collection)*

Front view of Montgomery's Union Station. Part of the train shed can be seen behind the station. (Postcard ca. 1908, from the author's collection)

The Pacific was a rare breed of locomotive on the Western Railway of Alabama. A 4-6-2 was delivered from Rogers in 1907, followed by another one from Richmond in 1910. These were sold, however, in 1934 and 1936, respectively. Meanwhile, a new Lima Pacific, No. 190, had been added to the roster in 1926. This engine, shown here at Atlanta in 1935, was assigned specifically to The Crescent Limited, and until it was retired in 1954, was the W of A's most modern passenger steam power. (From the author's collection)

Dining Room Private car Fritzi Scheff on The West Point Route between Atlanta and Montgomery.

THE
West Point
ROUTE

Fritzi Scheff was a notable turn-of-the-century opera singer and stage star. In this promotional picture issued by the West Point Route, Fritzi poses in the elegantly appointed private car that the railroad provided for her concert tours. (West Point Route advertising postcard, ca. 1907, from the author's collection)

rear, and the train was turned over to the West Point Route. "Old No. 97" sped out of the Peach State over the road built by Charles Pollard to make a connection with the L&N at Montgomery. From there, the Fast Mail headed for New Orleans under full throttle.[11]

In a 1905 *Atlanta Constitution* story, Roscoe W. Gorman captured the excitement this train generated. Gorman was privileged to ride in the cab of "Old 97" on a night when she overcame an untimely mechanical failure to set a speed record. This night's work was a historic success, but two years later a tragic mishap in Virginia would immortalize this train and inspire the famous ballad "Wreck of the Old 97."

Western of Alabama 4-8-2 No. 187, ready to highball out of Montgomery in 1936. In that year the W of A purchased three of these twelve-year-old Alco-Schenectady Mountain types, nos. 185–187, from the Florida East Coast Railway. They were added to a roster that already boasted of two Mountain types, nos. 180 and 181, that had been ordered new from Alco-Richmond in 1920. With over 44,000 lbs. of tractive effort, they were the W of A's most powerful passenger steam engines. (From the author's collection)

THE FLIGHT OF THE MIDNIGHT MAIL

A few nights ago No. 97, the fast mail on the Southern Railway, dropped down the Atlantic seaboard and reached Atlanta considerably late. It had done its work well. Leaving the great metropolis, it skimmed the Jersey marshes and thundered through towns and cities. Gathering momentum with each hour, it hurled itself through space like a catapult until the Gate City of the South was reached. Here, panting and quivering, it came to a stop, while the dust settled slowly around the wheels.

Engine No. 16 of the West Point Route, lithe and keen, stood under the west end of the old shed, and in the gloomy glimmering of the electric lights among the iron girders it looked like an iron greyhound. It stood about sixteen feet above the water line of the worm-eaten floor, and breathed like a thing of life. Back behind it, like the tail of a kite, there stretched four cars.

In the mail cars all was confusion. Brawny negroes hurled dozens of sacks of mail into the open doors, while the clerks worked rapidly. L. D. McDonald, a big blonde Scotchman, with clean blue overalls, oiled the mammoth machinery and caressingly wiped away a bit of grease here and there that interfered with the beauty of the 16. Jackson, the faithful fireman, touched up bolts and stirred around getting ready for the 175 miles down to the first capitol of the Confederacy. Up and down the shed Conductor John Harrison stirred, hurrying up everything and everybody, for the schedule was then thirty minutes to the bad, and he knew that the dispatcher was worried, and that the train sheet for No. 97 was the first thing that went under the president's eye in the morning. In the hands of these two men, McDonald and Harrison, lay the honor of the company that night. Strong, honest and handsome, they looked like the men such a company would select for such arduous and responsible duties. The schedule must be made. The mail must go into Montgomery and save the company the forfeit, and then, too, there were a number of passengers hurrying southward who had spent the last minute in Atlanta and the East and then took the last train.

There is a last hurried rattle of the mail trucks, a conglomeration of noises, and "All aboard"—the least jar, a puff of white smoke out of the 16's stack, a glimmer of steel in the electric light and Montgomery was eighteen feet nearer.

Down there a half-asleep hostler slowly backed a Louisville and Nashville engine on the turntable and began getting ready for 97 over the Louisville and Nashville for New Orleans. The Montgomery dispatcher was calling East Point, and then College Park, to know if 97 had passed, but it was winding through a mystic maze of green, red, and white lights through the Central railroad yard. A lone policeman on the Mitchell Street viaduct watched the electric light on the engine come into sight and fade into the red light on the rear end in another moment, and the city slipped suddenly away. High up in the air the red light changed to white at McPherson, when the 16 called for the semaphore, and the throb of the engine rose to a higher note.

East Point flared up in the darkness and a cloud of dust at the street crossing and all was still, while the calliope whistle asked the operator at College Park if all was well.

Off of the double track and out in the open 97 slipped into the night, Captain Harrison took up the tickets in the back coach, and the mail clerks worked with prodigious energy assorting the great pile of mail. The immense driving wheels were hammering the fish plates and the exhaust had grown into a titanic hum. The headlight cast ghostly glances athwart the landscape and the train seemed to be standing still, with the entire territory in front of it rushing toward it with feverish haste.

[The fireman] opened the furnace door and dropped in a few shovels of coal and the glow from the furnace door lit up the whole country in the rear. The heavy rails and the ballast held the cars steady, but the pace now and then threw the conductor or the mail clerks to one side or caused a piece of mail to miss the sack thrown at. There was a low hum of the calliope and 97 dropped into and out of Red Oak like a bird swoops through the air. The little tombstones in the country cemetery glimmered a moment in the light and disappeared, and the 16 steeled down like a horse with a good road and loosened bit until Fairburn, Palmetto and Coweta were passed and with a whir the train hustled into Newnan with a smoking hot box on a Pullman car and a record of 39 miles in 43 minutes.[12] Jacks and lever and brasses were thrown out. Willing men went to work. The train dispatcher at Montgomery was impatiently calling the operator at Newnan—"See that those fellows get a move on them and get out of there, at once." Newnan's eastbound freight trains were seeking sidings down the road. The station master at Montgomery was marking up 97 half an hour late. The 133 miles of silence that lay between Newnan and there were oppressive with their great distance. McDonald and Harrison worked as hard as men ever worked. The possibilities of missing connections were great. The United States mail was being delayed. Passengers were fretting. Armed with a permit from the proper officer, I climbed up into the fireman's seat and watched McDonald, serious and cool, climb into his, I saw his hand reach over and release the airbrakes, drop the lever forward and with hand on throttle lean out of the window and watch the gloom behind for a signal. At last the light stabbed the air as it waved him forward, the 16 jumped like a frightened bird. Newnan was slipping by!

The time card called for 97 to be in Montgomery in 135 minutes and it was 133 miles away. When 97 does not make the schedule, the cause for it must be shown on the president's desk next morning. We slowed down at the Carrollton crossing and in a moment whirled past the Pearl Springs park. As we took the curves, I leaned heavily inward to help balance the engine, which seemed to be instinct with life [*sic*]. Back in the night the green light glowed like the ghosts of stars and the dust there kept time to the general roar. All at once a bright light flashed into my face, there was a crash like a broken glass and Moreland went by to eastward. The switch light had destroyed my peace of mind with a jar that took my nerve. The momentum grew terrific. I tried to speak to the fireman, but my voice made no sound. I saw a twinkling of light, like fireflies on a dark background, or the moving of a man of war, and wondered, but the whistle told me it was Grantville. With three fingers on the throttle and his body half out of the window, McDonald leaned into the darkness and the whirlwind of sound and dust and leaves eddied into lovely little Hogansville and swept again into the outer world.

There seemed to grow in the darkness vast and fantastic shapes as forest or farms whirled into view and disappeared to make room for others. I felt someone looking at me, and McDonald was looking at his watch by the one small light. He smiled at the time card hanging in front of him and caressed the throttle seriously, looked at the fireman and the steam gauge and back into the night. Afar I saw the twinkling of many stars, as I thought, but in a moment LaGrange seemed to be coming madly up the hill and at us. I watched the brass handle turn and heard the hiss of air, and saw the sparks flying from the wheels, and, lurching half over, I caught myself as we drew up at the depot. There was a hurried alighting from the train, a few trunks off and on, and into the night 97 went again like a mad charger. Twelve minutes later we were peacefully getting water at West Point, and twenty minutes later Conductor Harrison was registering at Opelika, 22 miles away. Then again we were off, but I was in the back coach. Sixty-six miles away at Montgomery, the station master climbed up to the board and marked down the half hour sign to ten minutes. Down into Auburn 97 was falling like the stars fall in the sky. Its whistle awoke the echoes in the hills and startled the night birds from their haunts. Loachapoka was passed in a few moments, leaving a long freight with wondering crew looking after the apparition. Then Notasulga and Chehaw and Milstead came sliding up the steel rails toward 97, while the pace grew more furious. There was no time to talk. The coaches rolled uneasily as they took the curves, the whistle moaned uneasily above the hurricane of sound, while the roar was as of a great battle. And it was. It was the battle of business, where the diligent alone succeed. Down the hill at Chehaw we rushed, while under the engineer's call the red light was turned to white and the miles were rolled up under the 16 like thread on a spool. Thirty-nine miles in thirty-seven minutes was the record, and around the long curves leading into Montgomery this thing of steam and steel and human endurance swept, while the astonished depot employees could hardly believe their senses. The long night's ride was over and one of the world's records had been made. Every night over this superb road one of the mighty engines and brave engineers, with a gallant crew, makes exceptional speed, and here and there some phenomenal record is made.

Only the finest roadbed and the best rolling stock can stand the strain, and the West Point road is not egotistical when it claims the best.

When an ordinary passenger and mail train, without any preparation, puts its speed up to 5,280 feet every fifty-two seconds and holds it there for hours, it is something to talk about, and this record is in black and white on the train sheet in Montgomery, which tells the story of the lives and work of the heroes who make and keep the reputation of the midnight mail.[13]

Using the Old 97's route between Washington and New Orleans, the Southern Railway, Western Railway of Alabama, and L&N collaborated to usher in some of the most famous and beautiful trains in the world. The *Piedmont Limited* was inaugurated in 1925 and became a favorite for business travel between Atlanta and New Orleans. In April of the same year, the successor of the pioneer *Vestibule* went into operation when the all-Pullman, extra-fare *Crescent Limited* made its inaugural run from New Orleans to Washington over the same route. A beautiful two-tone green Southern K-4s Pacific was used between Washington and Atlanta and became so popular that the entire train of Pullmans was repainted in a similar gold-trimmed paint scheme in 1929. Unfortunately, the Great Depression caused the demise of the *Crescent Limited* and it was discontinued in 1934. A toned-down *Crescent* appeared in 1938 with air-conditioned coaches.[14]

The West Point–L&N route via Montgomery and Mobile was the most popular for trains bound for New Orleans from the East, but heavy passenger traffic also sped through Alabama en route to the Crescent City from the North. The L&N's South & North Alabama Railroad subsidiary should have captured much of this business, but Milton H. Smith disdained passenger trains and considered them to be a drag on more profitable freight operations. Indeed, he suffered little adornment of his equipment. It is said that he once refused to paint some rusty old switch engines, declaring that they would not haul one ton more of freight if a new coat of paint were applied. He was particularly overwrought when segregation policies required him to spend extra money furnishing separate accommodations in his coaches. Therefore, the Queen & Crescent Route happily filled the role abdicated by the L&N.[15]

Near the turn of the century the Queen & Crescent Route operated a New Orleans–Cincinnati through train known as the *Pan-American Special* which stopped at Birmingham's Union Station on northbound and southbound runs each day. Morning and afternoon Q&C "Limiteds" also lingered in Birmingham for five minutes on their journeys between Cincinnati and New Orleans. Other fast through trains stopping at Birmingham at that time were the Frisco's *Southeastern Limited* as well as the Louisville & Nashville's train nos. 1, 2, 3 and 4.

The iron boom brought a swell of immigrants to Alabama, and the ensuing bust only tempered the inflow. By the turn of the century, immigrant traffic into Birmingham was augmented by a growing number of passengers changing trains for other destinations. In 1903, sixty-two regularly scheduled passenger trains were carded into Birmingham's Union Passenger Station and it was obvious that expanded terminal facilities were

Mobile's Grand railroad station. (Postcard ca. 1915, from the author's collection)

necessary at the Magic City.[16] In 1907 Mobile answered her expanding passenger station needs by erecting a grand domed terminal.[17] Not to be outdone, Birmingham interests commissioned the design of the most lavish railroad palace in the South.

A consortium of railroads serving the Magic City appointed architect P. Thornton Marye to design a magnificent example of Byzantine architecture covering five city blocks, and organized the Birmingham

Terminal Company to manage the new station. The L&N and Atlanta, Birmingham & Atlantic railroads were not members of the consortium, choosing instead to continue using Union Station, six blocks southwest of the new station. Unfortunately, the contractor was unable to erect the building within the original budget and schedule, and after more than a year of delay, with costs spiraling relentlessly upward, the frustrated railroad consortium was forced to take up the construction business. The building had already cost the railroads much more than they had bargained for, so they dispatched their own crews to the construction site with orders to finish the job at the smallest possible cost. This meant that some of the office space and other planned amenities had to be deleted. Nevertheless, Terminal Station was a two-and-one-half-million-dollar sensation.[18]

The grand opening of this "Temple of Travel" on April 6, 1909, was one of the most auspicious occasions ever witnessed in the city. The coach yard was filled with the private cars of visiting dignitaries, and the station itself was gaily decorated with bunting and flags. The formal celebration began when two large balloons ascended from Capital Park and raced over the city. Next on the agenda was a "monster parade" that included seventy uniformed policemen, sixteen carriages bearing railroad officials, 150 couples from the riding club, an artillery battery, and several bands. Business establishments and residences along the parade route were lavishly decorated, and the crowd was large and enthusiastic.[19]

At the station, this crowd viewed an imposing facility bordered to the west by 26th Street, to the east by 28th Street, and enclosed by Second Avenue to the south and Seventh Avenue to the north. Stretching 785 feet between Fourth and Sixth avenues, the structure would have blocked Fifth Avenue, so a fifty-six-foot wide, seventeen-foot high subway was tunneled underneath the station in order to accommodate the wagon and automobile traffic. The subway emerged onto a plaza in front of the station.

At the rear of the station, the tracks led to a 40-by-271 foot con-

Terminal Station, looking West from 26th Street, Birmingham, Ala.

Birmingham's Terminal Station. (Postcard ca. 1910, from the author's collection)

course called the "Midway." To the north of the Midway was a large wing reserved for express companies; to the south an equally ample wing accommodated baggage and mail. Architect Marye shielded the station's tracks with a unique train shed that he described as a revolutionary design:

> The train shed, constructed of reinforced concrete, is 780 feet long, covering two platforms and four tracks, and 630 feet long, covering three platforms and six tracks. The total width is 210 feet over five platforms 19 feet 6 inches each in width, and two single and eight pairs of tracks.
>
> To avoid the "cutting" of trains and the crossing of tracks by the passengers a passenger subway twenty-eight feet in width, with nine feet clearance, is constructed under the train shed, with two stairways to each platform, and entrance and exit stairways with gateways on the midway. The passenger subway has an exit stairway to the Fifth Avenue subway. The roof of the midway is of reinforced concrete with skylights.
>
> The train shed is a series of connected "umbrella sheds." The sheds over the platforms are low, clearing the tops of the coaches only a few inches, while the sheds over the tracks have a clearance of twenty-one feet above the rail, and overlap the platform sheds, thus affording protection from weather and giving ventilation and light without the use of skylights.

Marye was convinced that this concrete shed would be far superior to traditional ones made of steel and wood, but with use, it proved to trap too much smoke and was eventually replaced by a conventional shed.

Entering the main waiting room from the Midway, the traveler found every imaginable convenience. As Marye describes, every effort was made to efficiently accommodate every member of the traveling public:

> In the center of the station building is located the general waiting room with smoking room, barber shop, ladies' waiting room, news and refreshment stands, telegraph and telephone booths, ticket office and information bureau adjoining.
>
> In front of the main waiting room and facing the plaza is an arcade twenty feet in width, with vaulted ceiling of tile, from which may be entered direct the smoking room and ladies' waiting room. This arcade is entered under cover of a marquise of iron and glass.
>
> To avoid congestion due to the waiting room being used as a passageway, two covered concourses, thirty feet in width, on the north and south of the main waiting room, connect the midway with the plaza. The refreshment stand, news stand, telephone and telegraph booths and information bureau are located on the east side of the main waiting room, so as to be accessible from the midway. To the left of the north concourse, as you enter, are located the lunch room, dining room, service rooms, kitchen, etc. The lunch

room, designed and thoroughly equipped for quick service, is reached from both the concourse and midway, the dining room being located in the front as far as possible from the noise of trains. Serving rooms are provided between the lunch room, dining room and kitchen, and connecting with the latter is a large store room and refrigerating department. On the right of the concourse is the station master's office.

To the right as you enter the south concourse is located the waiting room for colored people, with the smoking room, woman's retiring room, toilet rooms and lunch counter adjoining. The ticket office is located between the south concourse and the main waiting room, so as to be accessible to both white and colored passengers. The checking space of the baggage room opens both into the south concourse and midway, so as to be equally accessible to both races.

The necessity for separated accommodations for the two races, which is now required by statutes in most of the Southern States, creates a problem not met with in the planning of stations in other sections of the country. The accommodations for the colored race are required to be equal in every respect to those for the white people, and the economy of operation requires that they be so located as to be accessible to the ticket office, baggage rooms, etc., and prompt service rendered without material increase in the operating force of these departments.[20]

The doors of Birmingham's Terminal Station were thrown open just in time to welcome the golden age of the passenger train. Passenger trains had ascended from the mundane world of hauling travelers to become exalted stars of the rails. No longer were they "Limiteds" or "Fast Mails." Better, more descriptive names were required. Terminal Station now hosted the *Birmingham Special, Kansas City–Florida Special, Sunnyland, Cotton States Special, Robert E. Lee, Crescent City Special,* and *Seminole.*

The original *Birmingham Special* ran over the Southern Railway between Washington and the Magic City via Atlanta. Later, it was replaced on the timetable with the *Southerner* and *Washington, Atlanta and New Orleans Express,* which used the same route before going on to New Orleans. To save time, the *Birmingham Special* did not stop in downtown Atlanta and zipped into Alabama over the old Georgia Pacific route through Anniston. The name *Birmingham Special* was later assigned to train nos. 17 and 18 that entered Birmingham over Alabama Great Southern tracks via Lynchburg, Virginia, and Bristol, Tennessee. The Southern Railway also operated the *Memphis Special* and the *Tennessean* over the Lynchburg-Bristol-Chattanooga route, but they veered west at Chattanooga and followed David Hubbard's pioneer Tennessee Valley right-of-way into Memphis.[21]

Unusual concrete train shed at Birmingham's Terminal Station. (Postcard ca. 1910, from the author's collection)

Section of general waiting rooms, Terminal Station, Birmingham. (Postcard ca. 1910, from the author's collection)

The Frisco's *Kansas City–Florida Special* was handed over to the Southern at Birmingham and rolled into Jacksonville, Florida, via Atlanta and Macon. Another Frisco flyer, the *Sunnyland,* operated over the same route but terminated in Atlanta.[22]

The Seaboard Air Line also sent substantial passenger traffic to Birmingham. Shortly after the turn of the century the *Seaboard Mail* that ran between Portsmouth, Virginia, and Atlanta was extended into Birmingham with a sleeping car in tow. The sleeping car was switched to the Frisco for a fast run to Memphis. The *Seaboard Mail* maintained a regular schedule to Birmingham until the late 1920s. Later the *Seaboard Express* carried a café car as well as Pullmans into Birmingham from the Seaboard's main line junction at Hamlet, North Carolina. From Birmingham, the Frisco handled some of these sleeping cars into Memphis. In 1915 another Seaboard train known as the *Atlanta-Birmingham Special* ran to Birmingham. Then, in the mid-thirties, the Seaboard added the *Cotton States Special* and the *Robert E. Lee* to its Birmingham schedules. These luxurious air-conditioned trains carried a dining car, a lounge car, coaches, and sleeping cars. Seaboard advertisements proclaimed that "it's ten to fifteen degrees cooler in these two favorites— with noise, dirt and dust removed." The *Cotton States Special* stayed on the schedule until after World War II. Rounding out the SAL Terminal Station passenger offerings were the *Birmingham Owl* and *Atlanta Owl,* which provided overnight mail-express-passenger service between the two named cities. Each carried a Pullman sleeping car, and both were discontinued in the late 1930s. In addition to this extensive Birmingham timetable, the Seaboard also provided service to Montgomery by operating a daylight local between Savannah and the capital city.[23]

Over the years, through trains of the Queen & Crescent Route between New Orleans and Cincinnati bore names such as the *Cincinnati– New Orleans Limited, Crescent City Special,* and *Queen City Special.* Finally the *Queen & Crescent Limited* stopped briefly in Birmingham en route between the Queen and Crescent Cities. Connections to the East were

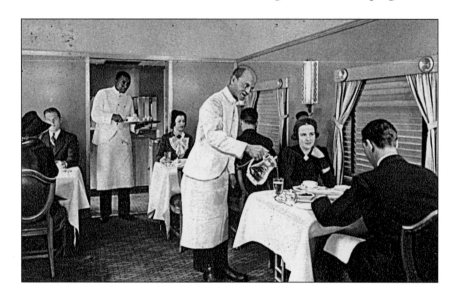

Frisco's Kansas City–Florida Special *carried a lounge-diner each way between Birmingham and Kansas City. (Frisco advertising postcard, ca. 1940s, from the author's collection)*

made at Chattanooga. In later years two of these trains ran through from New Orleans to Washington via Chattanooga.[24]

Louisville & Nashville passenger traffic in Alabama would not match that of its rivals as long as Milton H. Smith was president. After Smith's death in 1921, however, some of the most famous trains in the world were added to the Old Reliable's timetables. In the year of Smith's death the L&N inaugurated the *Pan-American,* train nos. 98 and 99, which carried Pullmans and coaches from Cincinnati to New Orleans via Birmingham, Montgomery, and Mobile. A dining car was included in the consist north of Birmingham. With daylight and evening runs, the *Pan-American* was so well patronized that new all-Pullman equipment was called for in 1925.

In the 1930s, Nashville's WSM Radio placed a microphone at trackside to pick up the sound of the *Pan-American* as it rushed by. The dramatic sound of the *Pan-American,* along with an announcement of the engineer in charge, was broadcast live every day except Sunday. For over a decade, Alabamians within range of this 5:07 P.M. broadcast were thrilled to hear the whistle of the *Pan-American* as it hurtled toward the state. When the train was late, subsequent programs would be interrupted while in progress to air the *Pan-American's* flight. But the train was rarely late and kept such a tight schedule that listeners could almost set their watches by the whistle.[25]

Delightful Meals are served in these Attractive L. & N. "Pan-American" Diners

Billed as "One of the World's Finest Trains," the Pan-American *advertised splendid dining car service. (L&N advertising postcard, ca. 1930s, from the author's collection)*

In 1935 the L&N placed another luxurious train on the main line from Louisville to Montgomery. The *Florida Arrow* pulled coaches and Pullmans to Alabama's capital, where the Atlantic Coast Line took over to guide the train to Jacksonville. Auxiliary tenders with the train's name proudly emblazoned across them in huge white letters were coupled behind the L&N's powerful L-1 Mountain type locomotives that were regularly assigned to the *Florida Arrow.* This distinctive feature made this train an endurance champion. Only one stop was made for coal between Louisville and Montgomery. Southbound, this was at Oakworth, Alabama.

Equipped with an auxiliary water tender, L&N 4-8-2 Mountain type locomotives powered the Florida Arrow *between Louisville and Montgomery. One of these locos, No. 416, is pictured being retired from service at Louisville after completing its final run with Train No. 10 on April 22, 1949. (Courtesy L&N Collection, University of Louisville Archives and Records Center)*

The *South Wind* ran over the same route beginning in December 1940. It ran every third day and whisked an all-coach consist from Chicago to Miami. To make the run as fast as possible, the Old Reliable tried to eliminate refueling stops completely. The most powerful Pacific type locomotive on the L&N roster was streamlined, fitted with an expanded capacity tender, and dedicated exclusively to this train. Tuscan red No. 295, equipped with roller bearing trucks, was one of three locomotives used on the *South Wind,* and set a world's record for avoiding coal chutes. The L&N boasted that the 490 miles between Louisville and Montgomery was the longest distance that any steam locomotive in the world ran with no fuel stop. Water was always needed at Nashville and Birmingham, however.[26]

In south Alabama, Flomaton was an important junction point and saw its share of passenger trains. In November 1924, at the height of the Florida boom, the *New Orleans Florida Limited* was carded over the L&N from River Junction, Florida, to New Orleans via Flomaton. The *New Orleans Florida Limited* was nationally renowned as the only train carrying a first-class coast-to-coast transcontinental sleeping car in America. The Pullman ran through from Jacksonville to Los Angeles over the Seaboard, L&N, and Southern Pacific lines.[27] The *Seaboard Mail and Express,* also carrying Pullman sleepers, operated between Jacksonville and New Orleans over the L&N's route through Flomaton. After World War II this train was replaced by the *Gulf Wind.*[28]

Meanwhile, the poor little Gulf, Mobile & Northern was struggling to provide passenger service to Mobile. Traffic to Mobile was extremely light over the GM&N and did not justify the expense of using steam-powered passenger trains. Therefore, in 1935 the GM&N replaced its passenger trains from Mobile to Jackson, Tennessee, with gasoline-powered motor coaches.[29] These motor cars appeared on other infrequently traveled roads as well and could be found on the Birmingham & Southeastern, the Bay Line, and the TAG Route.[30] Even the mighty Southern Railway used a similar diesel-powered car for local service in Alabama.

The GM&N caused quite a sensation across the South when it completely motorized all of its passenger operations, including the long-haul between Jackson, Tennessee, and New Orleans. The first streamlined diesel-electric passenger train to be placed in service in the South was assigned to this run. It was called the *Rebel,* and as the revolutionary streamliner slowly toured the country en route to GM&N tracks

Flomaton, Ala.

Flomaton, in South Alabama, was an important L&N junction point and a hotbed of railroad activity at the turn of the century. (Postcard ca. 1908, from the author's collection)

from its birthplace in Berwich, Pennsylvania, over 208,000 curious people lined up to see this new, highly publicized mode of travel. The GM&N claimed another "first" by employing hostesses on the *Rebel,* a feature that newspaper men along the line never tired of writing about. The *Rebel* was so popular that a similar streamliner called the *Mobile Rebel* was inaugurated in January 1938 to provide sleeper service between Mobile and Union, Mississippi. At Union, this new train connected with the older *Rebels* bound for New Orleans and northern destinations.[31]

These pioneer diesel-electric locomotives were the predecessors of many that were to follow. During World War II, demand for passenger service was so great that both steam and diesel power was used, but after the war the diesel was in ascendancy and new passenger trains would be exclusively diesel powered. One of the new diesel passenger trains that appeared shortly after the war was the L&N's *Humming Bird,* which ran between Louisville/Cincinnati and New Orleans.[32]

The Illinois Central Railroad had operated a through train from Chicago to Florida via Birmingham since 1909. The *Seminole Limited,* resplendent in its orange and chocolate livery, ran into Birmingham over IC tracks, where it was handed over to the Central of Georgia. Later, the *Seminole* was joined by the *Floridan* and the *City of Miami* to provide additional Pullman dining car service through Alabama en route to the Sunshine State. The *City of Miami* made its inaugural run in 1940 with a fast twenty-nine-and-one-half-hour every-third-day dieselized run between Chicago and Miami. This schedule produced a late-night meet of the northbound and southbound sections of this train near Alexander City, Alabama. The *City of Miami* complemented the every-third-day *South Wind* and *Dixie Flagler* that ran over a different route through Georgia. The *City of Miami* later handled Pullmans and alternated every second day with the *South Wind.* Initially, the IC provided the orange and chocolate motive power for the *City of Miami,* but the Central of Georgia eventually offered a matching unit.[33]

The *City of Miami,* along with the Seaboard's *Silver Comet* and the Southern's *Pelican,* was one of the final "name" trains to debut in Alabama. In 1947 Birmingham's Terminal Station was extensively renovated, but its usefulness was almost over. Automobiles and airplanes were insidiously and relentlessly eating into traffic, and the days of not only the name train but indeed all passenger business were numbered.

The Tennessee, Alabama & Georgia Railway owned two gasoline motor cars, No.
500, pictured here, and No. 501. (Photograph ca. 1930s, courtesy of Robert A.
Scarboro, Scarboro Photo Shop, Gadsden,
Alabama)

In 1947 the Bay Line purchased a new
EMD F3 diesel-electric locomotive, No.
1501, and assigned it to the passenger run
between Panama City and Dothan. All
passenger service on the A&SAB was discontinued on July 15, 1956. (Courtesy
of Quinton D. Bruner, Dothan, Alabama)

RIDE
"THE BAY LINE"
Gasoline Passenger Cars

▼

NO DETOURS
Takes You Direct to Your Destination

These all-steel passenger cars are operated on a
Double Daily Schedule between
Dothan, Ala., Cottondale, Fla., and Panama City, Fla.

▼

No Smoke, Cinders or Dust
Clean and Comfortable

▼

Ride these cars and avoid the dust,
dirt, the danger, crowded seats, and
close contact with diseased and un-
desirable persons encountered in
traveling by buses over the highway

Facts
About the Bay Line
Railway

▼

We pay $30,000.00 annually in taxes to Counties,
Cities and Towns.

Our annual pay roll is $130,000.00 which is spent
in the territory served by this road.

We buy annually $90,000.00 worth of material and
supplies and every item we can secure locally is bought
along our railroad.

▼

We furnish the public:

Double daily Mail Train Service
Double daily Express Service
Double daily Passenger Service
Daily Freight Service

▼

We provide Free Taxicab Service at Dothan and
Panama City to take passengers to and from trains and
their hotels or homes.

▼

When You Travel Ride
"The Bay Line"

When You Ship Use
"The Bay Line"

*This advertisement from the November 19,
1929, Atlanta & St. Andrews Bay Railway public timetable gave plenty of reasons for patronizing "The Bay Line."
(Courtesy of William Stanley Hoole Special Collections Library, The University
of Alabama, Tuscaloosa)*

GM&N's Rebel, *the first diesel-electric streamliner to operate in the South, was soon joined by the* Mobile Rebel, *which used the same kind of equipment. (Photograph ca. 1940, courtesy of the Birmingham Public Library Department of Archives and Manuscripts)*

The Gulf, Mobile & Ohio Railroad used distinctive Alco and Baldwin diesel-electric locomotives on its Southern Division when the road was dieselized in the 1940s. In this scene at the Mobile roundhouse, the Alco DL-109 diesel at the far left is flanked by three 1500-horsepower Alco FA1 freight locos and an Alco switcher. (Photograph ca. 1940s, courtesy of the Alabama Department of Archives and History, Montgomery, Alabama)

First-generation L&N diesel units show-cased against Birmingham's skyline in the early 1950s. (Courtesy of the Birmingham Public Library Department of Archives and Manuscripts)

Final Louisville & Nashville steam-powered passenger train leaves Birmingham's Union Station on January 27, 1951. This quaint local was a fixture on the Alabama Mineral Railroad for many years. It left Birmingham each morning, looped through Anniston and Gadsden, and returned to Union Station in the afternoon. (Courtesy of the Birmingham Public Library Department of Archives and Manuscripts)

During its heyday, fifty-four daily passenger trains stopped at Terminal Station. By the 1960s this figure had fallen to 26. One by one, the name trains were discontinued. The *Kansas City–Florida Special,* the *Silver Comet,* the *Seminole,* and the *Pelican* could no longer survive on their dwindling patronage. By 1967, all Frisco passenger trains ceased to run into Birmingham. Finally, on September 22, 1969, the wrecker's ball crashed through Terminal Station, signaling its demise.[34] Only a handful of passenger trains still served the state. Among those was the *City of Miami.*

Shortly after midnight on May 1, 1971, the Central of Georgia agent at Sylacauga walked onto the nearly deserted station platform and waited in the cool early morning stillness. In his hand he carried a train order hoop with a loop of string hooked around its end. Attached to the string was a tissue-thin sheet of paper upon which were written instructions for train no. 14, the *City of Miami.* Soon, chocolate-and-orange engine no. 4021 glided out of the darkness, and without stopping, droned past the agent as he held up the train order hoop. The conductor leaned from the cab door, stretched out his arm, and caught the loop of string holding the order instructing southbound train no. 14 to meet the northbound *City of Miami* at Alexander City. This would be the final meet order issued for the *City of Miami.* The train was being discontinued. Within seconds, the last vestige of the southbound *City of Miami* vanished from sight. A short while later the lights of her northbound sister also faded away. A romantic era of railroading was ending. Soon, the Washington–New Orleans run of the Southern Railway was all that was left of the once-majestic passenger train in Alabama.

End of an era: The Central of Georgia operator at Sylacauga copies the final meet order for the City of Miami on May 1, 1971. (From the author's collection)

FORM 19	CENTRAL OF GEORGIA RAILWAY COMPANY		FORM 19

Train Order No. **7**   Date **MAY 1 1971**   19____

To   **C&E   NO 14** _____   At   **SYLACAUGA ALA**

X _____   Opr. _____   M

NO 14 FOURTEEN IC ENG 4021 MEET NO 13 THIRTEEN

IC ENG 4038 AT ALEXANDER CITY

JED

Made *Complete*   Time *1217AM*   *King*   Opr.

Chief Dispatcher

Conductor and Engineman must each have a copy of this Order

EPILOGUE

The *City of Miami* had scarcely cleared the main line on that crisp May morning at Sylacauga when the headlight beam of a modern Central of Georgia road switcher pierced the darkness as it pulled a cut of freight cars onto the high iron vacated by the passenger train. The symbolism was striking. The freight train replaced the passenger train; prosaic motive power replaced the glamorous first-generation diesel; and the new was replacing the old—not only at Sylacauga but throughout the state.

Even the paint scheme of the Central of Georgia road switcher portended change. It was clothed in the mundane black and white styling of the Southern Railway, indicating that consolidation was continuing to drastically reduce the number of independent roads serving Alabama. Central of Georgia colors had been lost forever in a merger with the giant Southern Railway System. Merger mania eventually claimed the Seaboard, Atlantic Coast Line, Gulf, Mobile & Ohio and Illinois Central logos. Even the venerable L&N became a fallen flag road.

The freight train disappeared into the night, leaving the Central of Georgia depot at Sylacauga enveloped in tranquil stillness. The train order hoop rested in a corner to be used less and less until modern signaling devices rendered it obsolete. Soon other icons of old-time railroading would be regarded as useless and expensive encumbrances. The depot itself would be condemned and razed, along with its L&N counterpart across the street. As the years wore on, depots throughout the state were swept into oblivion by demolition crews. Even the ubiquitous red caboose could not survive the modern era.

All the romantic old symbols of railroading were pushed aside to make room for signaling and track systems that enabled the huge national railway systems to efficiently consolidate and distribute growing volumes of freight throughout the country. Eventually, few mementos would remain to remind us of the state's railroad legacy, and recollections of the glory days would fade as surely as the sound of the *City of Miami* disappearing into the night.

But we can never forget that the state of Alabama was built with iron rails, and the influence of her railroads was felt in every corner of the country. If we allow our thoughts to wander back over a century and a half of Alabama railroading, and indulge a few speculative "what ifs," perhaps we can better appreciate the truly enormous impact Alabama's railroads have had on the course of southern and national history.

Many chords that were struck on Alabama railroads reverberated throughout the land and caused repercussions that changed the course of history. The initial land-grant legislation underscores this resonant linkage between the railways of Alabama and the national railroad system. What if Alabama lawmakers had not offered decisive support for this legislation in 1850? If Alabamians had not taken action at this critical time, land-grant authorizations, especially for southern routes, might have been lost in the rapidly shifting prewar political agenda. Alabama railroad promoters aggressively pursued land grants, however, and set a precedent that assured the development of the greatest national rail system in the world.

What if Alabamians in the antebellum period had followed the lead of Alabama's sister states and provided state aid for railroad construction? Within a few years, the state might have offered the Confederacy a substantially built system of iron roads connecting with adjoining systems at vital points, instead of the poorly constructed patchwork of rusty rails that hampered the South throughout the war. If an even higher degree of progressive thinking had taken hold, the momentum of railroad building might have spurred development of the state's iron industry so that enough iron could have been provided to the Confederacy to effectively alleviate wartime shortages. Such a scenario would have undeniably strengthened the Confederacy, and might have materially influenced the course of the war.

Sadly, the exclamation point marking the end of the Civil War was etched with the wreckage of Alabama's railway system. Even more regrettable is the fact that much of the destruction was unnecessary. What if General Wilson had exercised more restraint at Montgomery and in the Chattahoochee Valley in mid-April 1865? Even though General Lee's army had surrendered at Appomattox Courthouse three days earlier, Wilson showed no mercy when he attacked the defenseless Montgomery & West Point Railroad on April 12 and 13. Fully a week after the surrender at Appomattox, the Federal army continued its rampage against the railroad at Columbus and West Point, Georgia. This belated violence destroyed most of the Black Belt's railroad resources and forced Charles T. Pollard to divert his attention from consolidating and extending the state's postwar railway system. Had Pollard been free of rehabilitation worries, he might have fully focused his resourceful energy upon the task of creating a viable, integrated railway system in Alabama. As it was, the wanton destruction inflicted by the Union army only served to fuel animosities that would last for decades, and left Pollard to share completely in the bitterness of Reconstruction.

Of the dozens of significant railway developments that followed the Civil War in Alabama, none was more profoundly important than the L&N's redemption of the South & North Alabama Railroad. What if the L&N had turned its back on the South & North—and on the state of Alabama? If the L&N had deserted the South & North, Chattanooga interests almost certainly would have gained control of north Alabama's coal and iron resources, and these minerals would have flowed over the Alabama & Chattanooga Railroad to nourish the Tennessee city into one of the greatest commercial and industrial centers in the South. Postwar Chattanooga had already established herself as the gateway to the South, with exclusive connections from the North and West to the eastern Cotton Belt states of Georgia and South Carolina. The Alabama & Chattanooga Railroad would have extended Chattanooga's sphere of influence all the way to New Orleans and would have placed the Birmingham District, the Anniston District, and the Sheffield District within easy reach. Furnaces would likely have been built in Chattanooga instead of Alabama, and the mineral districts of the state would have languished as their mines became mere feeders for a growing industrial empire on the banks of the Tennessee River. John T. Milner envisioned the worst possible consequences when he said, "Without the aid of the Louisville and Nashville the South and North would never have become the factor it is in the State's development, and progress would have been staved off a century."[1]

But thanks to the farsighted planning of Milton H. Smith and the intervention of the Louisville & Nashville Railroad, industrial development did not elude Alabama's mineral districts, and the great boom of Birmingham proved that land grants could achieve their intended purpose. Thousands of settlers quickly followed the L&N Railroad into Jefferson County and other parts of the state, and Alabama served as a splendid model for the great westward expansion of America.

Indeed, a few distinguished men of vision like Milton H. Smith put Alabama on the American railway map. David Hubbard, Benjamin Sherrod, and David Deshler were among the first Americans to realize the tremendous potential of the iron horse, and backed up their conviction with a courageous, generous expenditure of their own resources. Through adversity after adversity, this trio assumed heavy financial risks in order to harness this new technology and hammer it into an efficient and reliable machine.

Charles T. Pollard deserves a place of highest honor among America's pioneer railroaders. He saw the shape of America's railway system and placed Alabama squarely in its path. A glance at a modern railway map shows that many of the main lines of the South now traverse routes laid out by Pollard almost 150 years ago. Pollard, like all great organizers, surrounded himself with the finest builders and brightest lights in the pioneer railroad firmament. The all-stars of Alabama railroading—Jones, Gilmer, Pratt, Dexter, and Milner—assembled under Pollard's leadership at Montgomery to begin the railroad movement in Alabama. All of these men shared the same qualities. They were practical and resourceful visionaries who possessed a relentless tenacity that could carry them through the worst of times. They believed in Alabama and its railroads and they did not quit until they had scaled the highest peaks of adversity to see that the railroads attained their potential. Through sheer perseverance, these men and others like them forged their dreams into a railroad framework that united the state and, with equal determination, overcame innumerable obstacles to nurture it to maturity.

But these successes could never have been achieved without the dedicated and often heroic efforts of the sledge-wielding gandy dancers, gallant engineers, courageous brakemen, dependable station agents, and all the thousands of other nameless railroad employees who toiled in diligent anonymity to provide for their families. With a resilience that matched that of their leaders, they surmounted one hardship after another to put together a reliable and efficient rail system.

While giving little thought to the important role they were playing on the stage of southern history, the builders and shapers of the state's railroads proved a fundamental principle: Although adversity comes along as regularly as a scheduled train, opportunity often springs from the depths of misfortune, and a better day will dawn for practical men of vision who refuse to give up their dreams.

And now, as our journey through Alabama's early railroad history comes to an end, a new day is dawning for the state's railroads. The state of Alabama is truly a product of her railroads, and the state's future as well as her past will forever be intertwined with steel rail. As cars, trucks, and airplanes choke the highways and airways, the nation

Proud vestiges of progress: The City of Miami *and Sloss Furnaces, ca. 1950. (Courtesy of the Birmingham Public Library Department of Archives and Manuscripts)*

may turn to modern steel steeds to solve pressing transportation problems. Then, resourceful Alabamians may invoke the spirit of their pioneering heritage to write more chapters in the continuing saga of Alabama railroads.

NOTES

INTRODUCTION

1. Ethel Armes, *The Story of Coal and Iron in Alabama* (Cambridge: Cambridge University Press, 1910), xxv.

2. Ulrich Bonnell Phillips, *A History of Transportation in the Eastern Cotton Belt to 1860* (New York: Octagon Books, 1968), 8–10.

3. N. P. Renfroe, Jr., *Beginning of Railroads in Alabama* (Auburn, Ala.: Alabama Polytechnic Institute Historical Studies, 1910), 6.

4. John F. Stover, *Iron Road to the West: American Railroads in the 1850s* (Chicago: University of Chicago Press, 1961), 99–100.

5. Robert S. Henry, "The Railroad Land Grant Legend in American History Texts," *Mississippi Valley Historical Review* 32, no. 2 (September 1945): 189–94.

6. Robert S. Henry, "Railroads and the Confederacy," *Railway and Locomotive Historical Society Bulletin* 40:46.

7. Aaron E. Klein, *Encyclopedia of North American Railroads* (New York: Bison Books, 1985), 84–85.

8. Maury Klein, *History of the Louisville & Nashville Railroad* (New York: Macmillan, 1972), 27–44.

1
THE TUSCUMBIA TRIO

1. Lucille Griffith, *Alabama: A Documentary History to 1900* (University: University of Alabama Press, 1972), 134.

2. Charles Desilver, "A New Map of Alabama with its Roads and Distances from Place To Place Along the Stage and Steamboat Routes" (Philadelphia, 1856).

3. Marie Bankhead Owen, *The Story of Alabama: A History of the State* (New York: Lewis Historical Publishing Co., 1949), 2:171–72.

4. Thomas McAdory Owen, *History of Alabama and Dictionary of Alabama Biography* (Chicago: S. J. Clarke, 1921), 854.

5. Armes, *Story of Coal and Iron in Alabama,* 36–37.

6. John Halbert, "Shoals Railway was a First," *Birmingham News,* March 8, 1968.

7. Ernest F. Patterson, "Alabama's First Railroad," *Alabama Review* 9, no. 1 (January 1956): 33–34.

8. Richard C. Sheridan, "Tuscumbia Landing," *Journal of Muscle Shoals History* 8 (1980): 71.

9. Quoted in Griffith, *Alabama,* 213.

10. Sheridan, "Tuscumbia Landing," 71.

11. Mrs. W. G. Henry, "First Alabama Railroad Was Completed a Century Ago," *Anniston Star,* December 15, 1934.

12. Renfroe, *Beginning of Railroads in Alabama,* 2–3.

13. Patterson, "Alabama's First Railroad," 35–36.

14. Henry, "First Alabama Railroad Was Completed a Century Ago."

15. Owen, *History of Alabama,* 1547–48.

16. Patterson, "Alabama's First Railroad," 36–37.

17. Quoted in ibid., 37.

18. Quoted in Renfroe, *Beginning of Railroads in Alabama,* 5.

19. Henry, "First Alabama Railroad Was Completed a Century Ago."

20. Quoted in ibid.

21. Quoted in Renfroe, *Beginning of Railroads in Alabama,* 4–5.

22. Clara Foote Adams, "Alabama's First Railroad—Third in the U. S. A.," *Birmingham News,* March 17, 1929, 3.

23. Steam locomotives are identified by their wheel arrangement. A sequence of numbers, usually three, indicate the number of powered and unpowered wheels. The first and last numbers of the sequence tell how many undriven wheels are used to support the weight of the locomotive at the front and rear, respectively. The middle number tells how many wheels actually receive power from the steam cylinders via connecting crank rods. Thus, a 2-2-0 is a primitive wheel arrangement in which two wheels are unpowered at the front of the engine, two are powered, and there are no wheels at the rear of the locomotive. During the nineteenth century the most common engine was the 4-4-0, called the American type. It had a four-wheel truck at the front (two wheels on each side of the engine), four drivers (again, two on each side), and no trailing truck. The powered wheels (or *drivers*) of the 4-4-0 and later types of steam locomotives were larger than the leading and trailing wheels. Fast engines generally had the largest driving wheels, while smaller drivers were usually needed when a great deal of power was to be brought to bear to haul heavy loads over steep grades. In the twentieth century, the Pacific, or 4-6-2, was one of the most common passenger locomotives. It had a four-wheel leading truck, six large drivers, and a two-wheel trailing truck underneath the firebox. One of the most popular freight engines of the twentieth century was the Mikado, which had a 2-8-2 wheel arrangement, with eight drivers that were usually smaller than the six powered wheels of the Pacific locomotive.

24. Quoted in Patterson, "Alabama's First Railroad," 38–39.

25. Henry, "First Alabama Railroad Was Completed a Century Ago."

26. Patterson, "Alabama's First Railroad," 43.

27. Armes, *Story of Coal and Iron in Alabama,* 38.

28. Henry, "First Alabama Railroad Was Completed a Century Ago."

29. R. E. Prince, *Southern Railway System, Steam Locomotives and Boats* (Millard, Nebr.: Richard E. Prince, 1970), 18.

2
PIONEER POLLARD

1. Owen, *History of Alabama,* 1163; Owen, *Story of Alabama,* 116.

2. Owen, *Story of Alabama,* 114–17.

3. Walter L. Fleming, *Civil War and Reconstruction in Alabama* (New York, 1905), 588.

4. Renfroe, *Beginning of Railroads in Alabama,* 5–6.

5. Owen, *History of Alabama,* 1116–17.

6. Marshall L. Bowie, *A Time of Adversity—and Courage* (Montgomery, Ala.: Western Railway of Alabama, 1961), 1.

7. Mildred Beale, "Colonel Charles Teed Pollard, Sketch." *Alabama Historical Quarterly* 1, no. 4 (Winter 1930): 389–90.

8. Matthew P. Blue, *City Directory and History of Montgomery, Alabama* (Montgomery, Ala.: T. C. Bingham, ca. 1878), 13.

9. Renfroe, *Beginning of Railroads in Alabama,* 10–11; Owen, *Story of Alabama,* 114, 122–23.

10. Beale, "Charles Teed Pollard, Industrialist" (1930), 395–96.

11. Renfroe, *Beginning of Railroads in Alabama,* 6–7.

12. Beale, "Charles Teed Pollard, Industrialist" (1930), 400.

13. Renfroe, *Beginning of Railroads in Alabama,* 7–10.

14. Beale, "Charles Teed Pollard, Industrialist" (1930), 400–403.

15. Thomas T. Taber, "Locomotive Rosters" (Muncy, Pa.: Railway and Locomotive Historical Society).

16. Bowie, *A Time of Adversity,* 2.

17. Mildred Beale, "Charles Teed Pollard, Industrialist," *Alabama Historical Quarterly* 2, no. 1 (Spring 1940): 72.

18. Taber, "Locomotive Rosters."

19. Renfroe, *Beginning of Railroads in Alabama,* 14–15.

20. Bowie, *A Time of Adversity,* 2–3.

21. Owen, *Story of Alabama,* 231.

22. Quoted in Bowie, *A Time of Adversity,* 3.

23. Quoted in Renfroe, *Beginning of Railroads in Alabama,* 15–16.

24. Quoted in ibid., 16.

25. Quoted in ibid., 15–16.

26. Ibid., 17.

27. R. E. Prince, *Georgia Railroad and West Point Route Steam Locomotives and History* (Green River, Wyo.: Richard E. Prince, 1969), 18.

28. Bowie, *A Time of Adversity,* 5.

29. Robert C. Black, *Railroads of the Confederacy* (Chapel Hill: University of North Carolina Press, 1952), 50.

30. Bowie, *A Time of Adversity,* 3–5.

31. Owen, *Story of Alabama,* 147–48.

32. Ibid., 232; Beale, "Charles Teed Pollard, Industrialist" (1940), 78.

33. Owen, *History of Alabama,* 1387–88.

34. Owen, *Story of Alabama,* 233.

35. Walter M. Jackson, *The Story of Selma* (Birmingham, Ala.: Birmingham Printing Co., 1954), 134.

36. Owen, *Story of Alabama,* 160; Albert Burton Moore, *History of Alabama* (University, Ala.: University Supply Store, 1934), 311; Beale, "Charles Teed Pollard, Industrialist" (1940), 80.

37. Beale, "Charles Teed Pollard, Industrialist" (1940), 79–80; Moore, *History of Alabama,* 311.

38. Blue, *City Directory and History of Montgomery,* 34.

39. W. W. Screws, Jr., "The Story of Montgomery Railroads," *Montgomery Advertiser,* December 16, 1906.

40. Owen, *History of Alabama,* 1207.

41. Ibid., 656–57.

42. Screws, "The Story of Montgomery Railroads."

43. Armes, *Story of Coal and Iron in Alabama,* 106–7.

44. Blue, *City Directory and History of Montgomery,* 34–35.

45. Owen, *Story of Alabama,* 126.

46. Ibid., 161.

47. Taber, "Locomotive Rosters."

3
LAND GRANTS

1. Grace Lewis Miller, "The Mobile and Ohio Railroad in Ante Bellum Times," *Alabama Historical Quarterly* 7, no. 1 (Spring 1945): 38–42.

2. Owen, *History of Alabama,* 1168.

3. Quoted in ibid., 1168.

4. Miller, "Mobile and Ohio Railroad," 48–51.

5. Owen, *History of Alabama,* 1171; Miller, "Mobile and Ohio Railroad," 48–51.

6. Taber, "Locomotive Rosters."

7. James Hutton Lemly, *The Gulf, Mobile and Ohio* (Homewood, Ill.: Richard D. Irwin, 1953): 309–10.

8. Owen, *Story of Alabama,* 193.

9. Quoted in Lemly, *Gulf, Mobile and Ohio,* 310.

10. Owen, *Story of Alabama,* 126.

11. Jackson, *Story of Selma,* 106–10.

12. Ibid., 111.

13. Quoted in ibid., 111–12.

14. Ibid., 112–13.

15. Quoted in ibid., 113–15.

16. Owen, *Story of Alabama,* 143.

17. Jackson, *Story of Selma,* 115.

18. Owen, *Story of Alabama,* 144.

19. John Witherspoon Dubose, *Alabama's Tragic Decade: Ten Years of Alabama, 1865–1874* (Birmingham, Ala.: Webb Book Company, 1940), 174; James Harold Clark, "History of the North East and South West Alabama Railroad to 1872, a Thesis" (master's thesis, University of Alabama, 1949), 1–9.

20. Quoted in Clark, "History of the North East and South West Alabama Railroad," 9.

21. Ibid., 13–31.

22. Henry, "Railroad Land Grant Legend," 185, 194.

4
MINERALS AND MILNER

1. Owen, *History of Alabama,* 1164.

2. Owen, *Story of Alabama,* 153–54.

3. Stover, *Iron Road to the West,* 77.

4. William Webb, *Southern Railway System: An Illustrated History* (Erin, Ontario: Boston Mills Press, 1986), 19.

5. Owen, *History of Alabama,* 1572–73.

6. Kincaid A. Herr, *Louisville & Nashville Railroad 1850–1963* (Louisville, Ky.: L&N Public Relations Department, 1964), 46.

7. Stover, *Iron Road to the West,* 86.

8. Klein, *History of the Louisville & Nashville Railroad,* 115–16.

9. William Letford, "Alabama Railroads, April 1861," map (Montgomery, Ala.: Alabama Department of Archives and History, January 6, 1961).

10. Phillips, *History of Transportation in the Eastern Cotton Belt,* 1–10.

11. Quoted in Minnie Clare Boyd, *Alabama in the Fifties* (New York: Columbia University Press, 1931), 88.

12. Quoted in Armes, *Story of Coal and Iron in Alabama,* 116.

13. Phillips, *History of Transportation in the Eastern Cotton Belt,* 9–10; Boyd, *Alabama in the Fifties,* 77.

14. Quoted in Armes, *Story of Coal and Iron in Alabama,* 115–16.

15. Owen, *Story of Alabama,* 118–19.

16. Quoted in ibid., 119.

17. Ibid.

18. Armes, *Story of Coal and Iron in Alabama,* 100–106.

19. Quoted in ibid., 103.

20. Ibid., 105.

21. Ibid., 106–9.

22. Ibid., 109–10.

23. Quoted in ibid., 112.

24. Quoted in ibid., 113.

25. Quoted in ibid., 114.

26. Ibid., 115–17.

27. Quoted in ibid., 116.

28. Quoted in ibid., 116–17.

29. Ibid., 118

30. Owen, *Story of Alabama,* 267.

31. Quoted in Armes, *Story of Coal and Iron in Alabama,* 118–20.

5

THE CIVIL WAR

1. Armes, *Story of Coal and Iron in Alabama,* 124.

2. Black, *Railroads of the Confederacy,* 50.

3. Ibid., 51.

4. Ibid., 74.

5. Ibid., 75–76.

6. Ibid., 139–42.

7. Quoted in ibid., 139.

8. Ibid., 143.

9. Ibid., 153–58.

10. Ibid., 201–4.

11. Ibid., 205–7.

12. Ibid., 180–84.

13. Quoted in Armes, *Story of Coal and Iron in Alabama,* 163–64.

14. Jackson, *Story of Selma,* 116.

15. Grace E. Jemison, *Historic Tales of Talladega* (Montgomery, Ala.: Paragon Press, 1959), 128.

16. Armes, *Story of Coal and Iron in Alabama,* 173.

17. Quoted in Bowie, *A Time of Adversity,* 11–12.

18. Ibid., 7–8, 10.

19. Quoted in ibid., 10.

20. Edwin C. Bearss, "Rousseau's Raid on the Montgomery and West Point Railroad," *Alabama Historical Quarterly* 25, no. 1 (Spring–Summer 1963): 7–12.

21. Ibid., 12–30.

22. Ibid., 31–34.

23. Ibid., 35–41.

24. A *wye* is a track configuration that allows locomotives as well as complete trains to reverse direction without the aid of a turntable. A single track branches into two legs, forming a Y shape. A connecting track joins the left and right branches. A train moving along the single track can take either branch and, by backing along the connecting track, end up pointed in the opposite direction.

25. Ibid., 42–47.

26. Quoted in ibid., 48.

27. *Reports of the Committees of the House of Representatives made during the Second Session, Thirty-Ninth Congress, 1866–67* (Washington, D.C.: Government Printing Office, 1867), 866.

28. Armes, *Story of Coal and Iron in Alabama,* 190–94.

29. Prince, *Southern Railway System,* 17.

30. Armes, *Story of Coal and Iron in Alabama,* 181.

31. *Reports of the Committees of the House,* 896.

32. Blue, *City Directory and History of Montgomery,* 38.

33. *Reports of the Committees of the House,* 885.

34. Quoted in Bowie, *A Time of Adversity,* 12–13.

35. Quoted in *Reports of the Committees of the House,* 896.

36. Ibid., 909.

37. Lemly, *Gulf, Mobile and Ohio,* 311.

38. Quoted in Bowie, *A Time of Adversity,* 13.

6
AFTERMATH

1. Quoted in *Reports of the Committees of the House*, 877.

2. Ibid., 880–81.

3. Ibid., 884.

4. Webb, *Southern Railway System*, 39.

5. *Reports of the Committees of the House*, 857–58.

6. Ibid., 867.

7. Ibid., 906–9.

8. Ibid., 895–99.

9. *Mobile Register*, September 9, 1870.

10. *Reports of the Committees of the House*, 857.

11. Quoted in *Reports of the Committees of the House*, 912.

12. Mary K. Bonstee Tachau, "The Making of a Railroad President: Milton Hannibal Smith and the L&N," *The Filson Club History Quarterly* 43, no. 2 (April 1969): 128–32.

13. Owen, *Story of Alabama*, 233.

14. *Mobile Register*, September 15, 1870.

15. U.S. Congress, House, *Memorial of the Selma, Rome and Dalton Railroad Company, Misc. Doc. no. 33*, 40th Cong., 3d sess., February 1, 1869, 2–3.

16. Richard E. Prince, *Louisville & Nashville Steam Locomotives* (Green River, Wyo.: Richard E. Prince, 1968), 24.

17. Quoted in *Memorial of the Selma, Rome and Dalton Railroad*, 3.

7
RADICALS AND RASCALS

1. Clark, "History of the North East and South West Alabama Railroad," 42–46.

2. Owen, *Story of Alabama*, 128–31.

3. Clark, "History of the North East and South West Alabama Railroad," 43–47.

4. Fleming, *Civil War and Reconstruction in Alabama*, 591.

5. Quoted in Owen, *Story of Alabama*, 132–33.

6. Owen, *Story of Alabama*, 134.

7. Fleming, *Civil War and Reconstruction in Alabama*, 604–5; Moore, *History of Alabama*, 495.

8 Owen, *Story of Alabama*, 187; Dubose, *Alabama's Tragic Decade*, 166.

9. Fleming, *Civil War and Reconstruction in Alabama*, 605.

10. Dubose, *Alabama's Tragic Decade,* 162–63.

11. Ibid., 163; Owen, *Story of Alabama,* 140.

12. Owen, *Story of Alabama,* 165–66.

13. Ibid., 150, from the Mobile & Alabama Grand Trunk Railroad charter, which was granted by the Alabama legislature on February 23, 1866.

14. John C. Jay, "General N. B. Forrest as a Railroad Builder in Alabama," *Alabama Historical Quarterly* 24, no. 1 (Spring 1962): 16–20.

15. Ibid., 20–22.

16. Waller's recollections are reported in ibid., 23–26.

17. Ibid., 27.

18. Ibid., 27–28.

19. Clark, "History of the North East and South West Alabama Railroad," 64.

20. Ibid., 60–63.

21. Ibid., 60–61.

22. Ibid., 63–64.

23. Ibid., 64–65.

24. Ibid., 65–66.

25. Fleming, *Civil War and Reconstruction in Alabama,* 604.

26. Clark, "History of the North East and South West Alabama Railroad," 66.

27. Ibid., 67–69.

28. Quoted in ibid., 71–73.

29. Ibid., 73–74.

30. Quoted in the *Jacksonville Republican,* April 29, 1871.

31. Clark, "History of the North East and South West Alabama Railroad," 69–70.

32. *Jacksonville Republican,* April 29, 1871.

33. Clark, "History of the North East and South West Alabama Railroad," 75.

34. *Jacksonville Republican,* June 17, 1871.

35. Clark, "History of the North East and South West Alabama Railroad," 76–79.

36. Ibid., 79–80.

37. Ibid., 80–83.

38. John F. Stover, *The Railroads of the South, 1865–1900* (Chapel Hill: University of North Carolina Press, 1955), 92; Dorothy R. Adler, *British Investment in American Railways* (Charlottesville: University Press of Virginia, 1970), 128–29.

39. Stover, *Railroads of the South,* 94.

40. Moore, *History of Alabama,* 495.

41. Herr, *Louisville & Nashville Railroad 1850–1963,* 58.

42. Stover, *Railroads of the South,* 61.

43. James Doster, *Railroads in Alabama Politics, 1875–1914* (University: University of Alabama Press, 1957), 46–51.

44. Moore, *History of Alabama,* 496.

45. Ibid., 448.

46. Quoted in Clark, "History of the North East and South West Alabama Railroad," 83.

8
L&N TO THE RESCUE

1. Owen, *History of Alabama,* 659.

2. Quoted in Armes, *Story of Coal and Iron in Alabama,* 215–16.

3. Klein, *History of the Louisville & Nashville Railroad,* 118.

4. Quoted in Armes, *Story of Coal and Iron in Alabama,* 216.

5. Quoted in ibid., 216–17.

6. Ibid., 217.

7. Ibid., 217–18.

8. Prince, *Louisville & Nashville,* 18.

9. Armes, *Story of Coal and Iron in Alabama,* 218.

10. Ibid., 218–20.

11. Ibid., 220–22. The twelve charter members of the Elyton Land Company were Josiah Morris, J. R. Powell, Sam Tate, Campbell Wallace, H. M. Caldwell, Bolling Hall, J. N. Gilmer, B. P. Worthington, Robert N. Greene, W. F. Nabers, John A. Milner, and William S. Mudd.

12. Ibid., 222–32.

13. Quoted in ibid., 243.

14. Klein, *History of the Louisville & Nashville Railroad,* 13.

15. Quoted in Armes, *Story of Coal and Iron in Alabama,* 247.

16. Klein, *History of the Louisville & Nashville Railroad,* 121.

17. Quoted in Armes, *Story of Coal and Iron in Alabama,* 249.

18. Tachau, "Making of a Railroad President," 132–34.

19. Quoted in Owen, *Story of Alabama,* 202–3.

20. Klein, *History of the Louisville & Nashville Railroad,* 122, 129.

21. Ibid., 355.

22. Ibid., 135.

23. Griffith, *Alabama,* 606–7.

24. Quoted in Armes, *Story of Coal and Iron in Alabama,* 234.

25. Quoted in Klein, *History of the Louisville & Nashville Railroad,* 124.

26. Ibid., 129.

27. Quoted in Owen, *Story of Alabama,* 203–4.

28. Quoted in Armes, *Story of Coal and Iron in Alabama,* 252.

9
"THE FOOLS DOWN IN ALABAMA"

1. Quoted in Armes, *Story of Coal and Iron in Alabama,* 254.

2. Ibid., 238, 253.

3. Quoted in ibid., 257.

4. H. H. Chapman, *The Iron and Steel Industries of the South* (University: University of Alabama Press, 1953), 101–3; Klein, *History of the Louisville & Nashville Railroad,* 132–33; *Alabama Blast Furnaces* (Woodward, Ala.: Woodward Iron Company, 1940), 26.

5. Quoted in Armes, *Story of Coal and Iron in Alabama,* 258.

6. Quoted in ibid., 259.

7. Ibid.

8. *Alabama Blast Furnaces,* 26.

9. Klein, *History of the Louisville & Nashville Railroad,* 135; quoted in Armes, *Story of Coal and Iron in Alabama,* 266.

10. Quoted in Armes, *Story of Coal and Iron in Alabama,* 279–80.

11. Quoted in ibid., 267–72.

12. Quoted in ibid., 272–73.

13. Ibid., 273–74; Klein, *History of the Louisville & Nashville Railroad,* 134.

14. *Birmingham Age,* September 23, 1886.

15. Tachau, "Making of a Railroad President," 138; Klein, *History of the Louisville & Nashville Railroad,* 232.

16. Prince, *Louisville & Nashville Steam Locomotives,* 24.

17. Herr, *Louisville and Nashville Railroad 1850–1963,* 59.

18. Quoted in Klein, *History of the Louisville & Nashville Railroad,* 137.

19. Jean E. Keith, "Sand Mountains and Sawgrass Marshes," *Alabama Review* 7, no. 2 (April 1954): 100; Klein, *History of the Louisville & Nashville Railroad,* 157.

20. Herr, *Louisville and Nashville Railroad 1850–1963,* 62.

21. Ibid., 58–60.

22. Armes, *Story of Coal and Iron in Alabama,* 283–84.

23. Ibid., 284–85.

24. Ibid., 287–88.

25. Ibid., 287, 293.

26. Quoted in ibid., 275.

27. Keith, "Sand Mountains and Sawgrass Marshes," 100–101.

28. Klein, *History of the Louisville & Nashville Railroad,* 135.

29. Tachau, "Making of a Railroad President," 143.

30. Quoted in Armes, *Story of Coal and Iron in Alabama,* 290–91.

31. Ibid., 306–7; Klein, *History of the Louisville & Nashville Railroad,* 268.

32. *Birmingham Age,* September 9, 1886.

33. Herr, *Louisville & Nashville Railroad 1850–1963,* 52.

34. Quoted in Armes, *Story of Coal and Iron in Alabama,* 278.

35. Ibid., 298.

10

THE IRON BOOM

1. Armes, *Story of Coal and Iron in Alabama,* 291–93.

2. Ibid., 295–98.

3. Ibid., 299–301.

4. Ibid., 330–46.

5. Ibid., 295–97.

6. Ibid., 313–15; Grace Hooten Gates, *The Model City of the New South: Anniston, Alabama, 1872–1900* (Huntsville, Ala.: Strode Publishers, 1978; reprint, with Preface to the Paperbound Edition, Tuscaloosa: University of Alabama Press, 1996), 17–27.

7. Gates, *Model City of the New South,* 37–39.

8. Ibid., 86–87.

9. Prince, *Southern Railway System,* 14–18.

10. *Birmingham Age,* September 22, 1886.

11. Prince, *Southern Railway System,* 14.

12. Gates, *Model City of the New South,* 87–90.

13. Ibid., 87–89.

14. Ibid., 90.

15. Owen, *Story of Alabama,* 101.

16. Jemison, *Historic Tales of Talladega,* 130–31.

17. Gates, *Model City of the New South,* 99–101.

18. Record of the Elyton Land Company, quoted in Armes, *Story of Coal and Iron in Alabama*, 344–45. Armes identifies the author of the record only as "Caldwell"; presumably this is H. M. Caldwell, one of the charter members of the Elyton Land Company.

19. Herr, *Louisville & Nashville Railroad 1850–1963*, 78–81; Klein, *History of the Louisville & Nashville Railroad*, 317–19.

20. "Magic City Letter," *Gadsden Times*, June 11, 1886.

21. Prince, *Georgia Railroad and West Point Route*, 60–61.

22. R. E. Prince, *Seaboard Air Line Railway Steam Boats, Locomotives and History* (Green River, Wyo.: Richard E. Prince, 1969), 87.

23. Doster, *Railroads in Alabama Politics*, 59–60, 70.

24. Herr, *Louisville & Nashville Railroad 1850–1963*, 84.

25. Armes, *Story of Coal and Iron in Alabama*, 360–62.

26. Klein, *History of the Louisville & Nashville Railroad*, 267–69.

27. Quoted in ibid., 270.

28. W. Forrest Beckum, Jr., and Albert M. Langley, *Central of Georgia Railway Album* (North Augusta, S.C.: Union Station Publishing, 1986), 9; Owen, *Story of Alabama*, 190.

29. Herr, *Louisville & Nashville Railroad 1850–1963*, 88.

30. Kincaid A. Herr, *Louisville & Nashville Railroad 1850–1959* (Louisville, Ky.: L&N Magazine, 1959), 80.

31. Herr, *Louisville & Nashville Railroad 1850–1963*, 88–89.

32. Herr, *Louisville & Nashville Railroad 1850–1959*, 53.

33. *Alabama Blast Furnaces*, 160–61.

34. *Gadsden Times*, November 19, 1886.

35. Ibid., March 20, 1887.

36. "Grand Gala Time at Gadsden," *Gadsden Times*, October 2, 1888; Prince, *Southern Railway System*, 18.

37. Armes, *Story of Coal and Iron in Alabama*, 320.

38. *Gadsden Times*, July 31, 1890, March 15, 1895.

39. Quoted in "Etowah on Wheels," *Gadsden Times*, December 6, 1888.

40. Ibid.

41. Owen, *Story of Alabama*, 220–21.

42. Klein, *History of the Louisville & Nashville Railroad*, 264–65.

43. *Gadsden Weekly Times and News*, March 17, 1887.

44. Etowah Centennial Committee, *The History of Etowah County* (Gadsden, Ala.: Etowah Centennial Committee, 1968), 92.

45. *Alabama Blast Furnaces*, 42.

11
MATURITY

1. Armes, *Story of Coal and Iron in Alabama,* 423–25.

2. Quoted in ibid., 425–26.

3. Quoted in Klein, *History of the Louisville & Nashville Railroad,* 273.

4. Armes, *Story of Coal and Iron in Alabama,* 427.

5. Herr, *Louisville & Nashville Railroad 1850–1963,* 333.

6. Richard Reinhardt, *Workin' on the Railroad: Reminiscences from the Age of Steam* (New York: Weathervane Books, 1970), 274.

7. "The American Railroad," *Harper's New Monthly Magazine* 49, no. 291 (August 1874): n.p.

8. Reinhardt, *Workin' on the Railroad,* 274.

9. Ibid., 102–4.

10. Klein, *History of the Louisville & Nashville Railroad,* 334–35.

11. Philip Taft, *Organizing Dixie: Alabama Workers in the Industrial Era* (Westport, Conn.: Greenwood Press, 1981), 8–10.

12. Quoted in Robert David Ward and William Warren Rogers, *Labor Revolt in Alabama: The Great Strike of 1894* (University: University of Alabama Press, 1965), 105–7.

13. John H. Bracey, *Black Workers and Organized Labor* (Belmont, Calif.: Wadsworth Publishing Company, 1971), 47.

14. Taft, *Organizing Dixie,* 10.

15. Ibid., 25–30.

16. Herr, *Louisville & Nashville Railroad 1850–1959,* 74–76.

17. Quoted in Klein, *History of the Louisville & Nashville Railroad,* 297–301.

18. "History of the Tennessee, Alabama & Georgia Railway Company," May 5, 1939, in vertical files, Gadsden Public Library.

19. Klein, *History of the Louisville & Nashville Railroad,* 301.

20. "History of the Tennessee, Alabama & Georgia Railway Company."

21. Klein, *History of the Louisville & Nashville Railroad,* 303.

22. W. Forrest Beckum, Jr., and Albert M. Langley, *Central of Georgia Railway Album* (North Augusta, S.C.: Union Station Publishing, 1986), 5–6, 9.

23. Robert W. Mann, *Rails 'Neath the Palms* (Burbank, Calif.: Darwin Publications, 1983), 168–69.

24. Owen, *Story of Alabama,* 139–40.

25. Ibid., 230.

26. R. E. Prince, *Atlantic Coast Line Railroad Steam Locomotives, Ships and History,* (Green River, Wyo.: Richard E. Prince, 1966), 21.

27. Dudley Johnson, "Early History of the Alabama Midland Railroad Company," *Alabama Review* 21, no. 4 (October 1968): 276–83.

28. Prince, *Atlantic Coast Line Railroad,* 30.

29. Quoted in Johnson, "Early History of the Alabama Midland Railroad," 284.

30. Prince, *Atlantic Coast Line Railroad,* 30.

31. "Tenth Annual Report of the Railroad Commisioners of Alabama for the Year Ending June 30, 1890" (Montgomery, Ala., 1890), ix–xi.

32. Lemly, *Gulf, Mobile and Ohio,* 312.

33. Owen, *Story of Alabama,* 196.

34. Prince, *Seaboard Air Line Railway,* 81–82.

35. Ibid., 87.

36. Quoted in Klein, *History of the Louisville & Nashville Railroad,* 311–12.

37. Mann, *Rails 'Neath the Palms,* 195–96.

38. Carlton J. Corliss, *Main Line of Mid-America: The Story of the Illinois Central* (New York: Creative Age Press, 1950), 331–33.

39. Prince, *Atlantic Coast Line Railroad,* 71–72.

40. J. J. Newman, *Life on the Hootaloocceo and Beyond, 1888–1913, as told to Margaret Newman* (N.p.: Privately published, n.d.), 28.

41. Prince, *Atlantic Coast Line Railroad,* 72–73.

42. Lemly, *Gulf, Mobile and Ohio,* 10, 291–95; Saffold Berney, *Hand-Book of Alabama* (Birmingham: Roberts & Son, 1892), 379.

43. Quoted in ibid., 295.

44. I. B. Tigrett, *My Railroad Saga* (New York: Newcomen Society of North America, 1952), 1–14.

12
REGULATION

1. James F. Doster, "People vs. Railroad at Ashville: A Community Squabble of 1881," *Alabama Review* 9, no. 1 (January, 1956): 46–53.

2. Doster, *Railroads in Alabama Politics,* 36–40.

3. Ibid., 60–66.

4. Ibid., 67.

5. Ibid., 8–9.

6. Ibid., 11–26.

7. Ibid., 26, 82.

8. Ibid., 26–45.

9. Ibid., 87–111.

10. Ibid., 112–28; quotation by B. B. Comer in ibid., 119–20.

11. Ibid., 128–40.

12. Ibid., 140–45.

13. Quoted in Newman, *Life on the Hootaloocceo and Beyond,* 27.

14. Doster, *Railroads in Alabama Politics,* 146–75.

15. Ibid., 175–97.

16. Ibid., 197–210.

17. Ibid., 210–13.

18. Quoted in Klein, *History of the Louisville & Nashville Railroad,* 392–93.

19. Doster, *Railroads in Alabama Politics,* 214–25.

20. Quoted in ibid., 225.

13

SHORT LINES AND LOGGING RAILROADS

1. Moore, *History of Alabama,* 532.

2. Dwight M. Wilhelm, *History of the Cotton Textile Industry of Alabama, 1809–1950* (Montgomery, Ala., 1950), 77.

3. Owen, *Story of Alabama,* 191.

4. Quoted in Newman, *Life on the Hootaloocceo and Beyond,* 28.

5. Owen, *Story of Alabama,* 191.

6. Ibid., 173–74.

7. Michael J. Dunn III, "The Birmingham & Southeastern Railroad," *Alabama Historical Quarterly* 27, no. 1 (Spring–Summer 1965): 59–64.

8. Ibid., 64–79.

9. Richard W. Massey, Jr., "Logging Railroads in Alabama, 1880–1914," *Alabama Review* 14, no. 1 (January 1961): 41.

10. Ibid., 41–44.

11. Taber, "Locomotive Rosters."

12. George W. Hilton, *American Narrow Gauge Railroads* (Stanford, Calif.: Stanford University Press, 1990), 159–61.

13. Massey, "Logging Railroads in Alabama," 48.

14. Ibid., 47–49.

15. Ibid., 45–46.

16. Ibid., 44–46.

17. Ibid., 44, 47.

18. Taber, "Locomotive Rosters."

19. John Krause with H. Reid, *Rails Through Dixie* (San Marino, Calif.: Golden West Books, 1965), 130–31.

20. Fred S. Watson, *Hub of the Wiregrass: A History of Houston County, Alabama, 1903–1972* (Anniston, Ala.: Higginbotham, Inc., 1972), 179–80.

21. Taber, "Locomotive Rosters."

22. Ibid.

23. Ibid.; *The Bessemer,* November 5, 1887.

24. Ibid.; Thomas Lawson, Jr., H. Reid, and William S. Young, "Last of the Last," *Railroading Magazine* 28 (June 1969): 10–12.

25. Krause, *Rails Through Dixie,* 128–29.

26. Taber, "Locomotive Rosters."

27. Ibid.; Virginia O. Foscue, *Place Names in Alabama* (Tuscaloosa: University of Alabama Press, 1989), 21.

28. Taber, "Locomotive Rosters"; Annie C. Waters, *History of Escambia County, Alabama* (Huntsville, Ala.: Strode Publishers, 1983), 98.

29. Taber, "Locomotive Rosters"; Foscue, *Place Names in Alabama,* 81.

30. Taber, "Locomotive Rosters"; Foscue, *Place Names in Alabama,* 86, 118.

31. Taber, "Locomotive Rosters."

32. Ibid.; Foscue, *Place Names in Alabama,* 132.

33. Owen, *Story of Alabama,* 217–18.

34. Waters, *History of Escambia County,* 389–90.

35. Taber, "Locomotive Rosters."

36. Ibid.; Foscue, *Place Names in Alabama,* 14, 99.

37. Taber, "Locomotive Rosters."

38. Massey, "Logging Railroads in Alabama," 44–47.

39. Taber, "Locomotive Rosters."

40. Ibid.

41. Herr, *Louisville & Nashville Railroad 1850–1963,* 159; Owen, *Story of Alabama,* 217.

42. Owen, *Story of Alabama,* 175–79.

43. Information provided by Quinton D. Bruner, retired executive of the Bay Line Railroad, Dothan, Alabama; Owen, *The Story of Alabama,* 176–79.

44. Betty Dickenson Ivey, "From River to Rail in Pickens County," *Alabama Review* 7, no. 1 (January 1954): 53–64.

45. Foscue, *Place Names in Alabama,* 10, 15, 25, 52, 60, 79, 85, 90, 107, 123, 125, 138, 139, 143.

14
ALABAMA VARNISH

1. Lance Phillips, *Yonder Comes the Train* (New York: A. S. Barnes, 1965), 324.

2. Ella S. Witherill, "Trains Frightened Natives at First," undated clipping from unidentified newspaper, in "Railroads" folder, vertical files, Anniston Public Library.

3. Phillips, *Yonder Comes the Train,* 322, 353.

4. Prince, *Louisville & Nashville,* 25–26.

5. Ibid., 139, 141.

6. *Gadsden Times-News,* June 20, 1893.

7. Ibid., December 1, 1893.

8. Webb, *Southern Railway System,* 70.

9. Prince, *Louisville & Nashville,* 142.

10. *Montgomery Advertiser,* May 21, 1982.

11. Prince, *Southern Railway System,* 128.

12. A *hot box* is an overheated journal bearing. The axles of railroad cars protrude outside the wheels and are contained in an enclosure called a *journal* or *journal box.* Inside the journal, the axles rotate against lubricated bearings. If for any reason the lubrication becomes insufficient, excessive friction will cause the bearings to overheat and the journal will begin to smoke. When a hot box is detected, it must be cooled and lubricated immediately or else the axle may wring off and cause the train to derail.

13. Quoted in Prince, *Georgia Railroad and West Point Route,* 68–69.

14. Webb, *Southern Railway System,* 70, 72.

15. Klein, *History of the Louisville & Nashville Railroad,* 331.

16. "Time Table No. 229 in effect June 14, 1903—Arrival and Departure of all Trains at Union Passenger Station, Birmingham, Alabama," vertical files, Birmingham Public Library.

17. *Mobile Press,* January 15, 1987.

18. Heart of Dixie Railroad Club, *Birmingham's Terminal Station, 1909–1969* (Birmingham, Ala.: Heart of Dixie Railroad Club, 1969), 4.

19. Ibid., 11–12.

20. Ibid., 9–10.

21. Prince, *Southern Railway System,* 128.

22. Ibid., 128.

23. Prince, *Seaboard Air Line Railway,* 204, 214–15, 219.

24. Prince, *Southern Railway System,* 128.

25. Prince, *Louisville & Nashville,* 147.

26. Ibid., 161–65.

27. Ibid., 147.

28. Prince, *Seaboard Air Line Railway,* 222.

29. Lemly, *Gulf, Mobile and Ohio,* 139.

30. Dunn, "Birmingham & Southeastern Railroad," 65.

31. Lemly, *Gulf, Mobile and Ohio,* 137, 145–46.

32. Klein, *History of the Louisville & Nashville Railroad,* 470.

33. Beckum and Langley, *Central of Georgia Railway Album,* 116.

34. Heart of Dixie Railroad Club, *Birmingham's Terminal Station,* 4, 6, 13.

EPILOGUE

1. Quoted in Armes, *Story of Coal and Iron in Alabama,* 298.

BIBLIOGRAPHY

BOOKS

Adler, Dorothy R. *British Investment in American Railways.* Charlottesville, Va.: University Press of Virginia, 1970.

Armes, Ethel. *The Story of Coal and Iron in Alabama.* Cambridge: Cambridge University Press, 1910.

Beckum, W. Forrest, Jr., and Albert M. Langley. *Central of Georgia Railway Album.* North Augusta, S.C.: Union Station Publishing, 1986.

Berney, Saffold. *Hand-Book of Alabama.* Birmingham, Ala.: Roberts & Son, 1892.

Black, Robert C. *Railroads of the Confederacy.* Chapel Hill: University of North Carolina Press, 1952.

Blue, Matthew P. *City Directory and History of Montgomery, Alabama.* Montgomery, Ala.: T. C. Bingham, ca. 1878.

Boyd, Minnie Clare. *Alabama in the Fifties, a Social Study.* New York: Columbia University Press, 1931.

Bracey, John H. *Black Workers and Organized Labor.* Belmont, Calif.: Wadsworth Publishing Company, 1971.

Chapman, H. H. *The Iron and Steel Industries of the South.* University: University of Alabama Press, 1953.

Corliss, Carlton J. *Main Line of Mid-America: The Story of the Illinois Central.* New York: Creative Age Press, 1950.

Doster, James. *Railroads in Alabama Politics, 1875–1914.* University: University of Alabama Studies, 1957.

Dubose, John Witherspoon. *Alabama's Tragic Decade: Ten Years of Alabama, 1865–1874.* Birmingham, Ala.: Webb Book Company, 1940.

Etowah Centennial Committee. *The History of Etowah County.* Gadsden, Ala.: Etowah Centennial Committee, 1968.

Fleming, Walter L. *Civil War and Reconstruction in Alabama.* New York: Columbia University Press, 1905.

Foscue, Virginia O. *Place Names in Alabama.* Tuscaloosa: University of Alabama Press, 1989.

Gates, Grace Hooten. *The Model City of the New South: Anniston, Alabama, 1872–1900.* Huntsville, Ala.: Strode Publishers, 1978. Reprint, with Preface to the Paperbound Edition, Tuscaloosa: University of Alabama Press, 1996.

Griffith, Lucille. *Alabama: A Documentary History to 1900.* University: University of Alabama Press, 1972.

Herr, Kincaid A. *Louisville & Nashville Railroad 1850–1963.* Louisville, Ky.: L&N Public Relations Department, 1964.

———. *Louisville & Nashville Railroad 1850–1959.* Louisville, Ky.: L&N Public Relations Department, 1959.

Hilton, George W. *American Narrow Gauge Railroads.* Stanford, Calif.: Stanford University Press, 1990.

Jackson, Walter M. *The Story of Selma.* Birmingham, Ala.: Birmingham Printing Co., 1954.

Jemison, Grace E. *Historic Tales of Talladega.* Montgomery, Ala.: Paragon Press, 1959.

Klein, Aaron E. *Encyclopedia of North American Railroads.* New York: Bison Books, 1985.

Klein, Maury. *History of the Louisville & Nashville Railroad.* New York: Macmillan, 1972.

Krause, John, with H. Reid. *Rails Through Dixie.* San Marino, Calif.: Golden West Books, 1965.

Lemly, James Hutton. *The Gulf, Mobile and Ohio.* Homewood, Ill.: Richard D. Irwin, 1953.

Mann, Robert W. *Rails 'Neath the Palms.* Burbank, Calif.: Darwin Publications, 1983.

Moore, Albert Burton. *History of Alabama.* University, Ala.: University Supply Store, 1934.

Newman, J. J. *Life on the Hootaloocceo and Beyond, 1888–1913, as told to Margaret Newman.* N.p.: Privately published, n.d.

Owen, Marie Bankhead. *The Story of Alabama: A History of the State.* Vol. 2. New York: Lewis Historical Publishing Co., 1949.

Owen, Thomas McAdory. *History of Alabama and Dictionary of Alabama Biography.* Chicago: S. J. Clarke, 1921.

Phillips, Lance. *Yonder Comes the Train.* New York: A. S. Barnes, 1965.

Phillips, Ulrich Bonnell. *A History of Transportation in the Eastern Cotton Belt to 1860.* New York: Octagon Books, 1968.

Prince, R. E. *Atlantic Coast Line Railroad Steam Locomotives, Ships and History.* Green River, Wyo.: Richard E. Prince, 1966.

———. *Georgia Railroad and West Point Route Steam Locomotives and History.* Green River, Wyo.: Richard E. Prince, 1962.

———. *Louisville & Nashville Steam Locomotives.* Green River, Wyo.: Richard E. Prince, 1968.

————. *Seaboard Air Line Railway Steam Boats, Locomotives and History.* Green River, Wyo.: Richard E. Prince, 1969.

————. *Southern Railway System, Steam Locomotives and Boats.* Millard, Nebr.: Richard E. Prince, 1970.

Reinhardt, Richard. *Workin' on the Railroad: Reminiscences from the Age of Steam.* New York: Weathervane Books, 1970.

Reports of the Committees of the House of Representatives made during the Second Session, Thirty-Ninth Congress, 1866–67. Washington, D.C.: Government Printing Office, 1867.

Reports of the Railroad Commissioners of Alabama. First through Eleventh Annual Reports, 1881–1891. State Archives, Montgomery, Ala., 1890.

Stover, John F. *Iron Road to the West: American Railroads in the 1850s.* Chicago: University of Chicago Press, 1961.

————. *The Railroads of the South, 1865–1900.* Chapel Hill: University of North Carolina Press, 1955.

Taft, Philip. *Organizing Dixie: Alabama Workers in the Industrial Era.* Westport, Conn.: Greenwood Press, 1981.

Ward, Robert David, and William Warren Rogers. *Labor Revolt in Alabama: The Great Strike of 1894.* University: University of Alabama Press, 1965.

Waters, Annie C. *History of Escambia County, Alabama.* Huntsville, Ala.: Strode Publishers, 1983.

Watson, Fred S. *Hub of the Wiregrass: A History of Houston County, Alabama, 1903–1972.* Anniston, Ala.: Higginbotham, Inc., 1972.

Webb, William. *Southern Railway System: An Illustrated History.* Erin, Ontario: Boston Mills Press, 1986.

Wilhelm, Dwight M. *History of the Cotton Textile Industry of Alabama 1809–1950.* Montgomery, Ala., 1950.

Woodward Iron Company. *Alabama Blast Furnaces.* Woodward, Ala.: Woodward Iron Company, 1940.

PAMPHLETS

Bowie, Marshall L. *A Time of Adversity—and Courage.* Montgomery: Western Railway of Alabama, 1961.

Heart of Dixie Railroad Club. *Birmingham's Terminal Station 1909–1969.* Birmingham, Ala.: Heart of Dixie Railroad Club, 1969.

History of the Tennessee, Alabama & Georgia Railway Company. Vertical Files, Gadsden Public Library.

Milner, Willis J. *Some Historic Reminiscences of the Building of the First Railroad into Pensacola.* Vertical Files, Alabama Department of Archives and History, Montgomery, Ala.

Renfroe, N. P., Jr. *Beginning of Railroads in Alabama.* Auburn: Alabama Polytechnic Institute Historical Studies, 1910.

Tigrett, I. B. *My Railroad Saga.* New York: Newcomen Society in North America, 1952.

U.S. Congress. House. *Memorial of the Selma, Rome and Dalton Railroad Company, Misc. Doc. no. 33.* 40th Cong., 3d sess., February 1, 1869.

ARTICLES, REPORTS, AND THESES

"The American Railroad." *Harper's New Monthly Magazine* 49, no. 291 (August 1874): n.p.

Beale, Mildred. "Colonel Charles Teed Pollard, Sketch." *Alabama Historical Quarterly* 1, no. 4 (Winter 1930): 389–93.

————. "Charles Teed Pollard, Industrialist." *Alabama Historical Quarterly* 1, no. 4 (Winter 1930): 394–405.

————. "Charles Teed Pollard, Industrialist." *Alabama Historical Quarterly* 2, no. 1 (Spring 1940): 72–85.

Bearss, Edwin C. "Rousseau's Raid on the Montgomery and West Point Railroad." *Alabama Historical Quarterly* 25, no. 1 (Spring–Summer 1963): 7–48.

Clark, James Harold. "History of the North East and South West Alabama Railroad to 1872, a Thesis." Master's thesis, University of Alabama, 1949.

Doster, James F. "People vs. Railroad at Ashville: A Community Squabble of 1881." *Alabama Review* 9, no. 1 (January 1956): 46–53.

Dunn, Michael J. "The Birmingham & Southeastern Railroad." *Alabama Historical Quarterly* 27 (Spring–Summer 1965): 59–79.

Henry, Robert S. "The Railroad Land Grant Legend in American History Texts." *Mississippi Valley Historical Review* 32, no. 2 (September 1945): 171–94.

————. "Railroads and the Confederacy." *Railway and Locomotive Historical Society Bulletin* 40 (1936): 46–52.

Ivey, Betty Dickenson. "From River to Rail in Pickens County." *Alabama Review* 7, no. 1 (January 1954): 53–65.

Jay, John C. "General N. B. Forrest as a Railroad Builder in Alabama." *Alabama Historical Quarterly* 24, no. 1 (Spring 1962): 16–31.

Johnson, Dudley S. "Early History of the Alabama Midland Railroad Company." *Alabama Review* 21, no. 4 (October 1968): 276–87.

Keith, Jean E. "Sand Mountains and Sawgrass Marshes." *Alabama Review* 7, no. 2 (April 1954): 99–112.

Lawson, Thomas, Jr., H. Reid, and William S. Young. "Last of the Last." *Railroading Magazine* 28 (June 1969): 10–19.

Massey, Richard W., Jr. "Logging Railroads in Alabama, 1880–1914." *Alabama Review* 14, no. 1 (January 1961): 41–50.

Miller, Grace Lewis. "The Mobile and Ohio Railroad in Ante Bellum Times." *Alabama Historical Quarterly* 7, no. 1 (Spring 1945): 37–59.

Patterson, Ernest F. "Alabama's First Railroad." *Alabama Review* 9, no. 1 (January 1956): 33–45.

Sheridan, Richard C. "Tuscumbia Landing." *Journal of Muscle Shoals History* 8 (1980): 70–81.

Tachau, Mary K. Bonsteel. "The Making of a Railroad President: Milton Hannibal Smith and the L&N." *Filson Club History Quarterly* 43, no. 2 (April 1969): 125–50.

LOCOMOTIVE ROSTERS

Taber, Thomas T. Various railroad locomotive rosters. Muncy, Pa.: Railway and Locomotive Historical Society.

INDEX

Burnett, Senator, 49

Burr, Aaron, 18

Bury, E. (locomotive manufacturer), 12

C

Cahaba Coal Mining Company, 127, 129, 158

Cahaba, Marion & Greensboro Railroad, 41, 53, 85

Calhoun, J. M., 49

Canby, E. R. S. (General), 65

Carrollton Short Line, 239–40

Cedar Creek Mill Company, 232

Central of Georgia Railway, 171, 173, 182–83, 190, 205, 208–9, 211–12, 214, 219–20, 235, 263, 270, 272

Central Railroad & Banking Company of Georgia, 27, 75, 84, 148, 171, 174–75, 200–201

Central Southern Railroad, 99

Chapman, Reuben (Governor), 44

Chattahoochee & Gulf Railroad, 171

Chattahoochee Valley Railway, 218–19

Chattanooga Southern Railroad, 167, 169

Choctaw Lumber Company, 230

Cincinnati-New Orleans Limited, 258

Cincinnati, Selma & Mobile Railway, 133

Cincinnati Southern Railroad, 137

City of Miami, 263, 270, 272

Clanton, J. H. (General), 59

Cleveland, Grover (President), 202

Clifton Iron Works, 135

Clifton Railroad, 135

Climax locomotive, 230–31

Cochrane, John, 239–40

Columbus & Pensacola Company, 21

Columbus & Western Railway, 148, 201

Comer, Braxton Bragg, 124, 158, 203–15

"Comerism," 212

Commercial Club of Birmingham, 203

Confederate Iron Commission, 54–56

Consolidated Coal & Iron Company, 152

Construction camp: description, 134. *See also* Georgia Pacific Railway

Cooperative Experimental Coke & Iron Company, 110, 111, 118

Cotton States Special, 256, 258

Coxheath Lumber Company, 225

Cram, Daniel H., 57–58, 65, 68

Cranford, Jordan, 136

Creek Indians, 9, 19–20

Crescent, 252

Crescent City Special, 256, 258

Crescent Limited, 252

Crook, James, 200, 202

Croxton, John Thomas (General), 63, 71

Cullman, John S., 105

Cunningham, Russell M., 209

D

Danner, A. C., 112–13

Davis, Jefferson, 76

Davis, M. L., Lumber Company, 233

DeBardeleben, Henry, 108, 111, 113–15, 117–18, 120–21, 123, 127–29, 157, 158–59

DeBardeleben Coal & Iron Company, 128, 138, 158

Debs, Eugene V., 162

DeFuniak, E. A., 207

Deshler, David, 13–16, 274

G

Gaines, A. S., 53–54

Galveston, Harrisburg & San Antonio Railway, 230

Garland, Professor L. C., 38–39

Gauge: change to universal, 140–42

Georgia & Alabama Railway, 177

Georgia Pacific Railway, 133–34, 135, 137, 142, 165, 203, 217, 256

Georgia Power Company, 182

Georgia Railroad & Banking Company, 75

Georgia Railroad Commission, 199–200, 204

German-American Lumber Company, 235–36

Gilmer, Frank, 28–29, 45, 56–57, 88–89, 97–99, 102–4, 108–9, 275

Gindrat, John H., 92–93

Goettel, August, 90–91

Goodrich, Levin S., 109–10

Gordon, John B. (General), 133

Gorman, Roscoe W., 249

Gould, Jay, 5

Graff, J. H., 69

Gulf Coast Development Company, 235

Gulf, Florida & Alabama Railway, 181, 232, 234

Gulf, Mobile & Northern Railroad, 187–90, 261–63

Gulf, Mobile & Ohio Railroad, 190, 272, 278

Gulf Wind, 261

Gurnee, W. S., 129, 137

Guthrie, B. F., 118

H

Hall, Bolling, 26–27, 101

Harding, W. P. G., 121

Hardy, John, 89

Harrellson, Jesse, 88

Harris, Cole & Company, 231

Harrison, Benjamin (President), 160

Harrison, John, 249–51

Hazelhurst, George, 28

Heisler locomotive, 223–25, 230–34

Henderson, Charles (Governor), 214–15

Hillman, T. T., 117, 126, 143

Hollins, Heflin & Sylacauga Railroad, 234

House of Morgan, 165

Houston, George S., 49

Hubbard, David, 6, 9, 10, 12, 16, 49, 256, 274

Huey, Captain, 62

Humming Bird, 263

I

Illinois Central Railroad, 3, 31–33, 176–77, 181–82, 190, 228, 263, 272

Inman, John H., 143–44

Internal Improvement Act of 1867, 79–82. *See also* Financial aid for railroad construction

International Paper Company, 238

Interstate Commerce Commission, 202

Iron Mountain Railroad, 105

J

Jackson, E. E., Lumber Company, 231

Jacksonville, Gadsden & Attalla Railroad Company, 137–38

James, C. E., 167–68

Janney, Eli, 160

Jemison, Robert, 79, 81, 101

Jennifer Iron Works, 135

M

N

ABOUT THE AUTHOR

Wayne Cline, an avid history enthusiast with a special interest in railroads, earned a master's degree from The University of Alabama. He taught in Alabama, Georgia, and Florida, later changing careers to become a stockbroker. After a number of years working in the securities industry, he returned to the classroom, most recently teaching electronics and mathematics for the Department of Defense.